'Fabulous … I really can't recommend this enough – especially if you are going on holiday' Tom Holland

'A sparkling mosaic … In six gloriously colourful chapters, Lethbridge explores everything from guidebooks to souvenirs, retelling these first tourists' tales with gleeful relish … A kaleidoscope of detail … impeccably researched' Dominic Sandbrook, *Sunday Times*

'Delightful … witty … Lucy Lethbridge has written a glorious romp of a book, expertly researched. She has skilfully marshalled her teeming cast of British eccentrics as they tiptoe into foreign parts. For anyone stuck in an airport, or sitting it out on a staycation, this is an inspired choice for your holiday reading' Kathryn Hughes, *Mail on Sunday*

'A lively history … bursting with first-hand detail gleaned from diaries, guidebooks, letters and memoirs … [Lethbridge] paints a poignant portrait of the British outside their comfort zones, never quite happy and often cramped up with constipation. She has an insatiable eye and ear for human dissatisfaction, discomfort, distaste and anxiety' Ysenda Maxtone Graham, *Times Literary Supplement*

'The kind of book I want to read in company, to have an audience for anecdotes. A touching, and frequently very funny, account of Brits venturing outside their comfort zones' Hannah Rose Woods, *New Statesman*

'So much varied research has contributed to this excellent book that it is a treasure-trove of many more significant facts than one can cite … She is surely right in her assessment that the hopeful tourist is forever in search of the lost pastoral world of our pre-industrial ancestors, the "real" foreign country, where authentic people make real things. Alas, as she concludes, "the prevailing paradox of tourism is that it so often destroys what it seeks." We are many centuries from the time when, as spring came, Chaucer's "folk did long to go on pilgrimage", but our urges, our inventiveness and our capacity for destruction have not changed' Gillian Tindall, *Literary Review*

'Full of human interest and fresh insights, *Tourists* offers a wonderfully enjoyable account of one of the defining phenomena of the past two centuries' David Kynaston

'Pleasingly nerdy … Lethbridge is as good on the sketchbook-carrying Victorians as she is on the Caravan Club of sturdy mobile homeowners' Caroline Eden, *Financial Times*

BY THE SAME AUTHOR

Servants: A Downstairs View of Twentieth Century Britain
Spit and Polish
A Deep But Dazzling Darkness (co-editor)

True Stories of Pirates
Napoleon
Florence Nightingale
Who Was Ada Lovelace?
Who Was St Francis of Assisi?
Who Was Annie Oakley?

LUCY LETHBRIDGE has written for a number of publications and is also the author of several children's books, one of which, *Who Was Ada Lovelace?*, won the 2002 Blue Peter Award for non-fiction. She is the author of *Spit and Polish* (2016) and *Servants*, published to critical acclaim in 2013. She lives in London.

Lucy
Lethbridge

Tourists

How the British Went Abroad to Find Themselves

BLOOMSBURY PUBLISHING
LONDON · OXFORD · NEW YORK · NEW DELHI · SYDNEY

BLOOMSBURY PUBLISHING
Bloomsbury Publishing Plc
50 Bedford Square, London, WC1B 3DP, UK
29 Earlsfort Terrace, Dublin 2, Ireland

BLOOMSBURY, BLOOMSBURY PUBLISHING and the Diana logo are trademarks of
Bloomsbury Publishing Plc

First published in Great Britain 2022
This edition published 2023

A catalogue record for this book is available from the British Library

ISBN: HB: 978-1-4088-5622-2; PB: 978-1-4088-5629-1;
EBOOK: 978-1-4088-5621-5; EPDF: 978-1-5266-5239-3

2 4 6 8 10 9 7 5 3 1

Typeset by Newgen KnowledgeWorks Pvt. Ltd., Chennai, India
Printed and bound in Great Britain by CPI Group (UK) Ltd, Croydon CR0 4YY

MIX
Paper | Supporting
responsible forestry
FSC® C171272

To find out more about our authors and books visit www.bloomsbury.com
and sign up for our newsletters

For Caspar and Anna

Contents

Introduction

'It's raining Englishmen!' wrote Prince Metternich in Paris in 1815, observing in astonishment the arrival of over 600 English a day in the French capital.

It had been more than ten years since the British had visited the continent in any number – in fact since the brief cessation of hostilities with the French under the Peace of Amiens in 1802. Lawyer John Carr, a Devonshire man, had gone to Paris that year, reporting on his disembarkation at Le Havre that everybody he met there looked overjoyed to welcome the British: 'They appeared highly delighted to see us, talked of our dress, Sir Sidney Smith, the blockade, the noble English, the peace, and a train of etceteras.'[1] With the outbreak of the Napoleonic Wars in 1803, mainland Europe was again cut off, and when it reopened twelve years later, after the rout of Napoleon at Waterloo, it was for a new generation of British tourists living in a period characterised by rapid industrialisation, steam technologies and commercial mass production; it was travel in the age of consumption and by an expanding middle class. A 'vast stream' of tourists was now pouring over the English Channel into Europe, noted the *Westminster Review*. 'It is the paramount wish of every English heart, ever addicted to vagabondising, to hasten to the Continent.'[2]

This book covers the subsequent century and a half of British vagabondage. Off the tourists went, in families, groups and households, by carriage, steam packet, train, then ferry, motor car and finally aeroplane, for jaunting, for health, for education and for curiosity; and, finally, in the ultimate benediction of modern leisure: for sea and sun. It will concentrate on Europe (with the occasional foray into Turkey, Egypt and Palestine) because, although global travel expanded vastly in this period, it was the continent that was the locus of popular tourism.

The Grand Tour had been the seventeenth-century finishing school which gave the final burnish to the classical education required by the young aristocrat. The tour was as much about reading, talking and encountering important people as looking at important sights. It was about making connections that broadened the mind and consolidated a shared culture. Richard Lassels, a tutor, or 'bear leader', who accompanied several wealthy young men to Europe during this time, wrote that the chief object of a young man on the Grand Tour should be to experience 'the rare discourse we hear from learned men';[3] on his return, the idea was that he would then reread the works of the ancient philosophers with a deeper sophistication. By the end of the eighteenth century, however, the Grand Tour was associated more in the public imagination with debauchery, with spoiled and entitled young milords and their entourages behaving badly away from home.

We are all tourists now – despite what superior claims we may make for our travelling – and for two centuries the Grand Tour has laid down the foundations of the European sightseeing canon. Yet all manner of intricate snobberies about the masses on the move was present from the first. There is nothing so undesirable for the high-minded traveller as the sight of his or her own countrymen and women following their guidebooks along the same path. The poet Samuel Taylor Coleridge was among many dispirited by the sight of 'Delinquent Travellers' as a mass distraction, observing in 1818 that the hoi-polloi was on the move: 'peace has set John Bull a-gadding'.[4] Innumerable cartoons during this period depict the well-fed, coarse-grained British with their untidy entourages, their vulgar manners and baskets of provisions descending on the cities of Europe. These ruddy-cheeked caricatures are reminders that class distinctions are not left behind when travelling abroad; in fact they are, for the most part, reinforced.

For Coleridge, as for many commentators, the new tourists were trippers and lightweights – mere 'excursionists'. They were gadabouts and vulgarians, empty vessels 'agog' for new experience, unreflective and undisciplined consumers, 'with leaky purse and open mouth'.[5] These restless jaunters blurred distinctions between what was truly valuable and what was merely popular. The idea of the Grand Tour, either to Italy or, in its cheaper version, to the Low Countries, was co-opted by the middle classes as a sign of status: in *Little Dorrit*, written in the mid-1850s, it is the Dorrits' extended tour across the Alps which most vividly indicates their rising fortunes. Naturally, this ruined a view that many had thought exclusively their own. In 1825 the Marquis of Normanby deplored the sight of undefined hordes of 'Jenkinsons and Tomkinsons tumbling down the Alps in living avalanches'.[6] Tourists were and are often described in dehumanising terms: they come in 'swarms', 'herds' or 'flocks'. Later in the nineteenth century they were compared to mass-produced items on an industrial conveyor belt, as if the presence of a crowd by definition robbed individual experience of any distinguishing features. The expensive tourist experience became marked by its most important clear difference to the cheaper experience: the luxury of privacy and separation from the hell of other people like oneself. 'Real' travelling, in this paradigm, is marked by exclusive knowledge, by the bespoke and the handmade rather than the mass-produced, by discerning pleasures rather than simple ones. As Evelyn Waugh remarked wryly, observing how the English tourists on his cruise ship sorted themselves into social categories, 'the tourist is the other fellow'.[7]

In a foreshadowing of current anxieties about the corrupting distractions of online media, Coleridge thought that movement itself, made increasingly convenient by industrial technology, led to spiritual impoverishment and reduced attention spans:

Keep moving! Steam or Gas or Stage,
Hold, cabin, steerage, hencoop's cage –
Tour, Journey, Voyage, Lounge, Ride, Walk,
Skim, Sketch, Excursion, Travel-Talk –

For move you must! 'Tis now the rage,
The law and fashion of the Age.[8]

It was a social movement, however – and with it new attitudes towards what once seemed pre-ordained by social contract – that brought the real change. And the shift in the experience of work was echoed in new ideas about the definition of leisure. The historian J. A. R. Pimlott has pointed out that the numbers of traditional holy days – or days off work for religious feasts – enjoyed by clerical and industrial workers actually reduced dramatically in the first half of the nineteenth century. With narrow factory routines replacing more ad hoc or seasonal arrangements, and with no legal trades unions, employers could whittle down the traditional holidays that had been part of working life for centuries. The Bank of England, for example, closed on 47 days in 1761, on 44 in 1808, on 40 in 1825, on 18 in 1830 and on only 4 days in 1834. The first statutory bank holidays were not introduced until 1871. It is from a society in which work-free days were confined for the most part to Sundays that Thomas Cook, the progenitor of modern tourism and the package tour, emerges as one of the most remarkable figures of an era of remarkable self-made individuals.

The idea of the holiday gradually came to embody the idea that change – of scenery, air, climate and culture – was beneficial to health and spirit. And just as the tourist is the audience of a foreign culture often especially preserved for them to observe, so its familiar features can be packaged up in anticipation of the tourist's arrival. The rise of popular tourism runs parallel with that of consumerism and the transformation of experience into merchandising opportunities. The tourist business put the cultures of the world up for sale in a shorthand of enticing symbols: a pyramid, a palm tree, a Roman ruin, a peasant or a mountain peak. The history of tourism is therefore inseparable from the history of mass-produced bric-a-brac in the guise of holiday souvenirs. In 1909, the *Journal of Decorative Arts* wondered at the ways in which the diverse cultures of the world could be reduced to repeating images: 'Every portion of the habitable globe, from the Arctic regions to the Torrid zones, from the tea gardens of Tokyo to the

Peak of Teneriffe . . . has been ransacked to provide entertainment in the first place for the patrons of wallpaper showrooms.'⁹

Alongside the development of the standardised tourist experience – bringing with it improvements in sanitation, desirable air-conditioning and food that although interestingly different is still sufficiently familiar as to be palatable – is another, poignant strand of 'vagabondising': the recreation of the pastoral. This is the holiday that requires (an element of) physical hard work: it is about hiking, cycling, knapsacks, campfires and caravanning. The self-improving spirit of touristic curiosity unleashed by Thomas Cook and the madcap theatricality of Albert Smith are combined in the camping holiday or the hiking tour: it is a happy illusion of splendid solitude and ancient skills. What better delivers the wild romance of the open road as well as the cosy safety of the traditional cottage than the caravan?

This book's subtitle, 'How the British went abroad to find themselves', I think is best answered by this kind of pastoral fantasy. The famous sociologist Erik Cohen once referred to the modern 'drifter' tourist as a 'nomad from affluence'.¹⁰ But even the sun, sea and sex resort bubbles of the package holiday are a response, changing over a century and a half in style but in their essence the same, to the industrialisation and standardisation of the West. The tourist industry is dependent on a technology that it also explicitly repudiates. In many ways, it is a story of both optimism and disappointment, of hopes raised by the promise of the view at sunrise and dashed by the cloud, or the crowd, that obscures it.

I've used, as far as possible, the voices of ordinary people, from the nineteenth century to the 1970s. For the rise of popular tourism is about the ascendancy of the middling classes, and changing attitudes to travel, to work, to leisure, to the canon of established culture. It is about the desire to be different and the reassurance of being the same. Most of all it's a search for arcadia. Like the medieval pilgrims from whom the tourist descends, the modern vagabondiser hopes in some way to be enlarged by a brush with something more spiritual, more primitive, than life at home – and returns, not with a cockleshell as a trophy, but with a status-enhancing suntan.

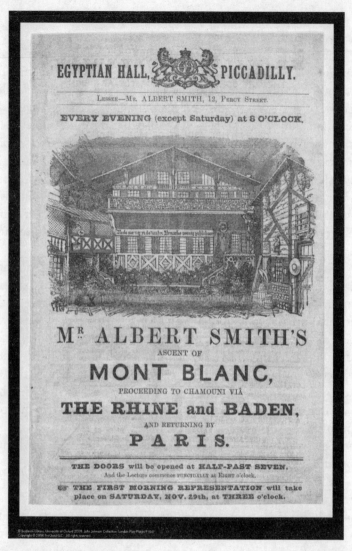

Albert Smith's enactment of his ascent of Mont Blanc was one of Victorian London's great entertainments.

I

'Where Shall We Go Next?'

'THE ALPS IN A BOX'

'Where shall we go next?' wrote Jemima Morrell in her diary in the early summer of 1863.[1] And what a question it was. Her grandparents neither would nor could have asked it. But for the British middle classes in the age of steam and railway, travelling the world really did seem suddenly possible. The earth had become a spectacle, a pageant of many nations with their wares on display for the happy shopper.

All the Victorian pioneers of popular tourism sold the idea of travel as a containable adventure to which there was a clear beginning and a defined end. Thomas Cook and Henry Gaze, the founders of the package holiday, we will meet later on; but arguably it was Albert Smith, the grand panjandrum of the panoramic spectacle, who did more than any other nineteenth-century figure to package up new experience itself. For Smith, the great landscapes of Europe could be reduced to scenes in a thrilling pantomime, their features to a single evocative image.

In 1850, Charles Dickens wrote a fictional sketch of a retired banking clerk called Mr Booley who has roamed the world in search of wild adventures. Elderly and corpulent, Mr Booley has travelled hundreds of miles since he left England for the first time at the age of sixty-five, 'alone and unattended': his 'powers of endurance are wonderful. All climates are alike to him. Nothing exhausts him; no alternations of heat and cold appear to have the least effect upon his hardy frame . . . Though remarkable for personal cleanliness, he has carried no luggage; and his diet has been of the simplest kind. He has often found a biscuit, or a bun, sufficient for his support over a vast tract of country.' As it turns out, however, Dickens's Mr Booley has never left Britain; in fact, he rarely leaves London. All his travelling is done via the 'gigantic-moving-panorama and diorama modes of conveyance'. All his travelling is 'pictorial'.[2]

The 3D thrill of 'pictorial travelling' was embodied in one of the great spectacles of Victorian London, the nearest thing most people then would have got to the excitement of real travel. First the diorama, and then the panorama offered an experience of heightened reality for all the senses, similar to today's IMAX cinema. They distilled into a single space all the largeness, fearfulness and dangerous exotica of popular imaginings about foreign places. Like Mr Booley, members of the armchair-travelling audience of a panorama could buy for pennies a simulated experience of the adventure of abroad: its battles, its weather, its mountaintops, rivers and peoples. While the rest of the world was being opened up to the public via new steamships and the rapid expansion of railways, the panoramas delivered the once-unimaginable image of travel as a series of instantly consumable, quantifiable, romantic, decorative, theatrical images – the globe in a nutshell.

The panorama is a development of the bird's-eye view of landscape – in which perspective is altered by a high viewpoint to take in a wider range of features than would be experienced by the human eye. It is an encapsulation of a place rather than a completely accurate representation of it. It was the Scottish painter Robert Barker who first exhibited a landscape painting in a 360-degree circular surround view, lit from above. Barker refined and patented his technology and opened his first panorama to the public – a view of Edinburgh from Carlton Hill – in 1792. For those early viewers, the experience of the image was extraordinary, immersive, as though they themselves were inside the picture frame. In order to get to the viewing platform, visitors had to walk through a dark tunnel at the end of which they suddenly found themselves surrounded by light and image, the artificial creation of stepping into a painted scene. Barker stressed that the overwhelming effect of his panorama was not trickery or illusion but simply a radical extension of the boundaries of art: 'There is no deception of glasses, or any other whatever,' he wrote, 'the view being only a fair sketch, displaying at once a circle of a very extraordinary extent, the same as if on the spot; forming perhaps one of the most picturesque views in Europe. The idea is completely new, and the effect produced by fair perspective, a proper point of view, and unlimiting the bounds of the Art of Painting.'[3]

In 1793, Barker and his son Henry Aston Barker, also a painter, travelled to London and later that year set up in a purpose-built exhibition space near Leicester Square, which they called 'The Panorama'. It was very successful. By the turn of the nineteenth century panoramas were among the most popular entertainments in the country, representative of a new appetite for illusion, automata, waxworks and magic shows.[4] Most excitingly of all, panoramas conveyed with what seemed like thrilling accuracy the feelings and atmosphere that might be experienced by participants in voyages of exploration and archaeological discoveries. In 1812, William Bullock commissioned the Egyptian Hall, a pharaonic temple-like structure in Piccadilly, in which to exhibit his large collection of natural history specimens and curiosities – including some brought back from the South Pacific by Captain Cook. In 1822, capitalising on the vogue for all things Arctic following the expeditions of Captain Ross and Sir William Parry in 1818, Bullock exhibited a family of 'real-life Laplanders' who danced, sang and amazed the public with their stories of the hardships of life in the icy wastes. The show incorporated a real reindeer, a shelter constructed of stones and moss, and a Lapp sled harnessed to a dejected elk. This *tableau vivant* was set against a painted panorama of snow-capped mountains and ice pinnacles. Bullock's Lapland extravaganza took £100 a day for the first six weeks of its run alone.[5]

Battle-scene panoramas proved a particular draw for Victorian audiences and, naturally, the most popular of all was the one which

recreated the field of Waterloo. In 1821, a young girl on her first visit
to London wrote in her diary that at the top of her sightseeing list
were the panoramas in Leicester Square of the Bay of Naples and
the Battle of Waterloo ('not near so pretty as Naples, it seemed all
confusion').[6]

New innovations in the development of ever more spectacular
shows were enthusiastically taken up. In the early nineteenth
century the French photography pioneer Daguerre invented
the diorama. These added extra thrills to the panoramic circular
experience, with their vertiginous illusion of distance, including
a background wall, a middle view and a foreground in which
objects were placed as if to suggest human habitation. The first
dioramas, in Paris and London, displayed gasp-inducing natural
landscapes and examples of dramatic architecture. One took the
viewer into the soaring medieval ceiling of Canterbury Cathedral's
Trinity Chapel. In another, of the Sarnen Valley in Switzerland, the
summer sky appeared to the audience to become more and more
overcast, threatening an approaching thunderous storm. The effects
were so lifelike that some spectators reportedly refused to believe
they were not real. In a later diorama by Daguerre himself, of the
Rhineland Castle of Stolzenfels, the effect of rain was so realistic
that spectators put up their umbrellas.[7] Other similar spectaculars
went even further – the relatively short-lived pleorama, pioneered
by Karl Wilhelm Gropius in Berlin during the 1830s, incorporated
actual movement. Viewers found themselves seated on a rocking,
boat-like contraption in a pool of water representing the Rhine –
while scenery moved past them as if they themselves were floating
down the river. In 1834, in London, spectators got a taste of the
sensations delivered by train travel when they sat in railway carriages
while watching through the windows a moving panorama of scenes
between Liverpool and Manchester (the line between the two cities
having opened four years before).

The journalist Edmund Yates remembered the discordant riot
of panoramas and dioramas in the London entertainment scene
of the 1840s. There was the Coliseum, for example, 'with its
wonderful panoramas of London by day and London by night . . .;

its glyptotheca [sculpture room], full of plaster casts; its swiss chalet, with a real waterfall, and a melancholy old eagle flopping about its "property rocks", its stalactite cavern . . . and its sham ruins near the desolate portico. . .'. Also on show there was the dramatically realistic representation of the earthquake of Lisbon: 'The manner in which the earth heaved and was rent, the buildings toppled over, and the sea rose, was most cleverly contrived, and had a most terrifying effect upon the spectators; frightful rumblings, proceeding apparently from under your feet, increased the horror, which was anything but diminished by accompanying musical performances on that awful instrument, the apollonicon.' At St George's Gallery, Hyde Park, there was 'an extraordinary collection of the details of Chinese life, with some admirable wax figures representing the different ranks and classes', along with 'a Chinese junk . . . manned by a Chinese crew'.[8]

Max Schlesinger, visiting London from Germany in 1853, has left a vivid description of the lumbering and unwieldy paraphernalia of the panoramas which competed with each other by advertising their shows on flamboyant floats. 'Rolling down Oxford Street, three immense wooden pyramids – their outsides are painted all over with hieroglyphs and with monumental letters in the English language,' wrote Schlesinger:

These pyramids display faithful portraits of Isis and Osiris, of cats, storks and of the apis; and amidst these old-curiosity shop gods, any Englishman may read an inscription, printed in letters not much longer than a yard, from which it appears that there is now on view a panorama of Egypt . . . This panorama shows the flux and reflux of the Nile, with its hippopotamuses and crocodiles, and a section of the Red Sea . . . [and] here is another monstrous shape – a mosque with its cupola and blue and white surmounted by a crescent. The driver is a light-haired boy, with a white turban and a sooty face . . . The panorama of the Nile, the Overland Route, the Colosseum, Madame Tussaud's Exhibition of Waxworks, and other sights, are indeed wonder-works of human industry and skill, and invention; and in every respect, are they superior to the usual productions of the same kind. But, for all that, they must send their advertising vans into the streets: necessity compels them to strike the gong and blue the trumpet; choice there is none. They must either advertise or perish.[9]

But it was in the rackety vision of the great spectacularist Albert Smith that panoramic bewitchment reached its apotheosis. Smith was a consummate yarn-spinner who packaged up exaggerated versons of his real-life adventures in the painted set of the panorama and flogged them to sell-out crowds. Smith's extraordinary energy can be conjured just by looking at the index entry under 'Smith, A.' in the memoirs of his friend Edmund Yates.[10] Here, a few taken at random indicate the range of his activities (and the flamboyant persona he cultivated to sell them): 'his return from the Nile with a beard'; 'a candidate for the Garrick Club'; a 'month at Constantinople'; 'anecdote of Louis Napoleon'; 'dinners at the "Shades"'; 'balloon ascent'; 'burlesques at the Lyceum'; 'editor of the Man in the Moon'; 'his admiration for my mother'; 'we swear friendship'; 'ascent of Mont Blanc'.

Smith was in turn a hack, entertainer, traveller, mountaineer, man about town, and eccentric dandy. He was a clubbable raconteur who also managed to fall out with almost all his friends and colleagues. He climbed Mont Blanc and was a founder member of the Alpine Club. He was a playwright, a rhymester, satirist and creator of burlesque theatricals. He wrote more than thirty books, thousands of articles and hundreds of comic songs. His novels were bestsellers, his talks were packed out, his panoramas drew crowds of thousands. Smith's appetite for life proved too much even for him: he was dead by the age of forty-four.

Smith was ten years old when he was taken to see the entertainments in London's Vauxhall Gardens, then seedily past their heyday, in 1826. He was there enchanted by a panorama of the Battle of Waterloo complete with musket fire replicated by cascading fireworks. He never forgot it. Born in Chertsey, Surrey, Smith qualified at the age of twenty-two as a surgeon – the profession of his father. Shortly afterwards, a trip to Switzerland ignited his enthusiasm for mountains, and on his return he discovered, by giving 'descriptive lectures' on the Alps to local literary societies in Surrey, that he had a talent for showmanship; he could work an audience. To add further colour to his talks, Smith even devised a crude Alpine panorama. 'The Alps in a box', he called it, using a previously written account of an ascent of Mont Blanc, with his brother holding a candle behind the screen to represent the moon shining on the route up the mountain known as the Mulets.

By the early 1840s, Smith had given up his medical practice and was working as a journalist, turning out scores of articles for a range of periodicals. Not only did he land the job of drama critic of the *Illustrated London News* but he edited his own monthly magazine called *The Man in the Moon*, which specialised in political titbits, a sprinkling of arch satire and some Grub Street gossip. To publicise it, he made several balloon ascents above Vauxhall Gardens, during one of which the balloon burst and he had to use the deflated silk as a parachute. Delighted by the copy opportunity this presented, Smith laughed off the danger with a quip for his audience: 'We almost wanted a few perils to give excitement to the trip.'[11]

In 1849 (1848's 'year of revolutions' in Europe having prevented the British from continental travel), Smith took a trip to Constantinople and Egypt and on his return devised a panoramic show, with himself in the role of comic narrator, called 'The Overland Mail' – about adventures and travails on the overland route to India. Smith was not the first journalist to put his travel adventures on the stage, and this one was a thinly disguised imitation of 'The Overland Route', which was already a popular panoramic representation of 'all the principal places between Southampton and Calcutta . . . delivered with a clear, concise and most pleasantly delivered descriptive comment on the passing scene' by a Mr Stocqueler.[12] Smith, however, characteristically pitched his performance several steps further in terms of extravagance, employing William Beverley, the foremost scenery artist of the day, to produce a backdrop of astonishingly realistic 3D-effect landscapes.

The 'Overland Mail' opened at Willis's Rooms in King Street on 28 May 1850 and was billed as a 'Literary, Pictorial and Musical Entertainment'. In *The Times*, the reviewer's faint praise was not quite damning: Smith, he wrote, 'brings forward a quality which is always popular with an English audience – unfeigned good humour. Profundity he does not attain, but he gives in as pleasant as form as possible the impressions which a series of new objects produces upon a traveller determined to enjoy himself after his own fashion and little disposed to be influenced by those who have gone before him.'[13]

The technique employed in Smith's panoramas was a beguiling mix of colourful foreign anecdotes with all those interesting practical details which make a journey really come to life. He'd had a knapsack made to his own design for his 'travels', 4 inches deep, 13 inches broad, and 12 inches long, not too cumbersome in size, yet large enough to hold a coat, waistcoat and trousers of thin black tweed, for occasions when something like evening dress was necessary; a pair of light French boots; four coloured shirts for everyday use and a white one for great occasions; a 'housewife' and an oil-silk toilet bag; four handkerchiefs, two black silk ties, four pairs of socks and a brush and comb. He did not pack a shaving kit, for he had started to grow a beard. On top of the knapsack he strapped a tin case for easy access to his Seidlitz (laxative) powders, laudanum (opium), Brokedon's compressed soda, and sticking plasters. The knapsack was 'tolerably heavy when charged', but Smith reckoned there was still room for whatever few souvenirs he might collect on the way. He wore a broad-brimmed felt hat for protection against the sun and, in place of a jacket, a blue blouse with pockets. A pouch holding a map, drawing board, knife, matches and string hung at his side.[14]

It proved an irresistible formula. Encouraged by a sell-out run, in 1851 Smith set off to climb Mont Blanc, the highest peak in Europe and subject, at third hand, of his earliest forays into entertainment. His intention was to create a magnificently dramatic panoramic account of his ascent on his return.[15] Smith departed for the summit at seven on an August morning, accompanied by three friends and eighteen porters, the largest climbing party ever to leave the village of Chamonix. According to his own legend, Smith packed in his knapsack spare boots, lambswool socks, thick scotch plaid trousers, a 'templar' worsted headpiece and a peasant's blouse. The eighteen porters meanwhile carried: '60 bottles of vin ordinaire, 6 bottles of Bordeaux, 10 bottles of St George, 15 bottles of St Jean, 3 bottles of cognac, 1 bottle of syrup raspberries, 6 bottles of lemonade, 2 bottles of champagne, 20 loaves, 10 small cheese, 6 packets of chocolate, 6 packets of sugar, 4 packets of prunes, 4 packets of raisins, 2 packets of salt, 4 wax candles, 4 legs of mutton, 4 shoulders of mutton, 6 pieces of veal, 1 piece of beef, 11 large fowls, 35 small fowls.'[16]

The ascent was perilous for an urban journalist, even one with Smith's feckless courage, and by the time the party were in sight of Mont Blanc's summit, he was barely conscious. Floyd, one his companions, loyally reported: 'AS was perfectly done up and had to be dragged the rest of the way. His courage was such as I have never yet seen.' At the top, the group celebrated by cracking open the champagne that had been heaved there by the porters, and smoking cigars.[17]

In March the following year, 1852, 'Mr Albert Smith's Ascent of Mont Blanc' opened with great fanfare at the Egyptian Hall, on a stage on which Smith's Swiss chalet had been recreated by woodworkers especially brought over from Chamonix. According to Yates, the opening night was as lavish as might be expected. 'There was a liberal supply of champagne; Mr Rule, the well-known *écailler* of Maiden Lane, and his sons, presided over a grog counter, and served out oysters and bread and butter; and hot baked potatoes were dispensed by a man described in the programme mysteriously as "Tatur Khan".' Real St Bernard dogs roamed the aisles during the interval, their collars hung with barrels full of chocolates. There was a waterfall with real water, a mill wheel and a lily pond. The stage was decked with Alpine plants, the lampshades were covered with edelweiss and the walls were hung with chamois skins. Smith interspersed his account of the climb itself with humorous songs, accompanying himself on the piano, while behind him a painted diorama rolled by on wheels to show each cliff-hanging moment of the ascent. He had a genius for extemporising patter, incorporating something topical every night to keep the show fresh and lively. Even his critics conceded that he had 'the rare art of rendering even the poorest stuff amusing'.[18]

One of the keys to Smith's success was his realisation that the audience's interest in information about foreign parts had limitations – but that their appetite for humorous caricatures of fellow travellers was boundless. The show therefore concluded with a barnstorming account of Smith's time in Paris which starred a hilarious impersonation of Brown, a young English tourist, ordering dinner at the Palais Royal restaurant and making an idiot of himself. Smith supplied mocking anecdotes featuring a range of comic stereotypes, many of which had been already tried out in his Overland panorama. There were Americans, for example, who did not know the difference between Byron and Mazeppa, or timorous ladies who pulled down the blinds of the stagecoach whenever they approached a precipice. An old woman who kept losing her luggage was guaranteed to raise a laugh, as was an 'undecided Mr Parker' – a 'Maltese commercial traveller'; 'an English engineer and his complicated dilemmas'; a Greek Genius and his tin fiddle', and 'an American showman travelling for curiosities'. All of these cartoonish types, out of their depth outside their own sphere of understanding, made fools of themselves when abroad – raising in Smith's audience not only a frisson of superiority but also fellow feeling.

Smith also realised that British audiences liked to see the themes of social class at home played out abroad. The highfalutin claims of the tourist experience were thus cut down to size. Yates described the merriment when, pretending to gaze into his recreated Rhine, Smith didn't see 'crystal caves and lovely nymphs' but 'a bed of black mud relieved by mosaics of old shoes and dilapidated pipkins'.[19] A physician who had been to a Smith panorama (the cold weather was recreated by buckets of iced water placed around the hall) and later visited the Rhine observed that the real-life experience lived up to expectations: 'All those who have seen the pictures which, for some years, accompanied Albert Smith's entertainment, have a very correct idea of Rhine scenery, as I found on visiting the said river.'[20]

This cheerful populism, with its familiar array of stock characters and pantomime archetypes, encouraged Smith's audience to believe that the pleasures of foreign travel were not beyond their reach. With his combination of lurid tall tales and sturdy practical advice, Smith established the tourist, in the public imagination, as an ordinary adventurer on a modest income rather than an idle dilettante with a private one. Smith had, after all, by his own account, climbed all the way to the top of Mont Blanc on a litre of wine, a bottle of brandy and a dozen hard-boiled eggs. Once, in a train, he said, he'd sat opposite a young Frenchman who was travelling all over the Alps taking nothing with him but a clean shirt, a knife and some string.

'The Ascent of Mont Blanc' made Smith an instant celebrity, one of London's great entertainments. The show ran for a record-breaking six years and finally closed in 1858 after nearly 2,000 performances, including a private one before Queen Victoria and the Prince Consort at Osborne House on the Isle of Wight.[21] Smith cannily merchandised the experience, expanding his repertoire to selling colouring books, fans, board games and miniature models of Mont Blanc. (On advertising and promotional material, at his own stipulation, the name Albert Smith appeared far larger than the words Mont Blanc.) At the height of his success, Smith liked to issue to chosen friends and acquaintances invitations made to look like passports:

We, Albert Smith, one of Her Britannic Majesty's representatives on the summit of Mont Blanc, Knight of the most noble order of the Grand Mulets, Baron Galignani of Piccadilly, Knight of the Grand Crossing from Burlington Arcade to the Egyptian Hall, Member of the Society for the Confusion of Useless Knowledge, Secretary for his own Affairs,

&c, &c. Request and require, in the name of His Majesty the
Monarch of the Mountains, all those whom it may concern,
ore especially the Police on the Piccadilly Frontier, to allow . . .
to pass freely in at the street-door of the Egyptian Hall, and
up-stairs to the Mont Blanc Room, on the evening of Saturday
1 December, 1855, at 8pm, and to afford him every assistance in
the way of oysters, stout, champagne, soda and brandy.[22]

Naturally, given his riotous popularity, Smith made enemies. The
writer and publisher Henry Vizetelly was among many who loathed
his 'huge self-conceit'.[23] John Ruskin, who had on two occasions
found himself in a then pristine Chamonix at the same time as
Smith, was appalled by what the panorama showman brought to the
Alps in his wake. To Ruskin, to make money from the mountains
as Smith did was more than just commercial exploitation, it was
a blasphemy against 'all the deep and sacred sensations of natural
scenery'. Ruskin was filled with gloom not only by the commercial
opportunism that seemed to be spreading like a disease over the
mountains ('a consuming white leprosy of hotels and performers'
shops') but by the way the Chamoniards themselves had been
so ready to take advantage of travellers, 'resolving the ancient
consistency and pastoral simplicity of the mountain life into the
two irregular trades of inn-keeper and mendicant'.[24] Smith's shows,
his 'Alps in a box' commercialisation, both exalted the mountains
and insolently cut them down to size; for Ruskin, he had corrupted
a sacred landscape by opening it up to the gawping of trippers.
The popularity of Smith's extravaganzas brought tourists streaming
into the Swiss valleys – and beyond. In 1856, a commentator in
the *Edinburgh Review* reported that once Smith's devotees had
finished with Chamonix, they moved on to other untouched
regions and mountain peaks such as the Matterhorn, bringing with
them 'cockneyism, the Albert Smithery, the fun, the frolic and the
vulgarity'.[25]

Anthony Trollope thought Smith a 'vulgarian' and so did
Thackeray: Vizetelly recalled that Thackeray found Smith's *mauvais
gout* more than he could stand. When brought into contact with

him he treated him with contemptuous toleration, showing him outward civility but the occasional sarcastic observations which he permitted to escape him, disclosed his true sentiments respecting Albert's mountebank ways'.[26] Accounts of Smith's 'unpleasant falsetto voice', his affectation of wearing a blue peasant smock, and the alarming dustiness of his rooms off Tottenham Court Road all added to the nose-holding disdain in which he was viewed by his literary peers. Stories abounded as to his charlatanry. The poet George Hodder cast doubt on his claim ever even to have reached the top of Mont Blanc. Hodder had been in Chamonix when Smith set off in 1851 and remembered later remarking to him that it was 'a bold thing for a man to do who had not been in training'. Smith had apparently rejoined: 'Pluck will serve me instead of training.' Pluck did no such thing, crowed Hodder, because Smith had been so 'deadbeat towards the end of the ascent, that he was unable to proceed any further and his stalwart guides had somehow or other managed to carry him to the summit between them'. Vizetelly whispered: 'Ill-natured people did not scruple to say that the adventurous author was carried up to the summit of the mountain in one of the big provision baskets.'[27]

But for Smith the only opinions that counted were those reflected in the box office. He earned £30,000 (well over a million today) in ticket sales alone in the six years that his Mont Blanc show ran in London. He continued to cultivate an unrepentantly spivvy public persona, favouring loudly checked suits, brightly coloured neckerchiefs, flat hats, and watch chains festooned with sparkly charms. A keen deflater of snobbery and pretension, he did a roaring trade in journalistic comic sketches of social 'types' (his 'Natural History of Stuck-up People' is typical) – the kind of witty little social summations which were also a speciality of many other popular writers, Thackeray and Trollope among them. He also enjoyed causing a stir in a respectable crowd by loudly claiming that high culture was nothing but a racket and Shakespeare 'all rot'.[28]

Smith often himself acted as a guide for the groups that by now thronged to Chamonix. A hut on the Mulets was soon erected to encourage yet more climbers and Smith inaugurated it by leading a huge party there, accompanied by a record thirty-four guides. By 1854 there were so many tourists and celebrities visiting Mont Blanc that Smith added new verses to the London show and new scenery – including a real-life Chamonix guide imported for the occasion, accompanied by ten St Bernards.

By 1856, *The Times* announced that it was all over for the mountains and the real travellers who alone could appreciate them: the Alps had lost their grandeur, the mystique which could only be maintained by inaccessibility. 'Mont Blanc has become a positive nuisance,' was the opinion of its leader writer. 'Its majesty is stale, its "diadem of snow" a mere theatrical gimmick, and its terrors under existing arrangements about as tremendous as the mysteries of the Thames Tunnel. We doubt not,' the piece declared, 'that as a pedestrian feat it may try the sinews of various adventurous gentlemen who have not yet walked off the "supremes" and iced champagne of a London season. What is it, however to the world in general that Brown, Jones and Robinson take a stiff breather up an inclined plane – ay, even if their daring spirits urge them on till they grow black in the face from exertion? The same result would follow if they ran a sufficient number of times round the Regent's Park before breakfast, but really the world in general cares very little about the matter.'[29]

Albert Smith perceived that his audience were reassured by the idea that travelling abroad was an exercise not only in new experiences but in deeply familiar ones. It was all very well to dangle above a mountain pass or feel stirred by a view of the Mediterranean – but the antics of one's fellow traveller might be the more abiding memory of the trip.

Smith is the railway-age chronicler of hopes and desires. A traveller abroad could encounter almost anyone in a train carriage, but would nonetheless be reassured to know that a fellow passenger was of a similar social class and type. Smith himself noted that the only way to meet real locals was by travelling third-class. The British tourist, however, he observed, preferred the more expensive carriages, 'wherein, by associating one with another, and not seeing much of the country they were passing, one of their great pleasures of travelling was obtained'.[30]

Smith died suddenly of bronchitis, at the height of his popularity, in 1858, shortly after returning from a trip to China (about which he had planned another spectacular), and six months after marrying the actress Lucy Keeley. He is buried in Brompton Cemetery. Although there were rumours that he persuaded hangers-on to sing his praises from the rooftops as part of a new show's pre-publicity (bribing them with hints that they would be included in his will), just eight friends were in attendance at his funeral.

Albert Smith's legacy was to democratise the tourist experience, establishing images of abroad in the public imagination in magic-lantern form. If you had been to a Smith panorama you knew what to expect from the Alps, or the cataracts of Egypt, or the Bay of Naples; the reality had to prove itself as thrilling as the artificial version (and quite often failed). Yates reflected disparagingly on the new kind of traveller that Smith's shows had engendered: ordinary middling types ('Brown, Jones and Robinson', in *The Times*'s disparaging description) wanting a jaunt, snatching an annual break from a dull and sedentary job, perhaps, in the expanding clerical bureaucracies of Victorian England. 'The Whitsuntide trip had a good deal of the Cockney element in it,' wrote Yates, 'and is composed of very high-spirited people, whose greatest delight in life is "having a fling", and who go to Paris, and rush through France, and through Switzerland to Chamonix, compare every place they are taken to with the views which formed part of the exhibition at the Egyptian Hall, carry London everywhere about with them in dress, habits and conversation, and rush back, convinced that they are great travellers.'[31]

But who exactly were they, these new travellers, these Jenkinsons, Tompkinsons, Browns, Joneses and Robinsons? 'A cohue of English who mostly looked as though they'd been disgorged from the Margate Hoy,' wrote Lady Lyttleton, encountering some in Italy; she imagined that they were all on commercial business.[32] They spanned the middle classes, from the modest lower middle to the almost upper middle, but most of all they were a new *type*. And more than anyone else, the one man who can be said to have enabled this new type to spill out from the confines of its own class and experience was Thomas Cook – the great, and visionary, travel agent, prophet, campaigner and founding father of the modern holiday.

'BROWN, JONES AND ROBINSON'

Aged thirty-one and unmarried, from Selby in Yorkshire, Jemima Morrell was a member of the Junior United Alpine Club, where discussions in 1863 on the subject of holidays were lively. 'What an anxious question this annual holiday is now becoming!', she wrote in her diary. Fellow member Mr Williams, flush with the success of a recent publication about income tax, suggested Norway but was overruled by those who objected to a holiday of only ten days when just getting to the destination would take six days. Morrell and her friends had their travel choices laid out before them in ways that were entirely new: holidays had become consumer desirables with a particular something tailored to suit every interest or hobby. 'Everybody has been to Scotland, some of us had done the Land's End, Ireland is not everybody's choice, the International Exhibition had tired us all of London, Scarbro' is only suitable for invalids and children, the Lake District done years ago, and Fleetwood is worse than Scarbro'.'[33]

This meeting of the Junior United Alpine Club gives us a small glimpse of the high Victorian moment of the professional middle classes: the new passion for mountaineering; the diversions of the self-made and the self-educated; the delights of the past harnessed to the technologies of the present; and, crucially, the security and excitement of the group. In Jemima Morrell and her friends, we have the new face of travel: 'holidays', agencies, convenience, leisure time and camaraderie. These were people who could spare only three weeks before they returned to work to worry, like Mr Williams, about income tax or, like Jemima, to a life that now offered more diversions than had previously been enjoyed by an unmarried youngish woman of the middle classes. The answer to the group's dilemmas was, by the mid-nineteenth century, the answer to most questions of travel: to go with Thomas Cook. 'This difficulty was unexpectedly solved by Mr Cook, of Excursion fame, announcing a preliminary tour in Switzerland "with cheap tickets to Mont Blanc",' Miss Jemima continued, recording in her journal that she would be delighted to join the group 'if suitably accompanied' by her brother William.[34]

Later in his career, Cook summarised his typical clients as 'ushers, governesses, practical people from the provinces, and representatives of the better style of the London Mercantile Community'.[35] Jemima Morrell's journal provides a snapshot of the English tourist group en fête. There is the obligatory jester, Tom, who insists, waggishly, on referring to the other members of the group by the Quaker *thee* and *thou*, 'to lighten the toils of the way'; the hilarity when Sarah's 'veritable Yorkshire tarts' are taxed at fifty cents at customs in Dieppe; the shared indignance at the extortionate price of souvenir alpenstocks; the closely observed class comedy among the English tourists they encountered (Miss Eliza and Mr James go missing: 'Mr HHM was sent in search, fell in with the son of the Lord Chancellor of England and the Hon. Miss Westbury'), and the nicknames bestowed on those they encounter, such as the vicar of the English church in Interlaken who, after an insufficiently rigorous sermon, became known as 'Poor Mr Littlegrace'.

High-minded, driven, frugal, self-educated and (most importantly) teetotal, Thomas Cook, who can be said almost singlehandedly to have enshrined the group jolly abroad in British culture, was an unlikely leisure tycoon. Yet the foundational success of his travel empire was built on the character of Cook himself and its reputation on his undoubted probity.

Cook was born in 1808 into a poor, strictly Baptist family in Derbyshire. Although he was originally apprenticed to a cabinet maker, by the age of twenty he was an itinerant preacher, travelling through the south Midlands distributing tracts and establishing Sunday schools. Cook married a Sunday school teacher, Marianne Mason, in 1833 and they settled in Market Harborough, Leicestershire, where he took up work as a wood turner. There he signed the pledge and became from that moment a temperance campaigner of evangelical intensity – utilising his natural skills not only for oratory but for management and organisation to provide

wholesome entertainments ('rational recreation' as he put it) as an
alternative to drinking. Sundays were working people's only day
off and cheap liquor was readily available: what was needed, Cook
saw, was distractions, hobbies, interests – to encourage people
whose horizons were naturally limited by education, geography or
poverty, to see what was open to them 'without the stimulus of
alcohol'. In 1841, after tramping fifteen miles to a meeting under a
hot sun, Cook organised his first railway excursion: 500 passengers
from Leicester to Loughborough to attend a temperance meeting.
The cost was one shilling per head and Cook negotiated the price
direct with the railway companies, block-buying tickets on the
cheap. It was a triumphant partnership of technology, capitalism
and evangelical ardour. At Loughborough, Cook roused the crowd
with an address which called for: 'One cheer more for Teetotalism
and Railwayism!!!'[36]

In 1841, the Cooks moved to Leicester where Thomas established
himself as a bookseller and printer of temperance literature. As
well as opening a temperance hotel, he continued to organise
excursions, persuading railway companies to offer group discounts
and always personally conducting the tours – to Liverpool, to
Snowdon and to Scotland. The presence of Thomas Cook himself,
so trustworthy, energetic and benevolent, would be a crucial
feature of what would later become, for tourists all over the world,
'the Cook experience'.

Over the course of one year, 1851, Cook arranged for a staggering
65,000 people to travel to London by train to visit the 'Great
Exhibition of the Works of Industry of All Nations'; travel,
accommodation (in temperance establishments of course) and
exhibition entry tickets were all included in the price. The Great
Exhibition was the temple in which the new wonders of industrial
consumerism were displayed. Exhibition-goers had there what was
usually their first glimpse of the world beyond their own immediate
experience: in its vast celebration of stuff, of things, of the wonders
of traditional craftsmanship as well as modern manufactories,
the exhibition encapsulated national differences in the objects
representing different countries. A kiwi's egg, for example, might

represent New Zealand, and a Colt firearm the western frontier-lands of North America. The conjuring of a place through a single image was to become a crucial component of the emerging business of popular travel, a sort of reassuringly predictable shorthand for not only the adventure of abroad but also its commercial potential.

Following the success of the Great Exhibition tours, in the same year Cook started a monthly magazine, *Cook's Excursionist*, a guide to the novice traveller on what to do and what to expect, its publishing costs met by advertisements for corn plasters, travelling bags and air cushions. Cook also, with characteristic far-sightedness into the importance of what we would now call brand loyalty and customer feedback, encouraged his travellers to supply the magazine with positive personal testimonies. 'It really is a miracle,' read one. 'Everything is organised, everything is catered for, one does not have to bother oneself with anything at all, neither timings, nor luggage nor hotels. And. Do you know, I have met the man who arranges it all. I have even said 'Good morning' to him. He is named Mister Cook and they say he is a saint!'[37]

Cook's own prose style, honed through those years on temperance pulpits, is delightful: crisp, clear and warmly authoritative. He advertises himself and his own role in the first edition of the magazine in 1851 thus: 'Our Herald will be an excursionist and excursion conductor and its aim will be to promote the comfort and pleasure of other Excursionists, by the indication of the best routes, descriptions of the most interesting objects along the way, and attention to the physical, social and financial circumstances of patrons and companions.' Note the language again – 'herald' and 'conductor' – suggesting not only a presence of almost angelic benignity ('he is a saint'!) but also a firm hand on the tiller. 'The Herald is a practical worker,' Cook continues, 'rather than a sentimental traveller; nevertheless he will be not be insensible to the lovely attractions of the verdant landscape, the majestic grandeur of the towering mountain, the music of the rill and the chorus of the rolling flood, the spring fragrance of Flora's flower and the reviving inhalation of nature's Universal Garden.'[38] In 1854, *Cook's Excursionist* had a monthly circulation of around 2,000, which grew to 58,000 by 1867 and by 1892 to 120,000. 'Hurrah for the Trip, the cheap, cheap Trip!' was its clarion call in 1854. It was a call to social revolution.

Cook had already understood that it would be the railways which would be the key to the promise of freedom. But because there were so many competing railway companies, the fares and timetables were off-puttingly complicated. What is more, how do you find a hotel in London if you have never been to the capital before? The answer was a package tour in which, for a single payment, Thomas Cook would look after the traveller. He offered the excitement of new experiences soothed by the reassuring mantle of paternal familiarity. Cook may have been (for the most part affectionately) nicknamed 'The General' by his excursionists but what he offered was security.

The first continental tour, to Paris, set off in August 1855. As was now customary, Cook published his customers' comments in the *Excursionist*. 'We find the greatest comfort in having such a friend as Mr Cook, to whom we look in every difficulty, to take us from the perplexity of selecting hotels, arranging with landlords, procuring railway tickets, exchanging money or learning the times of trains &c.,' wrote one passenger, while another extolled the convenience and camaraderie of the group over travelling alone: 'The greatest harmony prevailed amongst us – it was seldom so large a party was seen, and we always felt moved with compassion towards the solitary twos and threes who looked so isolated compared to ourselves.'[39]

Because the original success of his business depended so entirely on the character of the man himself, Thomas Cook, in his modest way, turned out to be a master of self-promotion. An article in the *Daily News* summed it up in 1869: 'Unprotected females confide in him; hypochondriacs tell him of their complaints; foolish travellers look to him to redeem their errors; stingy ones ask him how eighteenpence can be procured for a shilling; would-be dandies ask his opinion about dress; would-be connoisseurs show him their art treasures they have picked up; the cantankerous refer their quarrels to him, and the vacuous inflict on him their imbecility; but a great conductor never flinches.'[40]

By 1860, Cook had established an office in London. Three years later, under the Cook's wing, 2,000 British visitors had visited France and 500 Switzerland, among them Jemima Morrell and her companions. By 1868, the firm's offices were dealing with 30,000 letters and 50,000 enquiries every year.

Though Cook clearly had an acute business sense, the profit motive was not his main one; he was driven primarily by temperance zeal: 'The thought flashed through my brain, what a glorious thing it would be if the newly developed powers of railways and locomotion could be subservient to the promotion of temperance.'[41] With brass bands and fun outings, Cook aimed to persuade people that 'leisure' – an absence of work as yet not officially formalised need not inevitably involve the public house. Although a Cook's tour lost its explicitly temperance connotations early on, Cook himself often let Baptist or temperance passengers travel at reduced rates. It was his doggedly book-balancing and expansionist son John Mason Cook, whose life was entirely consumed by the business after his father's retirement in 1878, who turned the firm of Thomas Cook and Sons the excursionists into the world-dominating travel agency empire it became.

Cook is now the most celebrated figure in the popular travel revolution of the nineteenth century – but there were successful competitors from the beginning: it was a crowded field for similarly high-minded, nonconformist types with an interest in combining commercial opportunities with social improvement. A generation younger than Cook. Sir Henry Simpson Lunn, a Methodist former missionary, started the Co-operative Educational Tours in 1893 and was the founder of what became Lunn Poly. The firm of Dean & Dawson (also based in Leicester) was set up in 1871 and were the agents for the Central Railway Company, also offering, on the Cook model, inclusive tours in Britain and the continent. But it is the career of Cook's direct contemporary, Henry Gaze, which provides the most striking fable of fortunes made and lost in the tumultuous years of railway expansion across Europe. In fact, had any of Henry Gaze's sons been as remorselessly business-minded as John Mason Cook, the Gaze agencies might have survived and the

Cook empire been forgotten; in 1890, when Gaze retired, his firm had ninety offices round the world to Cook's eighty-five.

Gaze, who was born in 1825, was a Congregationalist who believed in the potential of travel to elevate the lives of those for whom it had been traditionally out of reach. Unlike Cook, he remained sensitive to any slights about the relative modesty of his origins as a bootmaker. Though a proud advocate of the moral uses to which commerce could be applied, he was pugnacious, chippy and bristling. Gaze's Southampton boot-making business became extremely prosperous (he patented the highly successful 'gutta-percha insole') and eventually received a royal appointment. He was a tireless proselytiser on a range of subjects – first as the author of books on chiropody (including *Hints on the Feet and their Coverings*, with a chapter on which he later drew for advice to foot-sore tourists, on corns, their cause and cure); then, as a popular lecturer on culture, history ('Southampton in Days of Yore' was typical) and, most popularly of all, travel.

Gaze had been from the mid-1840s a frequent visitor to the continent to research the latest styles of footwear and keep in touch with his French boot suppliers. He was an early adopter of photography, and his talks were illustrated with his own pictures and a talk by Henry Gaze on his continental adventures became a huge local event. Gaze's admiration for the eye-popping spectaculars staged in London a decade before by Albert Smith was evident in his own show-stoppers, which occupied ever-larger Southampton venues in the 1860s. Like Smith, he capitalised on dramatising his own cliffhanging (literally, sometimes) exploits, encouraging audiences to marvel at his physical stamina – he claimed, for example, to have covered 2,000 miles of the Alps in seventeen days in 1858 with his friend Ebeneezer Williams, a clerk in the Southampton post office. To create the atmosphere for a dramatic rendering of their Alpine travels ('Notes of a Tour Among the Alps of Switzerland and Savoy'), Gaze employed elaborate props, including animals and a tall figure dressed as a monk of St Bernard's Abbey. Music was supplied by a harmonium hidden behind the stage and colourful backdrops commissioned from a theatrical scenery painter. Nourished by hours of giving sermons, Gaze was a fluent speaker: the *Hampshire Advertiser* noted approvingly the effects on the audience of his 'free conversational style'.[42]

Gaze's theatrical productions paved the way for his forays into the business of real travel. Why shouldn't the hard-working, clerkly types who excitedly crowded the Southampton Polytechnic Institute for one of his extravaganzas not experience, in the short breaks their work allowed them, the thrill of the real mountains? He took his first guided tour to Paris in 1863: at a cost per head of five guineas for five days. Gaze knew his clients' desires and their limitations. A Gaze tourist had no time for leisurely wandering: what was required was a vigorous programme of education in the cities and robust exercise in the mountains: 'The overdone business-man, worn with eleven months' routine of duty, gains very solid advantages from the violent exercise and the risks he voluntarily encounters (sometimes at great expense too) in Switzerland.' In his promotional literature, Gaze pointed out that his kind of client was the opposite of the limp sybarite who travelled merely for diversion: 'There are those who on their travels chiefly seek the pleasures of the table, and who glide over the Continent in well-cushioned carriages, mixing in the society of their own countrymen, staying at English hotels, and returning with little more knowledge of the people through whose territory they have passed than if they had never been there,' Gaze declared, 'and there are some who raise objection because they do not desire to see those for whom these pages are prepared, too freely circulating in the picture galleries and ecclesiastical edifices of Belgium and Holland, or too numerously climbing the snowy sides of the Alps.'[43]

Gaze, like Cook, also made a selling point of his personal supervision, stressing the presence of his 'very intelligent' wife Mary. His advertisement for the first Paris tour indicates the reassuringly paterfamilias nature of the tour leader with his flock:

Mr H Gaze will accompany those who make the through journies on the Excursions, and will be in attendance during his stay in Paris at his office, at the Hotel de Paris et D'Albion, from 8.00 to

10.00 am, to assist in forming the day's plans and to afford any
aid in his power, as also from 5.0 to 7.0 pm (Sundays excepted).
He will also devote the intervening hours of the day to escorting
those who desire it to the sights of Paris. AND Special Facilities
for Ladies – Mrs Henry Gaze also intends to accompany the
Trips in order to promote the comfort of ladies travelling alone,
and to ensure the fulfilment of the Hotel arrangements.[44]

Gaze took a close interest in every tiny detail of his clients' diet,
wellbeing and comfort – particularly as regards the health of their feet.

'GUIDE, PHILOSOPHER AND FRIEND'

The paperwork and bureaucracy required both to leave Britain and
to move about on the continent was a time-consuming irritant.
Before the 1860s, all British travellers had to carry a passport in which
their destinations had been '*visé*-ed', or stamped, by the appropriate
embassy. These requirements were a legacy of the Napoleonic era
and were befuddlingly complicated. Such tribulations, observed
the journalist Alexander Innes Shand, looking back in 1887 at his
travels forty years earlier, 'become a farce, though a thorn in the
flesh and a perpetual nuisance'.[45]

Rules and regulations varied from country to country and
were bewilderingly inconsistent. In most places on the continent
you needed not only a passport for entry but one for exit too.
In 1818, the traveller 'W.E.F', trying to get to Paris, 'experienced
considerable difficulty in procuring a passport to quit Bruxelles;
my name having been included with that of General W which he
carried back with him to England. Our Ambassador was absent
and I was bandied about from Bureau to Bureau without success;
so that I began at last to think that I should be necessitated to
remain at Bruxelles all my life.'[46]

Travellers found the bureaucratic indignities irksome. Furious tales
abounded of jobsworths and box-tickers, of waiting interminably for
a 'sulky subordinate whose supper had disagreed with him'.[47] Having
secured the requisite paperwork from his own embassy, the traveller

then had to visit the embassy or consulate representing his desired destination to have it stamped by the correct official. Passports had to be produced not only for inspection at national borders but also when entering towns and cities – or sometimes simply for staying overnight in an inn. At all stopping points, tourists' passport details would be recorded in ledgers or registers.

For the new tourist, a helpful companion to the bureaucratic tangle was therefore indispensable and the history of popular tourism is also the history of an entire new genre of writing. This is the guidebook, with its comforting authority from a companion who has jumped through the hoops before you and knows how the system works. Mariana Starke was not the author of the first guidebook to travelling in Europe (James Howell's 1642 *Instructions for Forreine Travell* arguably has that honour) but Starke's guidebooks were the first to sell in tens of thousands. She was also the first author to categorise, in terms of value, the places and accommodation that the traveller would encounter, expanding widely the familiar canon of the classical tour. She conceded that the traveller might not be have enough leisure to commit to mistakes or time-wasting: with only a short stop in Naples or Leipzig, decisions needed to be made. Her categories are peppered with exclamation marks – !, !! or !!!, depending on her judgement of merit. Mrs Starke took the brisk view that the sites of classical antiquity and culture need not be so revered that they were exempt from a hierarchical tidying up.

Yet Mrs Starke's is also the first guidebook author to understand the reader's practical anxieties. Her list of basic equipment suggestions for the traveller setting out in 1818 is, to say the least, daunting. It includes leather sheets, pillows, blankets, calico sheets, pillowcases, mosquito nets, towels, tablecloths and napkins; a travelling chamber-lock, pistols, pocket knives, carving knife and fork; a silver teapot, Walkden's ink powder, pens, razors, straps, and hones, needles, thread, tape, worsted, and pins; a thermometer, a medicine chest, with scales; weights, an ounce, and half-ounce; measure for liquids, a glass pestle and mortar, a drop measure, tooth- and hair-brushes; Iceland moss, bark sal volatile, aether, sulphuric acid, pure opium, liquid laudanum, paregoric elixir, ipecacuanha, emetic tartar, prepared calomel, diluted vitriolic acid; essential oil of lavender, portable soup, Epsom salts and plasters.

Mariana Starke was indefatigable. By the time she published her guidebook, she was well into middle age and an author not only of two plays set in India but a well-received account, published in 1800, of her years spent in Italy taking care of a sick relative. When she first wrote to the publisher John Murray II in 1814, she was living in Exmouth, and had spotted an opportunity to market her expertise to the British tourists she forecast, correctly, would soon be flocking to the continent. She had, she told Murray, enlarged and expanded her *Travels from Italy* with that eventuality in mind. The new book, she wrote, covered all the most important countries of Europe and Scandinavia, divided into itineraries: 'My work therefore, in its present state, comprehends every kind of information most needful for continental travellers: as it seems reasonable to suppose the emigration from this Country will be immediate and immense, in case of peace, allow me to enquire whether, if that event occur, you would like to purchase the above named work, should you on perceiving, think well of it?[48]

Mariana Starke's book was eventually published in 1820 under the title *Travels on the Continent* and then, in an updated version, as *Information and Direction for Travellers on the Continent* (1824). Numerous updated editions followed. There was no region of the tourist's physical and spiritual welfare that Mrs Starke did not offer advice on; no problem, comfort or pleasure was left unanticipated. Her lengthy correspondence with Murray shows how furiously she worked at the endless task of correcting, updating and proofing (proofs being sent from Murray's offices in Albemarle Street, London, by 'water-carriage' to Exmouth), and she relied on correspondents abroad 'whose veracity I trust', to keep her informed as to any changes or errors. Mrs Starke left nothing to chance: in 1823, from Rome, she wrote: 'My general rule is never to print an account of anything I have not seen two or three times over.'[49]

Starke's attitude in her book to cultural destinations tends to come with a lofty wave of the authorial hand – in the spirit of her crushing exclamation marks. She makes merely a vague genuflection in the direction of Michelangelo's 'super-excellent' *Dying Gladiator*, say, but passes swiftly on without expansion. The idea of a Starke tour was to pack in as much as possible in a relatively short time, no loitering. Her many years of travelling before and after the Napoleonic Wars mean that her guidebooks paint an interesting picture of her own trenchant national prejudices. In the first edition of *Information and Directions*, for example, she observes:

> On revisiting Calais, in May, 1817, after an absence of twenty years, I discovered no apparent change, either in the town or its inhabitants; except that the latter, at least the lowest order of people have acquired a habit of smoking incessantly, like the Germans; while the former boasts a larger number of good inns than it possessed under the government of Louis XVI; and has been ridded of all its conventual institutions, and likewise of the host of mendicants by whom travellers were formerly annoyed.[50]

Starke's advice proved very popular for the new British tourists, and *Information and Directions* went into eight editions in four years. She understood that the underlying default position, even of the open-minded tourist, was of suspicion and fearfulness. Starke told her readers their fears were understandable and then, brusquely, how they might overcome them. Her book naturally had its detractors: a poem published in *John Bull* in 1836, for example, poked fun at Starke's middle-class insistence on prudence and haggling and her blithely inconsistent generalisations: 'She calls Italians "civil"/ Yet says "they often cheat";/ And that you "first must bargain"/ For all you buy and eat.'[51] But she set the style and content for every guidebook that has been published since.

Useful tips on haggling were not available in the also vastly popular *Classical Tour Through Italy* (1815) by Father John Chetwode Eustace – but if Father Eustace, also taking his readers in the footsteps of the grand tourist, looked after their spiritual and classical education, it was Mrs Starke who saw to it that they were not ripped off by the locals. In 1822, she pointed out to John Murray that hers was a road book and guide combined – a money saver for the thrifty traveller, teaching 'not only how to travel economically, but how to live frugally and healthfully on the Continent'.[52]

Soon guidebooks were the drivers of change, their ratings, rankings and recommendations encouraging local economies to accommodate British ideas about cleanliness and food. A disparaging comment or criticism in a guidebook – just one! – could finish business for an inn or a restaurant. In the 1850s, an American observer who only half-approved of the British obsession with comfort thought the British guidebook had bullied foreign hotels into submission: 'John Bull soon found it easier to make the Continent supply him with clean sheets – he has warmed the bed for the rest of the world.'[53] The matter of bedding continued to be a vexed one, however – with damp and dirty sheets a constant complaint – to say nothing of the mysterious continental habit of replacing sheets and blankets altogether with a down-filled 'feather mattress'. 'I'm not sure whether it was meant for us to lie on it or it on us,' wondered Hill the first-time tourist.[54] Mariana Starke advised her readers to bring their own sheets and blankets (and some travelling trunks advertised themselves as capacious enough for bedlinen). In 1843, while staying in a 'second-rate inn in rural Italy', Susan Horner (who had not brought her own) was pleased to find: 'our sheets very clean, as I do not think they had been slept in above once before'.[55]

Visitors to Paris had been using the English political journal *Galignani's Messenger* since 1814, but the purpose of Galignani's, the only English circulating library in the city, was to keep the British in touch with home rather than inspire them with new destinations abroad. Situated near the Palais-Royal, there were 20,000 English volumes in Galignani's which could be read in situ or lent out. The *Messenger* was published every day except Sunday:

> The greatest part of this Paper is dedicated to English news, the remainder to French and Continental; the Debates in the French House of Peers and Chamber of Deputies. The English news

is faithfully copied from all the London Newspapers, as well
Ministerial as Opposition. It contains the Parliamentary Debates,
Reports of Courts of Justice, Commercial and Provincial News,
Naval Intelligence, Price of Stocks and Exchange etc. etc. as well
as a short Analysis of Theatrical Criticism.

Galignani's also published a 'weekly reportery', a literary gazette
and a 'Journal of Belles-Lettres'.[56]

Galignani's quickly spotted an opening for producing guides of
its own. A travellers' guide to Switzerland was published in 1818,
translated from the German. It offered some practical tips – noting,
for instance, that the coach from Paris to Strasbourg took four
days and warning the wary that 'the inn-keepers are a very sturdy
gentry and will not readily make any reduction in their exorbitant
charges'. It advised that in rural northern France cheese and butter
were of poor quality, and cream was difficult to procure, and
recommended the visitor try a roasted leg of a chamois instead. On
the whole, however, the guide was full of buffeting generalisations,
all but useless for anyone pressed for time: 'The most economical
plan for a person who intends to remain any time in Switzerland is
to bring his own cattle with him as their keep is very moderate.'[57]

The Galignani guides were certainly not designed for ease of
use: what practical information there is immensely complicated and
detailed. Take the following section on hiring a carriage in Switzerland:

According to the last tariff, the post-masters are authorised
to demand of travellers one franc and fifty centimes for horse
an post, and sixty-five centimes for postilion and post. Every
courier, not accompanying a carriage, must have a mounted
postillion, to act as a guide. One postillion is not allowed to
conduct more than three couriers; if there are four couriers,
there must be two postilions. Carriages – as many horses
must be paid for as there are persons who go with the carriage
(without any distinction of age), either inside, outside, on the
coach-box, or behind, whether the horses be attached to it or
not. Two-wheeled carriages with poles, as well as cabriolets

with four wheels, must be conducted by a postilion, with not
less than two horses. If there be three passengers they must
have three horses and a postilion; but four horses are to be
paid for. Three passengers are to be driven with three horses,
and five are to be paid for. Postmasters are bound to attach
the third horse to two-wheeled carriages with two passengers;
but in case of an agreement made to attach but two they
can only demand half price for the horse not used. Carriages
upon four wheels, having but one passenger, with or without
trunk, vache or portmanteau, must have three horses
attached, and be driven by a postillion. Two passengers with
a vache, trunk, or portmanteau, must have three horses and a
postillion; two persons with one vache, trunk or portmanteau
between them, or with two of them, must be conducted by a
postillion, and though drawn by three horses, pay for four.[58]

It continues in this vein for another six pages. Similarly, Galignani's
later guide to Italy loses so much in translation that a tourist
turning to it for help would have found themselves thoroughly lost
and confounded. 'Italy's scenery rises far above rural beauty; it has
a claim to animation, and almost to genius,' it helpfully declares;
'one might suppose that nature, so prodigal towards Italy, placed it
in the midst of the seas in order that it might participate in all the
advantages of external commerce.'[59]

Mariana Starke maintained a gruelling schedule after the
publication of *Travels*. She travelled for several months of the year and
spent the time abroad harrying competitors such as Galignani's and
checking that pirated editions of her book were not in circulation in
continental bookshops. She died in 1838, aged seventy-six, in Milan,
en route to England following a research trip to Naples. In the year
of her death, Starke was finally eclipsed by the first in a series of
guidebooks that would dominate the British market for decades,
becoming the very symbol of British popular tourism and its quest
for what is new, old and reassuringly the same.

John Murray III, son of Mrs Starke's mentor, had seen an
opening for what he called a 'handbook' – like Starke's it would

be a combination of practical and cultural advice and although the first one was written by Murray himself, the plan was to develop a series, ranging far wider than Starke. They would be written by eminent literary figures and therefore each volume would have a companionable voice that was distinctively its own. In 1829, Murray had travelled to the Low Countries and found that there was no guidebook in existence for any of the places he particularly wanted to visit. 'The only Guides deserving the name were Ebel for Switzerland; Boyce for Belgium; and Mrs Starke for Italy.' It was rough travelling in the 1820s – and Murray wrote with some pride: 'I began my travels not only before a single railway had been begun, but while North Germany was yet ignorant of Macadam.'[60]

While in Germany, Murray began work on his handbook. 'I set to work to collect for myself all the facts, information, statistics, &c. which an English tourist would be likely to require or find useful. I travelled thus, notebook in hand.' He took large square sheets of paper which he divided into columns and 'noted down every fact as it occurred'. These were eventually sewn together into two large volumes, lettered on the spines 'H. B. Northern Germany Original Ms'.[61] On his return, Murray persuaded his father that the firm should publish a series of continental guidebooks which he would write himself. The project was codenamed, not exactly mysteriously, 'Handbook'. Murray III insisted on exhaustive research trips: not only would he make and write up preliminary journeys, but the different routes would then be further tested by friends who would report back. The books were not, he wrote, to be confined to 'plain matter of fact and practical information . . . not a mere compilation from other words, but the result of personal observation'. Descriptions were to be 'limited to the very condensed notices of the most remarkable places and to such facts only as are essential to enable a traveller in passing through a country to know what he ought to see why he ought to see it, in what manner he may see it best'.[62]

John Murray III's *Handbook for Travellers on the Continent*, finally published in 1836, carries a subtitle imposing even by Victorian guidebook standards: *Being a Guide though Holland, Belgium, Prussia and Northern Germany, and Along the Rhine, from Holland to Switzerland, Containing Descriptions of the Principal Cities, their Museums, Picture Galleries, &c.; – the Great High Roads; – and the Most Interesting and Picturesque Districts; also Directions for Travellers; and Hints for Tours with an Index Map*. It was followed later that year by his *Handbook for Travellers in Switzerland*.

It was their wide range of authors that made Murray's handbooks so companionable and gave each volume its own particular flavour. A Murray's handbook was more than a mere *vade mecum*; it was a journey with an enthusiast. Writers included the anthologist Sir Francis Palgrave on northern Italy and the hymn-writer Reverend John Mason Neale on Portugal. Although the style of the handbook was always expressive of the author, the tone had to be right – educated but accessible (though aimed squarely at readers with at least a basic education in the classics: in the 1853 guide to southern Italy, for example, all the classical authors were quoted in the original, without translation). Murray was exacting. 'What I require when I go to a foreign country,' he instructed his guide-writers,

> is what I can see here that I cannot see elsewhere, what is best worth notice & why it is worth notice. I am thankful to be told where there is a fine point of view & what are its peculiar characters & the objects which appear in it. I am equally obliged to the guide who will point out to me the interesting localities such as the spot where Mahomet passed the breach in the wall . . . & the square where the janissaries were annihilated by Hassin Pacha – I should be glad to be told a few interesting anecdotes connected with these two events, but I by no means wish to be burthened with all the details of the siege or the Reign of Sultan Mahomed . . . there is no reason in the world why a guide book should be dull & dry – although such works commonly enjoy the reputation of being so.[63]

Authors clamoured to write handbooks but Murray's standards were exacting. Trollope wanted to write a handbook on Ireland but was turned down. The Middle East expert Henry Parish (author of one for 'Travellers in the East') was criticised by Murray for bringing in too many references to contemporary politics ('The remarks directed against Russia would alone suffice to exclude our book from the Countries where that Power has rule, & therefore the impolicy of their introduction in a Guide Book must at once be obvious'[64]). Richard Ford's volume on Spain took him sixteen years to complete and he despaired of getting the tone required. 'Hand-book lingers. I have made no progress, and am tempted to give it up,' he wrote. 'I am all for the sublime and beautiful, sententious and sesquipedalian. I can't cool my style to the tone of a way-bill . . . I muddle on in my den, finding I compose every day with greater trouble.' A year later he was still at it, and complaining that the project was beneath him: 'I have been throwing pearly articles into the trough of a road-book.'[65] When it was finally published in 1847, Ford had managed to trim it down to 1,064 pages, but the first edition had to be destroyed as it was so rude about the Spanish.

Ford's deleted digressions were collected by Murray as *Gatherings from Spain*, which sold 600 copies on its first day of publication. In the *Quarterly Review*, Ford's friend George Borrow took the opportunity to add a dig both at the tourists so unlike himself – 'the fat English squire and his daughter' – and the business that handbooks were taking from the local guides with their exorbitant rates:

The various Hand-books which our friend Mr Murray has published at different times are very well known, and their merit generally recognised, we cannot say that we have made use of any of them ourselves, yet in the course of our peregrinations we have frequently heard travellers speak in terms of high encomium of their general truth and exactness, and of the immense mass of information which they contain. There is one class of people, however, who are by no means disposed to look upon these publications with a favourable eye – we mean certain gentry generally known by the name of valets de place, for whom we confess we entertain no particular affection, believing them upon the whole to be about the most worthless, heartless, and greedy set of miscreants to be found upon the whole wide continent of Europe. These gentry, we have reason to know,

look with a by no means favourable eye upon these far-famed
publications of Albemarle-street. 'They steal away our honest
bread,' said one of them the other day at Venice.[66]

Murray's handbooks with their instantly recognisable red covers were
soon indispensable. In 1850 a reviewer in *The Times* wrote in emphatic
capitals: 'Mr Murray has succeeded in identifying his countrymen all
the world over. Into every nook which an Englishman can penetrate
he carries his RED HANDBOOK. He trusts to his MURRAY as
he would trust to his razor, because it is thoroughly English and
reliable; and for his history, hotels, exchanges, scenery, for the clue
to his route and his comfort on the way, the RED HANDBOOK is
his guide, philosopher and friend.'[67]

Handbook enthusiasts wrote to Murray with suggestions or
modifications, drawing his attention to, for example, clean new
hotels or inns that may have been passed over or had sadly declined
in quality and cleanliness since publication. From the 1860s,
Murray published abridged versions, known as 'knapsack guides',
for those speeding through regions even faster than a Cook's tour.

Soon the ubiquity of a Murray's handbook made it a convenient
shorthand for the middlebrow travelling experience. Charles Lever,
the Irish novelist and consul in Spezia, took a pot-shot at the
tourists spoiling his view.

I cannot conceive of anything more frightful than the sudden
appearance of a work which should contradict everything in
the *Hand-book*, and convince English-people that John Murray
was wrong. National bankruptcy, a defeat at sea, the loss of
the colonies, might all be borne up against, but if we awoke
one morning to hear that the "Continent" was no longer the
Continent we have been accustomed to believe it, what a
terrific shock it would prove.[68]

Lever spoofed the Murrayite in *Arthur O'Leary: His Wanderings and
Ponderings in Many Lands*, his laboriously arch comic novel of 1844:

> And now, in sober seriousness, what literary fame equals John
> Murray's? What portmanteau, with two shirts and a nightcap,
> hasn't got one *Hand-book*? What Englishman issues forth
> at morn without one beneath his arm? How naturally does
> he compare the voluble statement of his valet-de-place with
> the testimony of the book. Does he not carry it with him to
> church. . .[69]

Everywhere, according to people of superior tastes, roamed British know-nothings, clutching their guidebooks like protective amulets, wandering over the continent, swallowing knowledge and experience in bite-sized but non-nutritious chunks. A Baedeker's guide to Switzerland (the German firm was Murray's chief competitor) wryly noted that the English 'give orders totally at variance with the customs of the country, and express great dissatisfaction when their wishes are not immediately complied with; others travel with a superabundance of luggage, which is often apt to embitter their enjoyment; and there is also a numerous class whose ignorance of foreign languages causes them frequent embarrassment and discomfort'.[70] These new types seemed to intrude themselves everywhere and every traveller seemed to have a misbehaving tourist in their sights. In St Peter's, newlywed Emily Birchall spotted 'one vulgar English tourist, who had seated himself, Murray in hand, on the top step of the High Altar itself'.[71]

Guidebooks became so ubiquitously the hallmark of the tourist that in real life Alfred Bishop recollected that when out on a walk in the Pyrenees, he came across a

> band of the most villainous-looking cut-throats round a camp-
> fire having their evening meal . . . Personally I felt alarmed.
> I took out the small guidebook of this tour given me in
> London and commenced picking flowers and laying them in
> the book as though botanising. I manged to remove my gold
> half-hunter watch, which I quietly slipped into the inside
> pocket of my waistcoat; also a sovereign case containing several
> pounds which I deposited in another pocket. I turned up the

collar of my coat and managed to bash in my hat and look as
poor and disreputable as I could.[72]

As tourism boomed, the social hierarchies represented by tourists
themselves seemed more on display. Increasingly, everywhere a
British tourist went there seemed to be another British tourist to
cause embarrassment. If exclusivity could no longer be defined by
experience, then other experiences had to be found that reinforced
particularity. In Naples, in 1873, the honeymooning Birchalls
thought they would avoid the crowds on Vesuvius by asking the
guide to take them to a volcanic side crater away from the main
view. 'He replied that he could shew us one, an hour's walk hence.
We decided at once to go thither, thinking it a nice unhackneyed
sort of thing to do, and rather out of the beaten track and golden
visions floated before our mind of the credit we should derive
from our discovery of the wonderful side-crater, which should
henceforth appear in all the Baedekers and Murrays.' As it turned
out the track was so miserably uncomfortable and unbeaten, even
with six porters trying to carry Emily's chaise through sliding soft
cinders, that they had to give up and head back to their hotel.[73]

Yet the handbooks were themselves keen to point out the
'boorishness' of undesirable fellow travellers, striving to separate the
Murray experience from that of the Cook's masses. In the fourteenth
edition of *Handbook for Travellers in France* (1877) there is an entire
section on 'The English Abroad' – and how to avoid them. The author
(John Murray III himself) berates those who 'through inattention,
unguardedness, wanton expenditure in some cases, niggardly parsimony
in others', bring their compatriots into disrepute. Stinginess – the sight
of well-fed tourists beating down local salesmen – was understandably
mortifying – even though John Murray himself had once been an
advocate of parsimony – foreshadowing the budgeting mania of the
dollar-a-day backpacker a century and a half later. Although early
handbooks assumed that their readers had lots of money – knapsack
readers were positively 'niggardly'.

Other, practical, guides followed the handbooks, lowering the
tone and crowding out the cultured. Travel agents often produced

their own: Henry Gaze aimed his sixpenny 'outline plans' squarely at the tighter budget. His booklets were convenient to carry and concentrated on value for money. In the 1861 *Belgium and Holland and How to See Them for Seven Guineas*, Gaze's frontispiece declares: 'A daily plan of progress, A reference to the principal routes, towns, public buildings, and noticeable places; the best modes of conveyance; the most recommendable hotels and A table of proposed expenditure', and directs the carrier to further reading as required: 'Those who desire more ample details as to the manufacturer of the knapsack or values, and side pouch or wallet, and general hints as to companionship, dress, luggage, language, sea-sickness &c. will find them in my larger Hand-books to Paris and Switzerland.' Gaze's guide to Switzerland, *How to See It for Ten Guineas* by 'One Who Has Done It', was satirised by *Punch* as 'A Week in the Moon for a Pound'.[74]

Other useful books were added to luggage already groaning with guides by the 1860s. 'Road books' dispensed for the most part with sightseeing and concentrated on the basics: food, accommodation and transport. Captain Jousiffe, in his 1840 *Road-Book for Travellers in Italy*, compiled lists of valuable addresses at every staging post and to cover every eventuality, from milliners, to banks, to corn-cutters. In 1858, Karl Baedeker's guidebooks were translated into English and rapidly overtook the sales and popularity of Murray's handbooks. Although Baedeker graciously acknowledged the inspiration of 'the most distinguished Guide-book ever published', his were different: they were all anonymous and therefore lacked the literary personality of a Murray; but they were also encyclopaedic with the strictest regard for hard fact: they did not list merely what the author considered the best hotels – they listed *all* the hotels. The avuncular sorting of wheat from chaff which made Murray's guides so reassuring was not part of the comprehensive Baedeker experience and this may reflected the growing confidence of the British traveller. In 1869, Gerald Codrington wrote home to his mother from Italy: 'I find my Murray very useful indeed; but now everybody has, instead, a book called "Baedekers", by a German of that name, it is supposed to be more correct.'[75] By 1874, Sir George Osborn was writing to

John Murray: 'I take the liberty to inform you that I was very much concerned to see how that most flagitious pirate Baedeker is flooding every nook and corner of the Continent with his guide book.'[76]

Fifty years after the publication of the first handbook, John Murray remembered testily that Baedeker had simply copied roughly translated sections from Murray's into his own guides. As a geology enthusiast as well as a stickler for accuracy, Murray was particularly incensed by a section of Baedeker's Switzerland which had lifted his own line 'the slate rocks are full of red garnets' and re-translated it back into English as 'the slate rocks are overgrown with red pomegranates'.[77] But by the end of the century, guidebooks were as ubiquitous as railway-station novelettes and there were bound to be repetitions in the information they imparted. But they had alternative uses. In 1889, Lillias Campbell Davidson in her *Hints to Lady Travellers at Home and Abroad* recommended that women railway travellers not overtax their eyes with heavy reading but suggested that a guidebook was handy if one was seated opposite a bore: they 'form a perfect library of themselves'.[78]

But to those who liked to think of themselves as true adventurers, the guidebook, with its bossy barometer of cultural value, its exclamation marks, stars and itineraries, remained the symbol of a hidebound spirit. 'I hate Baedeker a few degrees worse than Murray, so I never use either,' declared the author H. Ellen Browning in 1897. 'They always make the most beautiful places seem like items classified and ticketed in a museum, and I am Goth-like by nature as to detest museums.'[79] A decade later, the publisher Grant Richards remarked that guidebooks had no stability: they were just there to fill a gap and never made profits because of the 'lending habit': 'The average unintelligent person always borrows a guidebook when he can.'[80] The Reverend E. J. Hardy (author of the original *How to Be Happy Though Married*) thought in 1887 that guidebooks encouraged the same timid conformism in travelling as circulating libraries did to book reading in general:

Though everyone travels in these days, just as everyone reads, there are as few good travellers as there are good readers. The

people who ask at lending libraries for the very newest book only
to say 'they saw it, and liked it' are precisely those who rush to
and fro all over the earth, and return as empty as they set out . . .
Such globe-trotters neither improve themselves nor increase their
happiness. They never do anything they themselves care for, but
follow conventionalism as the best tourist's guide. They admire
by means of their Baedekers and Murrays and are 'charmed'
with the things with which they ought to be charmed. In picture
galleries, they do not look at the pictures, but read before them
out of a guide book for the sake of future conversation, a short
notice of the birth and death of this 'eminent artist'.[81]

Certainly guidebooks, with their increasingly exhaustive coverage,
can feel risk averse. Advice reached into every aspect of the
adventure of travel, inevitably rendering it less adventurous. Even
the *Railway Travellers' Handbook* felt it necessary to allay every
conceivable anxiety for even short journeys. Women should wear
sturdy veils and green spectacles for travelling. Gentlemen, it
suggested, should wear a suit, light in colour so as not to show the
dust, nor need brushing. The suit should be 'liberally furnished'
with pockets for books, newspapers, sandwiches, pocket-flasks etc.
Flannel shirts were better than linen on cotton because they were
warmer and didn't need to be changed so often, thus avoiding the
expense and inconvenience of laundering. Patent shoes and boots
were preferable to kid as they were easier to clean; a cap was better
than a hat, but if a hat must be worn a 'compressible' one (a 'gibus')
was recommended for ease of storage. Thick lambswool socks were
useful for long, cold journeys and so were strips of flannel and cork
that might be put inside shoes for extra warmth.

Guidebooks themselves are vivid chronicles of the impact of
tourism. In 1828, Galignani's had vividly warned readers of the
physical danger of crossing the Alps: 'The descent of these mountains
is uncommonly steep, and the path bordered by precipices on each
side; but if the traveller takes the precaution of sitting with his
back towards any particularly steep abyss, in the worst part of the
road, he may escape much of its horrors; and the lively songs of

the porters will scarcely fail to inspire him with confidence.'[82] In the 1892 edition of Murray's handbook to Switzerland, published ten years after the first Alpine railway was opened through the Gotthard Pass, there is an update on the speed at which modern conveniences have changed mountain life:

> The great annual influx of strangers is of the same importance as some additional branch of industry or commerce would be. It has been estimated that in 1880 there were over a thousand inns in Switzerland especially built for the use of travellers, the capital value of the buildings and their contents and sites being put at nearly 13 million pounds sterling.

The handbook noted how the Swiss had adapted themselves to British tastes in order to encourage tourism and the hotels now made a feature of serving 'the luxury of tea' and there were Anglican chaplains on tap: 'In many mountain inns, clergymen are offered free lodging with the same object, and the guests of other nations are ejected from the public sitting room while English service is performed.'[83]

The section of 'helpful foreign phrases' included in many guidebooks (though not Murray's) are an indication too of how the tourist experience is fraught with anticipated fears. The dangers in these glossaries of panic may have changed over the decades but they still constitute their own narratives of distress, disappointment and discomfort. In 1828, the English–Italian phrasebook put at the top of its list of useful phrases: 'He has hurt'; 'He bleeds'; 'Do not weep, it will soon be cured, it is but a scratch'; also 'I am ruined', 'I shall be scolded', 'I have not done my duty' and, poignantly, 'Poor little creature that I am! Where can I hide myself?'[84] Forty years later, in 1868, the popular tourist trail has been well beaten and the uses of conversation are strictly practical: 'These under-sleeves are too blue, they are not well washed'; 'I wish my hair crimped, be careful not to burn it'; 'Brush my hair. Gently, you hurt me, it is entangled.'[85] In 1874, the tourist continues to anticipate bad behaviour if not death: 'I shall demand reparation'; 'I am enraged beyond measure'; 'Stop, stop I tell you I want to alight!'; 'The carriage is near the precipice. One of the wheels is off. The axle-tree is broken'; 'It seems to me that the sheets are not clean – they have certainly been used already'; 'If fever comes on, I cannot answer for the consequence.' In 1897, Lucy James, travelling in Germany with a group, jotted down some useful phrases in the back of her diary: 'Have you any old china?'; 'Do not put my book near the fire'; 'Where can we cross the brook?' In the 1930s, in France, it was 'my wheelbarrow is broken', 'my shoes pinch' and, inevitably, 'the meat is not done'. Phrasebooks continued to tell a story of horrors into the mid-twentieth century: in the 1960s, the Letts phrasebook exhorted holidaymakers on the Italian Riviera to: 'Look out!'; 'Be quiet!'; 'Leave me alone'; 'I shall call a policeman' and 'I urgently need an ironmonger.'

Although Baedeker dominated the guidebook scene into the twentieth century, it remained a burgeoning market. Following the literary colour of a Murray's handbook, the views of guidebook authors began to spill out of their familiar boxes, beyond the confines of the asterisk or the star symbol. In the 1880s and 1890s, the Canadian novelist Grant Allen, for example, was a prodigious and influential penner of guides, covering all the major cities of Europe. Allen used the familiar formula to pour contempt on the conspicuous consumption of the wealthy habituées of Monte Carlo – a 'gambling hell' in which 'over-rich folk begot their diamond-decked women, and their clipped French poodles with gold bangles spanning their aristocratic legs. These are the spawn of land-owning, of capitalism, of military domination, of High Finance, of all the social ills that flesh is heir to.'[86] Although Allen was influenced by the philosopher Herbert Spencer's ideas about the need to develop 'self-evolution' through the practice of rigorously independent (objective) observation, his guides are didactic: he knew exactly how his readers should think about what he showed them and what they should find significant about it. His books offer no advice whatsoever on practical details, such as what to wear or where to stay. He is a pure proslytiser. 'The art of buttonholing' was how a friend described the Allen style.

For Allen, the value of sightseeing was about seeing in objects, buildings and monuments the 'material embodiments of the spirit of the age – crystallisations, as it were, in stone and bronze, in form and colour, of great popular enthusiasms'.[87] Allen's itineraries encouraged his readers to look beyond items of local interest to larger connecting themes and cross-references. In his *European Tour*, for example, he suggested that the tourist start with medieval cities, then move forward chronologically: 'You will find it best in practice to begin with what is nearest to you and your own civilisation.' He recommended setting off in the familiar surroundings of France and England,

> then go back to the Low Countries; and from the Low Countries,
> proceed to the Rhineland and so Romewards. Each country, as
> you come to it, teaches you something, and on the whole your
> progress is backward, from the known to the unknown . . . each
> step back helps to explain the steps you have already examined . . .
> you thus get in the end a more connected picture.[88]

It has always been popular among the travelling *cognoscenti* to abjure the guidebook – nothing, after all, quite so unambiguously pronounces the bearer to be passing through. Yet the ownership of a portable volume of information can be a useful substitute for slogging dutifully round a ruin under a scorching sun. Even Grant Allen's mentor Herbert Spencer, with his strong views on the value of empiricism and close observation, found the prospect of the real thing not always appealing. When Spencer joined the party of Canon Barnett (of Toynbee Hall, east London) for a tour of Egypt, he 'was much vexed by the interest shown by other visitors in the party on the tombs and temples of ancient Egypt, feeling it was much more effective and less tiring to gather the information from books'. Mrs Barnett thought it probably due to Spencer's inability 'to make the facts around him harmonise with his theories on Egypt'.[89]

'PLEASURE TRIPS DEFENDED'

By the mid-nineteenth century the press had bestowed on Thomas Cook a nickname: 'the Napoleon of Excursions'. It is a sobriquet which tells two stories: according to his admirers Thomas Cook went forth and conquered Europe; for his detractors he destroyed the very thing the tourists sought, his groups bringing with them the blandness of touristy standardisation. 'Cook's tour' became a byword for vulgarity, for swarms, hordes, masses, droves and herds. In the pages of *Punch*, these groups were variously described as 'Cook's vandals', 'Cook's hordes' and 'Cook's circus'. The rich, accustomed to having the continent to themselves, were appalled to find they often now had to share it with other *types*. 'Cook's' became representative of the sort of people who brought their small-town prejudices to foreign parts and ruined them for people with *real insight*. As one periodical journalist wrote as early as 1829: 'All sorts and conditions of his Britannic Majesty's subjects seem engaged . . . in steam-boats, omnibuses, and *acceleres*, on one common pursuit of perpetual motion; so that I verily believe that there are not in the entire parish of Cripplegate ten respectable housekeepers wholly disqualified for the traveller's club.'[90]

The sight of tourist groups even in the most inaccessible and exclusive places aroused fear of a giant and uncontrollable mass-movement about the intermingling of the classes, the exposure of the less educated to dangerous democratic ideas, and a general fraying of social edges. It was popular in the smarter journals to complain that Europe was being 'spoiled' by tourist groups, and by Cook's groups in particular.

In 1854, with characteristic dignity, Cook took on his critics in the *Excursionist*: 'To travel by train is to enjoy republican liberty and monarchical security. Railway travelling is cheap, common, safe and easy,' he wrote in 'Pleasure trips defended':

> 'But what does it amount to?' ask some, 'it neither fills the belly nor clothes the back.' Admitted; but it does infinitely more; it provides food for the mind; it contributes to the strength and enjoyment of the intellect; it helps pull men out of the mire and the corruption of old corrupt customs; it promotes a feeling of universal brotherhood; it accelerates the march of people, and virtue and love; it also contributes to the health of the body by a relaxation from toil and the . . .

of physical progress . . . A few years ago, a 'Visit to a watering
place' was a luxury beyond the reach of a toiling artisan
mechanic; his lot was to waste the midnight oil and his own
Vital Energies in pandering to the vitiated tastes of the sons
of fashion.[91]

In the same magazine there is a statement of the moral potential of
travel, how it uplifts, improves and expands the narrow confines of
provincial prejudice.

It was for the people to discover that war was a dangerous game;
a disreputable, a bad game, for any to play – that the hangman
was a bad teacher of the tender sensibilities of human nature,
and that in hanging there was crime, and no correction – that
in slavery there was no gain, but a loss of the world of men and
mind – and that to remain stationary in these times of change,
when all the world is the more, would be a crime![92]

In 1864, Charles Dickens, intrigued by the snobbery Cook's tours
engendered, sent the journalist Edmund Yates to interview the travel
agent for his periodical, *Household Words*. In Cook's Bloomsbury
office Yates found a man of simple, unshowy demeanour who seemed
blithely unconcerned, indeed proud, of the social range his tours
encompassed. Yates observed that the Cook's tours to Switzerland were
marked by two different types of person. The clients of the summer
tours, he noted, were respectably middle-class, keen sightseers
and guidebook wielders – Cook described them as 'ushers and
governesses, practical people from the provinces and representatives
of the better style of the London mercantile community'. The short
Whitsuntide break tour to Switzerland was a different matter. It was

mostly composed of very high-spirited people whose greatest
delight in life is "having a fling" and who do Paris, and rush
through France, and through Switzerland to Chamonix,
compare every place they visit with the views which formed
part of the Egyptian Hall, carry London everywhere with them

in dress, habits and conversation, and rush back, convinced
that they are great travellers.[93]

Often teetering somewhere between contempt and pride, these
caricatures of the British tourist are almost affectionate but not
quite. In reality, the 'practical people from the provinces' were also
appalled by the behaviour of what Yates called the 'roisterers'. The
railways had not eradicated social distinctions (indeed sometimes
exacerbated them) but travelling by rail jostled the classes up against
each other. 'Steam is a great leveller, not only of roads, but of social
rank,' observed the humourist Arthur Sketchley (who built an
entire writing career on jovial mockery of the lower middle class
at leisure, and then as an unofficial flag-waver for Cook's Tours) in
1870.[94] With the increasing popularity of ready-made clothes and
access to circulating library books, the outward signifiers of class
were more difficult to spot: it was disconcertingly hard to tell exactly
where a fellow passenger was positioned in the social pyramid. In
1865, George Heard, a Cook's tourist (presumably of the practical
provincial type), found himself sharing a compartment with a
man, 'who I took to be a well-to-do mechanic honeymooning with
his young wife. He was very talkative and seemed desirous to make
himself friendly. Judge my surprise, when on turning over one
of his books, I accidentally discovered his name with a prefix of
"Major". I saw my error at once and changed tactics altogether.'[95]

The stopping places of the Grand Tour, once the preserve of the
upper classes, were now available to anyone with sufficient funds to
book a trip with Cook or Gaze. In Sketchley's satire *Mrs Brown on
the Grand Tour*, the Brown family are cockneys recently come into
money. To celebrate their fortunes, the Browns decide to embark
on their own low-countries' Grand Tour and take a trip down the
Rhine. Immediately, to the hilarity of the narrator, Mrs Brown's
origins are revealed: she's a jumped-up washerwoman. 'As soon as
I know'd we was a-goin' to them forrin parts,' she says, 'I got all my
things werry nice, not to look out of the way afore forriners; and
not to take nothing but what was useful, and not spilt easy, for I'm
sure travellin' is downright ruin to your clothes.'[96]

The Browns are only one family on the long bookshelf of silly sightseeing upstarts. There is Thomas Moore's Fudge family and their hapless exploits in Paris, Thackeray's Kickleburys sailing down the Rhine, the adventures of Albert Smith's credulous ingenu Mr Ledbury and, in *Punch*, the flashy, parvenu Spangle-Lacquers, all show and no substance. Like Adolphus Crashem in *The Pickwick Papers* ('Shocking bad they build their wainscots in France'), these comic turns can't leave their commonplace opinions behind in Britain.

The depiction of the British tourist came to represent what was seen as a particular lack of real interest in the life and traditions of other countries. 'Many accusations have been made against travelling English families, touching that peculiarity of theirs in going hither and thither without an attempt to see and know the people of the countries they visit; and it is alleged, and truly alleged, that Frenchmen and Germans coming here do make efforts to come among us and see us, and learn of what like we are,' thought Trollope.[97]

Yet pretension was also mocked mercilessly. Mr Ledbury (a 'pale young gentleman' from Islington who plays the flute a little and drinks ginger beer) is typical of the non-roistering type: with his aspiration to culture, he finds foreign parts eventually are bound to disappoint. In Albert Smith's 1846 novel, *The Adventures of Mr Ledbury*, Ledbury returns to Paris and concludes he has seen it all:

Little occurred of especial notice on the road to Paris for
steamboat journeys across the channel are all alike; and when
you know one conducteur of a diligence, you are upon terms of
perfect intimacy with all, all over France; nor is there any great
diversity in the fashions of diligences. The boiled mutton and
French beans skated about the chief cabin table as usual, when the
able-bodied assembled to dine, halfway between the Chain Pier
and Dieppe Quais; the same lady of a certain age lay helpless on
deck with her head on a carpet bag, and her feet in an old cloak;
and now and then requested to be thrown overboard without
farther delay, and put out of her misery at once, as formerly.
There were apparently the very same soldiers and douaniers on
the pier at Boulogne; and the same incomprehensible soup, made

of cheese, lamp-oil, and hot water, shaken up together, awaited them; with the identical white crockery, blunt knives and wooden cruet-frames, in the Salle a manger of the ubiquitous Hotel d'Angletere, or 'de Londres' or 'de L'Europe' or whichever it was; but it was sure to be one of those.'[98]

In *Punch*, the Spangle-Lacquers are know-nothings who are always dropping names from their jaunt abroad: '"We bought that from Florence" or "when we were at Vienna" and the like speeches.'[99] Lady Helen Blackwood's 1863 satirical creation Impulsia Gushington reads the bestselling *Eothen* by Charles Kinglake and it thoroughly goes to her head: 'A delightful book! I fell asleep over it last night, and dreamt that, mounted on an ostrich, I was careering over the boundless sands of Arabia with the author by my side! . . . I gather from the book he is still unmarried . . . if so – why?'[100] The travel writer Mrs Gore even suggested that now the continent was full of clerks on their holidays, travel had lost any mystique. What was the point of travelling when every Tom, Dick and Harry was doing it and, worse, was coming home to bore everyone else with their anecdotes: 'mouthing their nothings, to our daily dismay at the London dinner-tables', she sniped. 'Who cares a fig for their exploits at Smyrna?'[101]

Many comic types are hopelessly led by their jolly but gross appetites always in search of a well-done *biftek* or, like Surtees's Jorrocks, made miserable by the unmanliness of the meat: 'Look, what stuff is here – beef boiled to rags! Well, I never, no never, saw anything like this before. Oh how I wish I was in Great Coram Street again.'[102]

The new kind of group jollification abroad was often viewed by detractors as an opportunity to demonstrate the vulgarity of the British provincial palette. Certainly food has always been a predominant feature of the holiday abroad (and increasingly so). Even Thomas Cook, in 1871, commented on 'that mysterious Scale of gluttony which so mysteriously sets in as we land in the Continent'.[103] There was also a not unnatural fear of going hungry because foreign food was either inedible or scarce. In 1767, the bookseller Samuel Paterson noticed that on Channel crossings his compatriots took precautions. 'The English of all people are the most provident upon those occasions, from a natural dread of being starved, which many of them are seized with the moment they lose sight of their native land – so that in the packets between Dover and Calais, or Ostend, it is no unusual thing to find as many fowls' tongues, pastry and liquors as would victual a ship for a month's voyage.'[104] For long carriage journeys, travellers were advised to take baskets of provisions, as there was no guarantee food would be readily available along the way.

Fears of contamination. In 1842, Mrs Dalkeith Homes reported on her overland travels to Florence that she and her companions were forced to order eggs in their shells as they were the only 'incorruptible kind of food, instead of sharing the greasy liquid and nameless ragouts which it pleased her to serve up before our companions'.[105] Softness, smothering and overcooking was a common complaint, as was the overuse of oil and garlic in Italy and France. Cuts of meat were unfamiliar and dismayingly difficult to identify. Reverend William Cole, who travelled to Paris in 1765, was appalled by the sight of the butchers' shops he saw there: 'monstrous black sausages, in great Guts of Bladders, hanging by many of their Shop windows; quantities of Sheeps' Heads boiled and partly dried in heaps on stalls'.[106] The British were used to roasting meat, but in France, where coal was expensive, they generally preferred to stew it on the hob. And for tourists used to meat in large and unapologetic quantities, the serving of varieties of little birds – thrushes, larks, lapwings and so on, with their fiddly bones – seemed a poor excuse for decent fare. The columns of the *Excursionist* in 1873 included customer feedback from a Cook's tour to Paris: and it wasn't friendly. The group had had the set menu: 'We dined at table d'hote at 6 o'clock this evening, we had soup, eels messed up, some kind of little birds, beef messed up, ices and dessert. No pudding at all.'[107]

Italian food was considered for many tourists a challenge, and macaroni had given its name in the mid-eighteenth century to an effete and dandified type with continental affectations. The custom of spreading tomato paste on flatbread, common to Naples and known as pizza, gets it first British mention in a travelogue in 1843 where it is described as a 'sort of cake made of flour, lard, eggs and garlick'.[108] Its second mention was in a 1903 *Gourmet's Guide to Europe* (the first tourist guide devoted to food travel). Lieutenant-Colonel Nathaniel Newnham Davies described it as a 'kind of Yorkshire pudding eaten either with cheese or anchovies and tomatoes flavoured with thyme'.[109]

For many tourists, the highest praise that any country's cuisine could be awarded was that it resembled the food of home. On finally arriving at Cannes, Henrietta Thornhill heaved a sigh of relief: 'They give us Capital food here, much more like our English living.'[110] Hotels tried from the beginning to adapt indigenous food to British tastes while conveying to diners the adventurous foreignness of the culinary experience. Many hoteliers were, in fact, British. Thomas Cook observed: 'Difficult to adapt a French dinner to a thoroughgoing roast-beef-and-pudding-eating Englishman . . . but many French hoteliers try.'[111]

The inexplicable foreign failure to make tea properly was a continuing trial: there are few subjects in the annals of British tourism that inspire such exasperation. Tea was both a real and symbolic consolation to the tired tourist. Tom Beswick endured 'Tea alias water boiled', on the boat to Valletta in 1840 – and was furious to be charged extra for it.[112] In Tenerife, Olivia Stone took the precaution of bringing her own tea leaves and 'requested that we might have boiling water, laying great emphasis on the boiling. It was boiled in a saucepan, and the tea made in the bottom of a coffee pot!'[113] 'Hill', the anonymous, and querulous, tourist abroad for the first time in 1867, was appalled on arrival at Boulogne to receive 'tea' that was 'simply hot water without one particcal [sic]of tea in it'. James Smith, however, was won over by café au lait enough to abandon, reluctantly, tea for his trip abroad: 'We found it so agreeable that without regret we bade adieu to Tea. I did not see Tea till I came to Geneva, and there I got Tea so trashy that I was glad to abandon all wish for it till I got across the Channel.'[114] The Quaker Catherine Braithwaite, on her first trip to the continent in 1892, with her friends the Thompsons, recorded in her diary that on arrival in their hotel in the Saxon city of Zittau, they 'got a very greasy, dirty dinner & something called tea, but what the mixture was, is yet a mystery'.[115]

Many, more experienced, tourists travelled with their own 'Etna' stoves, useful for brewing tea correctly or heating canned soup in adverse conditions.[116] In 1920, in her short story 'Tea on a Train', Katherine Mansfield described an elderly British couple, Edwardians in spirit, travelling to Menton. They reverently unpack their provisions for the journey, which included a large slice of Dundee cake that they cut with a penknife:

> 'This is the last of our precious Dundee,' said she, shaking her
> head over it, and cutting it so tenderly that it almost seemed an
> act of cannibalism.
>   'That's one thing I have learned,' said he, 'and that is never to
> come abroad without one of Buszard's Dundees.'[117]

There seemed no end to the 'types' who could be thoroughly pinned down on holiday abroad; it was as if no one could hide the truth of what they really were under the unforgiving spotlight of foreign climes. It seemed to smart observers that when abroad, a British tourist must reveal his true nature. No matter how rich or how well dressed, a coarseness, a true self, would eventually be revealed. Trollope, who wrote a series of light-hearted sketches of tourist types, saw only pathos in these glimpses: the young clerk, for example, who dreams of mountains but on finally reaching the Alps longs only for the comfortable routine of his office and his ledger; or the two ladies travelling together who cling to one another to avoid talking: 'Carry and Fanny mean to talk French boldly, but they intend to do so in railway carriages, at hotel dinners, and to the guides and waiters. No preparation is made for any attempt at social intercourse.' Or the slightly embarrassing ones who ask too loud 'in a tone of conscious superiority' questions that the poor guide cannot possibly answer.[118]

These literary caricatures reflect a wider discomfort about the extent to which the rise of popular tourism had changed the familiar class landscape. In a series of articles in the periodical *Temple Bar* in the 1880s, the journalist Charles Edwardes draws an imaginary picture of a newly built seaside hotel in a sun-bleached stretch of the Mediterranean. A motley crowd of English tourists pitches up to represent a range of class types through which Edwardes can express his mild anxiety about society on the move. The passing of an age is embodied in the only genuine aristocrat among them, a young man dying of consumption with a 'strange air of settled indifference'. There's a shy man of industry, a wealthy tycoon who drops his aitches and measures his travel experiences only by expense and distance, and a female adventurer – a rapacious man-eater of indeterminate past who does a midnight flit, leaving behind a bounced cheque. But most despicable of all, there is the type who appears to be trying to conceal his origins, the not-quite-gentleman in not-quite-placeable colourful clothes and a pith helmet. 'Is he a general on half-pay, or a retired Indian civilian?' 'No sir,' replied the manager, 'he has made money in coals.'[119]

Americans too had a particular place in the pantheon of ghastly fellow tourists. Their salient characteristics are that, like their uneducated British counterpart, they do not appreciate what they see because they do not have the 'background': they are plodders and the joy of serendipity is not open to them. Honeymooner Emily Birchall could not bear the American couple in the Birchalls' hotel in southern Italy: 'The Twains (Bates is their real name) have been for ages here in Naples, and yet had never once thought of ascending Vesuvius nor of visiting San Sebastiano, in fact we do not know of a single thing they have seen. What such people come to Italy for, it is difficult to perceive.'[120]

'Continental excursionists' were Charles Lever's favourite targets for derision. From his comfortable billet in Spezia, he knocked out furious but languid articles for *Blackwood's Magazine*, in which he prophesied that one day tourists would cover the world and ruin it. Lever viewed these groups as devaluing the real article, the one most happily epitomised by Lever and his enlightened expatriate circle. The problem for Lever was that these travellers were not staying in the box for which they were most happily fitted: the men were dreary and their wives were over-talkative. He compared tourists to the products of mass manufacturing, to those inferior British textiles that flooded the continental market and diminished the standing of Great Britain abroad. In 1865, in a particularly dyspeptic outpouring, he wrote:

> so the word English, which was once the guarantee for goodness, became the stamp of an inferior and deprecated article. So it has been with our travellers. These devil's-dust tourists have spread over Europe, injuring our credit and damaging our character. Their gross ignorance is the very smallest of their sins. It is their overbearing insolence, their purse-strong insistence, their absurd pretensions to be in a place abroad that they had never dreamed of aspiring to at home – all these claims suggesting to the mind of the foreigner that he is in the presence of very distinguished and exalted representatives of Great Britain.[121]

It was the idea of the group that seemed to irk tourism's detractors most. In his interview, Yates asked Cook: 'What was gained by remaining with the large body, and not rambling away by oneself?' But Cook believed that at least part of the pleasure of experience was experiencing it with other people. And he was also a paternalistic believer in the kindly hand on the tiller that the 'herald' provided. Although a Cook's tour had long departed by the 1860s from its temperance campaigning roots, it was still designed to uplift and distract, to open the eyes of its tourists to the larger picture. It was essentially paternalist and philanthropic. Cook replied, wrote Yates, that, 'His society and guidance were the advantages in question, he looked at me so sternly that I determined to press him with no further questions of that nature.'[122]

The commercial success of Thomas Cook saw off his critics more successfully than any verbal riposte could have done. Nonetheless, there was one occasion when he was moved to real anger. In 1875, the Prince of Wales stopped in Egypt on his way to a tour of India. The royal party was accompanied by the former Crimean War correspondent W. H. Russell, who later published an account of the trip in the form of a diary. When he was not fawning over his royal host, Russell took particular pleasure in mocking the British tourists the party encountered.

By 1875, John Mason Cook had established the company so successfully in Egypt that in 1890 the journalist G. W. Steevens remarked: 'The nominal governor is the Khedive, its real suzerain is Lord Cromer. Its nominal governor is the Sultan, its real governor is Thomas Cook.' This did not deter Russell, for whom the sight of Cook's groups presented an opportunity for some superior sneering. They were, wrote Russell, 'an aggregate of terrors'. What Russell found most contemptible about the tourists on the Nile was what he would have found contemptible about them at home: they appeared to him embarrassingly thrilled by royalty. It was so very lower-middle class, so 'worthy and respectable'. He throws up his hand in mock fear at the bourgeois rabble: 'the fear grew on us that the Cook's tourists might overhaul the flotilla'. Russell never questions his own slavish attitude towards the Prince of Wales, who appears (gratifyingly) to take no notice of him. Instead, Russell assumes the Cook's groups are unmoved by the sight of the pyramids when they might get a glimpse of the royal party:

> Mr Cook's tourists, who . . . were in full cry up the river after the Prince and Princess. Some of our companions had come from Brindisi with the British caravan, and gave accounts which did not tend to make us desire a closer acquaintance. Respectable people – worthy – intelligent – whatever you please; but all thrown off their balances by the prospect of running the Prince and Princess of Wales to earth in a pyramid, of driving them to bay in the Desert, of hunting them into the recesses of a ruin – enraptured at the idea of being able possibly to deliver an 'address' in the Temple of Karnak or of gazing at their ease on the royal couple, enclosed in their toils on the Island of Philae.[123]

Thomas Cook used the pages of the *Excursionist* to pen furious responses to both Russell and Lever, turning their snobbery back on them. The word 'toady' is a favourite Cookism – and he applied it liberally. He noted, for example, that Lever himself came from the class he excoriated in his article, that he wanted to preserve the culture and beauty available to the new traveller for the upper classes of which he himself was a hanger-on. 'Mr Lever is an Irish gentleman of the precise class to which the English clergymen, physicians, bankers, civil engineers and merchants, who honoured me by accepting my escort to Italy last year, indisputably belong,' Cook countered.

> By what right does he assume them incapable of properly enjoying and intelligently appreciating the wonders of nature, and the treasures of art, brought before them by travel? . . . It is surely a moot point whether the surroundings and moral tone of the curious little colonies of English people scattered up and down the Continent are so vastly superior to those enforced by public opinion at home, as to entitle the self-expatriated Britain to look down on us with contempt.

If Italy 'has been created for Mr Lever', he continued, 'and the social circle of which he is doubtless the literary lion, the drawing-room ornament, and the favoured jester, then have I committed a heinous crime in trespassing on his domain'. As for W. H. Russell:

> I am reluctant to think that either the Princess or your Royal Highness knew the entire contents of Dr Russell's 'Diary' as, apart from the general character of the book and its details, which I do not presume to criticise, there are in it numerous representations and statements, relating to myself and my tourists, of the most fabulous and imaginary character, the untruthfulness of which is well known to those immediately concerned . . . But I know for a certainty that many are influenced by such misrepresentations as those of Dr Russell;

many are deterred from accepting my proposals; whilst some of those who have the moral courage to encounter the jibes and sarcasm of contemptuous travellers abroad, feel it to be an annoyance thus to be marked by an inferior class of tourists. In the course of my long career in this peculiar work, I have been frequently assailed by uninformed or miss informed observers; but I never before was attached in such high quarters, under the immediate cognizance of Royalty.[124]

Note the use of 'my tourists'. It was Cook's insight that the group actually delighted in itself as a definable group. Here is the voice of a radical branch of mid-Victorian middle-class England: it doesn't pull rank, it dislikes patronage, it chafes at being left out of the pleasures and education of the elite; it is convivial and celebrates collective experience. The snobs are the ones with limitations.

Cook mentions two travelling aristocratic young men on the steamer, pointing out that although: 'amongst our party on board the steamer from Brindisi there was cordial intercourse and easy freedom, whilst these two gentlemen appeared to be disagreeably isolated, sitting in peculiar corners between midships, eating their meals alone, as though they were too timid to join the saloon parties at table d'hôte; and I believe I am right in stating that neither of them spoke to one of our party on the whole voyage'. As for Russell himself: 'We find him at Jaffa, where he meets his friend "Old Hamed" whom he engages as his dragoman to Jerusalem. Poor "helpless" soul! With all his power of language, speech and pen, he cannot travel in Palestine without the usual assistance of a dragoman; and yet forsooth he must ridicule those who avail themselves of my superintending arrangements, and the help of my good dragomans, whom I would not barter for "Old Hamed" or another other man!'[125]

Cook and his tourists triumphantly attained the upper hand. Several veterans of Cook's tours wrote to the *Excursionist* to express disgust at Russell ('dizzy with royal patronage'). According to 'A Continental Tourist':

To say that associated tours should not be allowed is,
practically, the same as saying that the great mass of the
English travelling public should not be allowed to travel on the
Continent. Such an idea is utterly preposterous. It might do
for an era of stage-coaches and heavy diligences, but it is utterly
inapplicable to a period of increasing railway enterprise . . . It is
impossible for us to travel too much abroad. We have all much
to learn. Were our artisans and skilled mechanics to see more
of continental working life, we should have fewer strikes and
fewer complaints of deficient scientific education.[126]

Thomas Cook retired in 1878, leaving John Mason to take up the reins
of the business. By the end of the century, there seemed no outpost
of the world, however remote, that didn't have a representative of
Cook's to smooth the way for the British tourist. In the late 1890s,
when the novelist Rider Haggard arrived in Beirut, the first person
to pop up was a Cook's representative: 'An emissary of the Beyrout
branch of the House of Cook arrived on board and asked us if we
had any revolvers or cigarettes. We had both. "Give them to me,"
he said, "And I'll see you through." '[127]

By the twentieth century, the Cook's tourist type is so
established and familiar in literature and satire that Evelyn Waugh,
commissioned to write a travel book while spending his honeymoon
on a cruise paid for by his publisher, both celebrated and sent up
the genre: he had to put aside his snobbery about circular tours and
pleasure cruises; for the purposes of the forthcoming book he was
one of them, a tourist of a 'new kind'.[128]

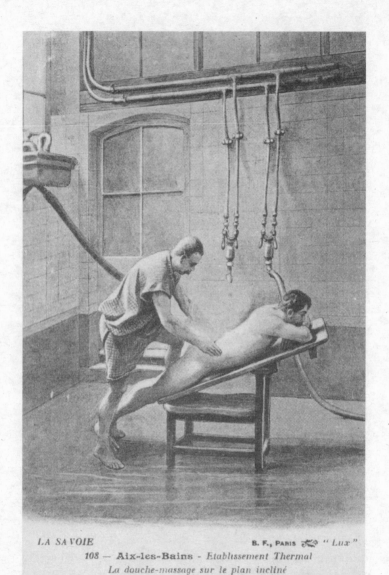

Preparing for a de-toxifying massage in the 'sulphurous and repulsive' vapour baths of Aix-les-Bains.

II

Water, Air and Movement

'KEEP MOVING!'

In 1825 the first public railway line in Britain opened between Stockton and Darlington. Its top speed was 8 miles per hour – about the same as the fastest horse-drawn stagecoach. Over the next century the new technologies of steam transport, both boat and rail, would radically change the nature of things that had once seemed fixed and certain. By 1830, steam trains could get up to 30 miles per hour and two decades later, in 1850, they were running at an average of 80 miles per hour.

The new speed was a source for many of intense anxiety about the breaking of communities and local identity and the threat of outsiders: one rural vicar worried that the coming of the railway would bring the end of 'stories'. But it established new ideas about the nature of movement, how change itself – change of scene, change of air, a jolting of old habits into new experiences – could cure both the sickness of the body and the sickness of the soul.

Early train travel was seen by some as encouraging idleness and day-tripping, flibbertigibbeting rather than moving with sturdy purpose. 'Honest travelling has been so rascally abused,' says the old hostler in Hardy's 1876 novel *The Hand of Ethelberta*. 'Tribes of nobodies tearing from one end of the country to t'other, to see the sun go down in salt water, or the moon play jack-lantern behind some rotten tower or other, that, upon my song.'[1] In 1850, the Reverend W. R. Williams, writing on 'Domestic Habits' in the *British Mother's Magazine*, argued that women 'jaunting from one locality to another' was a danger to domestic order. 'Wherever there are friends to entertain them they are sure to go. The carrier's van, the gig, the omnibus, the carriage, the railway train – every kind of road – every mode of travelling – and every species of conveyance, is pressed into the service of their roving disposition.'[2]

Others thought that the promises of travel and leisure were themselves illusory. The narrator of George Eliot's 1859 novel of rural life, *Adam Bede*, voices the concern that an increase in leisure time would only be filled with meaningless distraction, and that 'the great work of the steam-engine' would only create 'a vacuum for eager thought to rush in. Even idleness is eager now – eager for amusement; prone to excursion-trains, art museums, periodical literature and exciting novels. . .'[3] Certainly, people took to railway travel with extraordinary alacrity, and mostly with intense excitement. Anna Maria Twigg from Birmingham, travelling abroad for the first time with her family in the 1850s, described her rail ticket in her diary: 'a book of light pages, perforated, and bound in cloth, gold lettered, all very nice and knobbly. Back of the eight pages was for one stage of the journey. For instance, one would be "Newhaven to Dieppe" and another "Dieppe to Paris" and so on.'[4]

In 1840, just fifteen years after the inaugural steam train journey, 3,000 people travelled from Nottingham to Leicester in a train of sixty-seven carriages.[5] By 1858, when Dr Erasmus Wilson set out for a short trip to Cologne, the journey on the boat train to Harwich was cushioned by all sorts of purchasable new conveniences: 'Well, the passport obtained; the circular notes and letter of credit pocket-booked; the carpet bag locked; the railway wrapper buckled; and the blue canvas bag, containing the transcendent Bradshaw, travelling cap, *Times*, *Punch*, and *Black's* travelling atlas in hand; away glides the Doctor, at 8.30 p.m. on the 3rd of September, 1857, from the London Bridge terminus.'[6]

Ruskin, who as a child in the 1820s had travelled at 5 miles per hour through France and Italy with his parents in their specially designed horse-drawn carriage, was one of the loudest critics of the new speed. In 1851, in *The Stones of Venice*, he mourned the end of slow travel:

In the olden days of travelling, now to return no more, in which distance could not be vanquished without toil, but in which that toil was rewarded, partly by the power of deliberate survey of the countries through which the journey lay, and partly by the happiness of the evening hours, when from the top of the last hill he had surmounted, the traveller beheld the quiet village where he was to rest, scattered among the meadow beside its valley stream; or, from the long-hoped-for turn in the dusty perspective of the causeway, saw for the first time, the towers of some famed city, fain in the rays of sunset – hours of peaceful and thoughtful pleasure, for which the rush of the arrival in the railway stations is perhaps not always or to all men, an equivalent – in those days, I say, when there was something more to be anticipated and remembered in the first aspect of each successive halting place, than a new arrangement of glass roofing and iron girder.[7]

Ruskin had a particular loathing of trains, but others also thought that they fostered moral lassitude and idleness: with passengers required only to sit there staring out of the window, rail travel promoted the antithesis of the questing intelligence engendered by long, immersive travel. For the Ruskinites, life and culture had become as vaporous and insubstantial as steam itself. Rail travellers, wrote Ruskin, were mere 'steam-puffed tourists' who could not imagine the luxury of never being 'in a hurry'; passengers so comfortable slumped in their upholstered seats that they were seduced into sleep or indifference rather than aroused by curiosity.[8] And the more they travelled, said the critics, the more alienated from the world the new rail travellers became. The increasing popularity of reading in a train, and the resulting emergence of not only station bookstalls but a whole new genre of 'sensation' novels and periodicals, was seen by the train critics as another cause of the passengers' separation from the landscape through which they passed.

By 1862, *The Railway Traveller's Handy Book* seemed even to be encouraging this disengagement by recommending that passengers on long journeys might try passing the time by 'building castles in the air' or 'musing'. It suggested that 'the noise made by the train in its journey will accommodate itself to any tune, whether lively or sad, so that if a passenger choose to hum any of his favourite airs, he will find an accompaniment ready-made.'[9] When the writer E. F. Benson was a boy in the 1880s, however, railway travel was no longer burdened by moral anxiety about idleness: it was simply the easiest and most enjoyable form of travel. In fact, the Benson family, with their father Edmund who was Archbishop of Canterbury, saw their annual holidays in Switzerland as an opportunity to catch up on their reading. They took with them on the train a vast library:

> There were certainly half a dozen copies of Shakespeare, because of an evening after dinner we read Shakespeare aloud, each taking a character; and there was a quantity of Dickens which my mother read to us before dinner. Then each of us had some kind of holiday task except Arthur. Nellie had something about logic, and Maggie had her political economy, and I had a large Latin dictionary and a large Greek dictionary to elucidate Virgil and the *Medea* of Euripides, and Hugh had a Latin grammar and . . . everybody had a Bible and prayerbook and hymn-book. . . Then there were packs of cards for diversion, and my mother had a great medicine-chest in case of illness. Each of us had a paint-box and a 'Winsor and Newton' block.[10]

The view of rail travel as being insubstantial, or not quite 'real', remained a theme throughout the period, for many of the same reasons that going by train 200 years later often looks or seems more 'real' than going by air. Easy transportation took the adventure out of the experience. When the Brightwen family of Great Yarmouth went abroad in 1861, Hannah-Sarah noted in her diary that: 'Travelling by railroad, however convenient, extremely destroys the effect of entering a foreign town – were it not now almost impracticable I would far rather go a shorter distance by carriage than use the rail.'[11]

There were also early fears that moving at speeds of more than 30 miles per hour was injurious to physical health. There were theories that rapid movement could cause apoplexy and that the stale air that gathered in tunnels and cuttings would be harmful to weak chests. The fuss-pottish invalid Dr Augustus Granville thought that jolting could cause all sorts of ailments – and also that the insolence of railway staff might cause fits in those of a nervous disposition.[12]

But what if movement itself could actually improve health – by shaking the kaleidoscope and forcing a change in the picture outside the window? Rigid daily routines were thought to be debilitating and for centuries patients had been prescribed a change of scene as a pick-me-up. Even in the seventeenth century, Robert Burton's *Anatomy of Melancholy* had recommended lifting depressive spirits by visiting a new landscape. And in 1771, Ebeneezer Gilchrist, in *The Use of Sea Voyages*, had even argued that motion was healing. He thought that travelling by sea firmed the body's musculature by making it tense up prior to vomiting. Gilchrist thought that seasickness was actually a crucial part of any cure – a violent detox, 'a repeated friction and general kneading' of the internal organs.[13]

Violent movement was a feature of travel. The stomach-churning ghastliness of shipboard sickness was so common that even an excursionist jaunt to Gravesend could turn into a nightmare of 'blowing, and raining, and pitching, and tossing', as Dickens described it. His attempts to eat a meal belowdecks were ruined: 'The table vibrated and stated like a feverish pulse, and the very legs were convulsed – everything was shaking and jarring.'[14] On board, wrote Mary Browne in her diary in 1821: 'A great wave came over the ship, and wetted all the people at that side, who were obliged to run up higher. Mamma was so ill she looked like death. She said you might have thrown her into the sea, or done anything with her.' The whole deck, she noted, 'was covered with people lying in a heap like pigs'.[15] The Reverend Greatorex, travelling in 1878 from Shadwell to Gibraltar via Gravesend, experienced a 'terrible night. Pitching and rolling heavily. Felt seasick, so much so that I had breakfast on deck, could only take a mutton chop, potatoes and a cup of coffee . . . Felt too poorly to go below and had dinner on deck . . . the captain very kindly had my bed brought up to a cabin on deck forward where the motion of the ship was very much less.'[16]

Horse-drawn transportation along unpaved roads was bone-shakingly uncomfortable. Nona Bellairs, travelling in France in the 1850s, remembered hours of discomfort in a landau pulled by four 'lean wretched horses, tied with old ropes'. The vehicle (a landau was in fact a luxury, lightweight kind of carriage on elliptical springs) was a 'huge untidy, ill-shapen machine': 'off we go – dragging, tearing, jolting, jingling, crackling along the dusty roads'.[17] For passengers arriving at the coastal ports, the usual form of transportation was a lumbering covered stagecoach known as a diligence.

Few tourist experiences were as grindingly uncomfortable as the diligence. This behemoth of a vehicle held about sixteen passengers, moved at an average of 3 miles per hour, and instead of springs, the main body was attached by leather thongs to blocks of wood. It was divided into parts, seats in all of which were differently priced having (very) slightly different levels of comfort. Inside the front of the coach was the *coupé*, then in the middle the *intérieur* 'holding six persons and oppressively warm in summer', and behind that the *rotonde*, 'the receptacle of dust, dirt and bad company, the least desirable part of the diligence'. Cheapest of all seats was the *banquette*, which was up on the roof covered by a leather hood. But at least it afforded fresh air and a view of the countryside. For those inside the diligence there was no view at all, just the spectacle of one's miserable fellow passengers: 'It is impossible to have any idea of the grandeur of the scenery while sitting in a diligence,' wrote Charles Trollope in 1843.[18] The din was terrible. A governess, Miss W, remembered 'the outrageous noisiness of men and horses. We had 9 [horses at] once all neighing and jingling away together helter skelter up hill and down dale, and the whip snapping over their heads like a pistol.'[19] Poor Matthew Todd, stuck in the *rotonde* of a diligence in Switzerland, was in agonies. 'Kept moving on all night over rough roads, snow and ice, and very cold indeed – which I found began to affect my bowels, as it did also a French or Swiss gentleman travelling along with us, whose breath was extremely offensive, as also from the jolting of the carriage he was continually emitting voluntary posterior declamations, which made the carriage so offensive one could hardly keep one's head in for 5 minutes altogether.'[20]

Yet for many, the movement of travel, violent and unpredictable, was still seen as preferable to the soul-sapping repetitions of office work. There were concerns that the mechanical rhythms of modern urban life were the cause of sickness – both physical and spiritual. As he set off from his home in Shooters Hill, London, for his continental tour in 1831, the physician James Johnson 'turned round to take a parting look at Modern Babylon'. 'There is a condition or state of body and mind,' he continued,

> intermediate between that of sickness and health, but much
> nearer the former than the latter, to which I am unable to
> give a satisfactory name. It is daily and hourly felt by tens of
> thousands in this metropolis, and throughout the empire; but
> I do not know that it has ever been described. It is not curable
> by physic, though I apprehend that it makes much work for
> the doctors ultimately, if not for the undertakers. It is that wear
> and tear of the living machine, mental and corporeal.[21]

Nowadays, we would call what Johnson describes urban stress or environmental pressure. In the 1830s, it seemed for the first time that modern life had become a vast dislocating machine, the monotony of which drained bodies of their natural energies.

For Dr Augustus Granville in 1841, the answer was the introduction of regular holidays: but this was nearly a century before the Holidays with Pay Act first gave workers the right to a week's holiday a year.

> People who are the slaves of a certain routine are not usually
> considered to possess a high degree of working capacity and
> of health, but rather to suffer from depression of vital energy.
> This implies that the regular daily 'constitutional' is not
> enough; the daily change of air must be supplemented by a
> weekly change differing from that of every day; and to this

again should be added a half-yearly, or at least yearly, more complete change of air, such as is procured by holiday tours etc. the more thorough the change, the more fresh are mind and body maintained.[22]

Mid-nineteenth century self-help books stressed the importance of keeping on the move. There was a rapid growth in books for readers restlessly in search of the cure brought about by an alteration of perspective and unfamiliar encounters. The 1870 medical handbook *Every Man His Own Doctor* argued that even the workplace-related condition known as 'clergyman's sore throat' could be cured by a change of scene: 'This affliction calls for general treatment only. Relaxation, recreation and out-of-door life are far more efficacious than medicines, and the latter are of little use without the former. Pleasant travel or rural occupations are the necessities of such cases. Tonics must be taken in conjunction with hygienic treatment. Nutritious diet is called for.'[23] The idea was not to risk over-excitement with too much stimulation but simply to shake up routine by introducing an element of the unexpected.

The anonymous author of a long 1844 account of health-seeking went into great detail about the feelings induced by a shift out of familiar habits. 'The body has an astonishing faculty of accustoming itself even to a change, when that change preserves a certain uniformity; and this is equivalent to a diminution of the vital energy.' The sluggish, over-timetabled body was recharged by travelling.

The first beneficial influence of travelling is perceptible in the state of our corporeal feelings. If they were previously in a state of morbid acuteness, as they generally are in ill health, they are rendered less sensible. The eye, which was before annoyed by a strong light, soon becomes capable of bearing it without inconvenience; and so of hearing and the other senses. In short, morbid sensibility of the nervous system generally is obtunded, or reduced. This is brought about by more regular and free exposure to all atmospheric impressions and changes than before. . ..[24]

There were many who thought that the jolting and jerking endured in most methods of transport could be a cure for depressive ailments. For Henry Matthews, a popular chronicler of 'invalidism' (chiefly his own), there was 'nothing like the rattling of wheels to scare away blue devils'.[25] Steam travel was often described in terms of bone-juddering and organ-shaking, as if the engine was a body in convulsions. Henry Matthews, meanwhile, believed in the 'curative' qualities of shaking movement, because it might jar a patient back into an equilibrium, removing the imbalance which caused disease.

Certainly, Robert Louis Stevenson, travelling from resort to resort on the continent searching vainly for a cure for his consumption in the 1870s, found the roll of train wheels beneath him 'stimulated dull nerves into something of their old quickness and sensibility'.[26] Dr James Johnson took the view that when it came to overall wellbeing the British tourist was better off moving about than lounging in one place: he thought it suited the national character and alleviated the effects of modern living. It certainly suited the new culture of excursionism. In fact, according to Johnson, the biggest health risk to be found on a trip to the continent was what he warned was the danger of 'catching idleness from the Italians'. He had seen this happen in his youthful travels, he wrote, with young aristocrats on the Grand Tour who hung about Italy for too long doing nothing: 'This principle of inactivity', he claimed, 'was infused into the vigorous minds and bodies of Englishmen.'[27]

Such theories were, unsurprisingly, promoted by the railways. In 1862, *The Railway Traveller's Handy Book* flagged up all the many psychological advantages of a long rail journey: 'To the over-wrought brain, or the over-strained mental faculties, to the toiler who has sunk into a state of exhaustion, this rapid locomotion acts as a most agreeable fillip. Nor is this to be found alone in the journey itself; the bustle of the station, the incidents of the platform and waiting room, the chance chat in the railway carriage, all tend to arouse the faculties, and to impart to them a freshness which they lose in silent and persistent labour.'[28] For those in a really fragile mental state, however, the cure may have been worse than the disease. As one travel writer noted:

Continental travelling generally is a much more dirty and
dusty undertaking than travelling at home. The coal in general
use is of inferior quality and the engines emit dense volumes
of smoke, charged with soot and grit. To avoid this, you must
close the windows and rebreathe breathed air, possibly charged
with all sorts of horrors in the shape of microscopic organisms
left by your travelling predecessors.[29]

The author's advice was to keep handy a wet sponge with which to
douse face and hands, and an atomiser with menthol and eucalyptus
to spray into mouth and nostrils when required. There was a great
deal of advice available for invalids taking trains to watering holes
or southern climates. A particular concern was avoiding long breaks
without food, which could only damage fragile digestions. Dr
Edward Sparks in 1879 recommended packing a hamper of useful
comestibles: 'a well-cured ox-tongue is both palatable and easy to
handle, a chicken or pheasant . . . a plain cake, some grapes or pears
and a small bottle of claret or sherry and water. . .'[30]

The risk was that the excess of advice might induce an anxiety
that had the opposite effect than was intended. Henry Matthews
wondered if those of a really nervous disposition might not be
better off just staying at home:

What if a person is endowed with such exquisite sensibility
of the nervous system that the clumsy slamming of a door by
a careless footman at home or the tumbling down of a set of
fire-irons at once produce a start, a commotion and a headache
for the day. And if a lady be thrown into a fever and a state of
agitation at the sight of mere ordinary bustle – at the incessant
grinding of a carriage ploughing a gravelled road – or at the
rapid passage of objects before her – is such an individual fit to
travel by railway?[31]

James Johnson also wondered if the anxious traveller would be
better off staying put: at least at home the poor invalid will not be
'harassed by the douane, the passport, and the police – not liable to

be cheated by *vetturini*, poisoned with filth, infected with malaria, worried by beggars or murdered by bandits'.[32]

'Invalids' had once been conjoined to rest; now they were encouraged to move, restlessly in search of the medicine of new scenery. They were sometimes carried from place to place in the hope that a moving pageant of different cities and landscapes would produce a recovery. The physician Thomas Burgess was shocked in the early 1850s to see patients he considered 'positively moribund' conveyed about Florence on sightseeing tours, under the impression that they would be healed by a constant change of scene. What it really induced, he said, was psychological inertia.[33] It was not mental stimulation that created lassitude but 'mental agitation'– although agitations too often accompanied confined lives with small horizons. It was difficult to get it right; sickly wilting was tolerable but indolence was most definitely frowned upon.

Theories of the therapeutic nature of change was a major driver in the introduction of statutory bank holidays. Thomas Cook saw the break in working routine as vital. In his 1870 account of a Cook's tour, the journalist Arthur Sketchley reflected:

> No greater boon can be conferred on an overworked man, woman or child than a thorough holiday: for not only is it to be regarded in the light of a luxury, or treat, but as also an absolute necessity for all those who are busily engaged in the struggle of daily life; and how many are there who have sunk under the pressure of continued employment, whose health might have been preserved – nay, more, their lives prolonged – by timely relaxation from daily toil.'[34]

Encounters with the unexpected were also thought by many to be morally beneficial, healing irritability and sourness. Although there were those who viewed railways as promoting an unnatural mixing of social types and classes (Augustus Hare's mother used to get out at a station before her destination and travel the last part by carriage – so that her friends shouldn't know she'd been mixing with strangers), James Johnson took the opposite view and thought that conversing with fellow passengers – provided religion and politics were avoided, naturally – was 'one of the best remedies for irritability of temper'.[35]

Ruskin didn't win the battle for slow travel though his dislike of railways is in many ways a celebration of many of the pleasures sought by tourists. By the end of the nineteenth century, the movement generated by tourism was widely agreed to be beneficial in every way. It healed bodies and minds exhausted by modern life. When J. M. Dent, born in east London and at the beginning of his career as a printer and publisher, toured Europe in 1888 it was with the Toynbee Hall Travellers' Club, under the leadership of Toynbee founder Canon Barnett. Each member of the group (mostly clerks and schoolteachers) paid £13. For Dent, this introduction to new sights and places was balm. 'I was worn out physically with the reconstruction of my business,' he wrote, 'and as I was able to have my wife's sister at home, in desperation I took the opportunity to travel, and so began to widen my vision of the world and to develop any sense of the beautiful I had in me.'[36]

Though it was steam technology, courtesy of the railways, that took Dent to Europe, it was his encounter with pristine landscape and pre-industrial culture that helped heal him in ways that Ruskin would have appreciated. Of Florence, Dent later wrote: 'I can never make anyone understand what the revelation of this wondrous old world meant to me. Here was a city built before industrialism had destroyed the spirit of beauty, where man had lived by something other than money-making, luxury and power.' And of the Alps: 'Try and imagine what it was to come out of the East End of London (I had no knowledge of the West at the time, nor have I had much since) with its sordid grime, to cross the Alps in glorious sunshine with every mountain pinnacle draped in robes of Crystalline snow!' He felt cured of the diseases of money-making and materialism.

> Remember that I had come out of years of sordid struggle for
> a living, with hardly time to lift my eyes to the dull grey skies
> of the weary toilsome streets, of all the suffering and almost
> hopeless fight for dear life, and suddenly was lifted up and

carried by a magic carpet into a wealth of beauty and wonder
not to be surpassed in all the world.[37]

Many travellers believed that the people of 'abroad' had the right
work–life balance: there was poverty in other European countries
but it was seen to be old-fashioned rural poverty rather than the
ghastly, grinding, soul-destroying impoverishment of the mills and
factories of industrial Britain. Dr James Johnson reflected that the
British paid a heavy spiritual price for all their material comforts:

Is that which makes our fields better cultivated, our houses
better furnished, our villas more numerous, our cottons and
our cutlery better manufactured, our machinery more effective,
our merchants more rich, and our taxes more heavy than in
France or Italy. If we compare the Boulevards, the cafes, the
jardins, the promenades of Paris, with corresponding situations
in and around the British Metropolis, we shall be forced to
acknowledge that it is nearly "all work and no play" with John
Bull during six days of the week, and vice versa with his Gallic
neighbours.[38]

But paradoxically, it was routines, schedules and the reassuring
familiarity of order that became the most striking feature left
behind by the British holidaymaker. Leisure had been timetabled.
Ruskin had warned that speed of travel made a delightful exposure
to new experience swiftly become banal. Before long, those seeking
a truly new landscape had to go further afield to find it. The
wintering places of the Mediterranean became such established
British colonies that invalid visitors needed never to worry about
meeting anyone or anything strange or even foreign. In 1882, in the
Pall Mall Gazette, 'an exasperated exile' in Cannes complained that
'scorching, sun-baked boulevards' suitable for the perambulation
of invalid carriages had been built over the 'once shady, olive
tree lined lanes'.[39] From Nice, in 1857, Margaret Maria Brewster
wrote that 'there are English libraries, and English newspapers,
and English shops – billiard rooms – good table d'hôtes, plenty of

society – quantities of gossip, and a great deal of "dressiness"'. In Menton (in Italian, Mentone), the most popular southern resort for the British, there was a grocer called Willoughby who supplied familiar provisions to wintering consumptives. As Thackeray observed in *Vanity Fair*: 'Those who know the English colonies abroad know that we carry with us our pride, pills, prejudices, Harvey-sauces, cayenne-peppers, and other wares, making a little Britain wherever we settle down.'⁴⁰ The change of scene had very quickly begun to look like the home from home.

'A SORT OF END OF THE WORLD'

Sweating, steaming, freezing, steaming: there is no end to the curative uses of water. Mineral waters have been drunk in Europe since Roman times and before; sweating houses and hot vapour baths originated in Turkey and have been popular in western Europe since the seventeenth century; sea-bathing has been a health-giving exercise in Britain since the early nineteenth century.

The traditional water cure, or hydropathy as it came to be known, was further refined by nineteenth-century developments in technology. The Victorian culture of 'invalidism', much of it apparently provoked by the effects of industrial capitalism and rich food, expanded in the new hydro-technologies of the water cure. Fretful and ailing, the urban Victorian middle class took its mysterious digestive maladies to the once small spa towns that had become hugely profitable hydros. There they were purged by hot steam or torrents of cold water. In England, the mineral springs at Malvern and Buxton had been popular water-cure destinations since the eighteenth century, but in the nineteenth they burgeoned even more as centres dedicated to punitive and expensive treatments. It was cheaper to stay in Britain for a water treatment, but it was less cosmopolitan. In 1851, the pseudonymous 'A Moist Man' in his account of 'Three Weeks in Wet Sheets' described a stay at Malvern. Moist Man's ailments were typical: the anxious rumblings of sedentary office life, of 'bile, dyspepsia and nervousness' caused by 'confinement, by working too hard or eating too much'.[41] Taking the waters became associated not only with the restoration of health but with the moral lassitude which had so often led to ill-health in the first place. It led to watering holes being associated with seediness and undesirables. The spa promoter Dr Granville, whose books did much to encourage the water-cure trend, described Cheltenham in 1841 as populated by a transitory range of twilight people such as spinsters, Methodists, teetotallers, 'modish fribblers, male and female coquettes'. Without drive or purpose, they were 'those whose whole life is spent in devising one day how they shall spend the next day with as much enjoyment and as little expense as possible'.[42]

The surgeon Frederick Harrington Brett thought that the only cure for modern excesses was a dose of extreme hygiene: 'In a high degree of civilisation and luxury, in the turmoil of a busy city, people cannot or will not submit to a systematic discipline of Hygiene, which they are somewhat obliged to undergo at spas and watering-places, or at an hydropathic establishment.'[43] Plain water, clear and straight from the spring, was thought to be the antidote to the diseases of urban prosperity – boredom, nerves, stress, anxiety, gluttony and overindulgence in stimulants. Taking the waters therefore put the sufferer right both physically and morally. In Malvern, for example, Moist Man admits to needing help to recover from some 'backsliding as concerns excesses of the table', and finds that an hour in soaking wet sheets put him back on track: 'A packing or two has restored plasticity of mind and in the tranquilising repose of the Sitz bath, I have meditated on the blessings of temperance.'[44]

Water cures, with their diets and uncomfortable ministrations, thrived throughout the nineteenth century; the continent mushroomed with new spas and ancient watering holes expanded into cold-comfort wellness retreats. 'A gang of crafty adventurers thrive richly upon English credulity, and chuckle in their sleeve at English stupidity,' wrote a 'medical practitioner' who was the author of *Quacks and Quackery*, in 1844. He raged against the claims of what was now termed 'hydropathy', noting that traditional medicine had for centuries employed the cold affusion and the sweating bath, but by the 1840s, self-described hydropathists ascribed to these 'a universal remedial power'. Every small region of Europe was keen to capitalise on their own mineral springs and geysers. The tiny duchy of Nassau in Germany had 146 springs, many of which had been in use since Roman times – and all of which were quickly developed for the tourist in search of a punitive rest cure. By 1844, there were said to be more than 500 English residents permanently in the old spa town of Wiesbaden in Hesse. In 1802, in the brief pause in Anglo-French hostilities afforded by the Treaty of Amiens, it was said that Josephine Bonaparte was refused entry to the Belgian town of Spa, and told 'Madam, Spa is an entirely English town, that's all I can say.'[45] Spa had an English hunt and a factory dedicated to the manufacture of English-style buttons.

By 1893, France had 392 spas and 96 seaside health resorts. Over a century, tiny villages had ballooned into crowded tourist centres with large hotels, serious medical and spa facilities and bath-chair access. A visitor to the Bohemian spa of Marienbad noted that it was 'as if I had found myself in the North American forests where a town is built in three years'.[46] In the haste to capitalise on spa tourism, locals were often evicted or re-employed as colourful attractions. In many places, including Wiesbaden, to preserve the clean lines of the new spa aesthetic, all smelly or unsightly traditional crafts, working animals and labouring people were spirited away or concealed.

Continental spas became prosperous bubbles, their economies underpinned by residential tourism and, increasingly, gambling. 'The Rhine is the highway to the German health resorts,' observed the barrister and journalist Alexander Innes Shand, looking back at his time there in the 1840s and 1850s, 'which have enriched so many natives and ruined so many foreigners.'[47] Casinos in Germany were often run by entrepreneurial French who had crossed the Rhine after gambling was banned in France in the 1830s.

Shand looked back with typical nostalgia at the 'primitive' gaming tables once to be found at Spa where you could lose 'fabulous sums when taking a course of the springs for gout or dyspepsia'.[48] The physician Sir Erasmus Wilson (celebrated author of *Healthy Skin and Hair*), however, who visited Spa, Hamburg and Wiesbaden in 1857, was appalled by the goings-on: 'The atmosphere of the gaming rooms is always detestable, and the people grouped around the gaming tables equally so.' Particularly loathsome to Wilson were the female gamblers 'hot and eager', and the sight of the 'greedy and glittering heaps' of 'white crowns and shining napoleons'. At newly fashionable Baden-Baden he found that the new residents 'degrade the innocence of rural life by gambling'. Wilson shuddered to read in his guidebook that 'the gaming rooms are open from eleven in the morning to eleven at night'.[49]

The new spas catered for all material desires and also supported substantial industries for manufacturing soaps, lozenges, powders, salts, tooth powders and barley sugars. Their rapid development led to new planning laws and local tax structures that in turn encouraged the hotel industry, the promotion of luxury shops and the construction of desirable residential apartments. There were shops, coffee houses, and stores piled high with luxury goods. Open-air exercise was encouraged. A spa sojourn appealed to the healing power of nature but carefully expunged any hint of wildness: there were parks, flowerbeds, tree-lined boulevards, and the burbling source of the original spring was usually carefully contained within a surrounding frame of slip-free platforms. At Carlsbad, according to Dr Granville, visiting in 1837, there was no end of delights: 'concerts, balls, ventriloquists, jugglers, Tyrolean minstrels, rope dancers and fire eaters'.[50] At Schwalbach, according to Erasmus Wilson, there was a colonnade and series of bazaars in which stalls sold souvenirs, 'pretty trifles in bohemian glass; carvings in horn, wood and ivory; jewellery; prints and books; and [tales of] children's bravery'. In Baden-Baden, an English newspaper called the *Morning Paper for Sophisticated Classes* reported on just-arrived grandees and all the gossip. In 1830, when the spa had received 10,300 visitors (in 1800, it had had just 390), the paper surveyed the scene with satisfaction:

Among the eight to ten thousand strangers who visit Baden-Baden every year, there are barely two thousand really using the baths. Elegant houses equipped with magnificent appointments and conveniences, party grounds, brilliant soirees, concerts, balls, restaurants which compared to those in Paris, and innovations which came up one after another. In areas where before lonely strollers or harmonious groups were walking, one now meets luxurious carriages and horses, fine hired buggies, elegant equestrians of both sexes, some riding very valuable horses, and some on donkeys, which are especially chosen for children and timid ladies. This too, is characteristic of the changes in the community – that the number of children and women usually surpasses that of the men, giving the spa life an attractive diversity.[51]

But with the spa days broken by nothing but treatments, meals and shopping, life in a spa town, especially a small one, could also be mind-numbingly dull. Despite the trinkets, invalid Edwin Lee thought Schwalbach offered 'few resources for mental amusement'.[52] At Wildblad in the Black Forest (popular with gout sufferers), Alexander Shand found that although the tables were heaving with delicious food, and there was a crashing oompah band that awoke the sufferer 'at unholy hours', 'the system was boring to extinction, for after the early bath you were ordered to go back to the blankets, and above all things to avoid reading or thought'.[53]

There were bespoke treatments for every conceivable affliction, with physicians on hand claiming every specialism. There were bone doctors, worm doctors, wind and water doctors. Large claims were loudly made for amazing recoveries from life-threatening diseases – and at Wiesbaden, the houses were hung, as if they were votive offerings, with the crutches of invalids who had been cured by immersion in the naturally boiling springs. But the most effective cure for the nameless stress-related diseases of modern life seems to have been a combination of luxurious self-indulgence and punitive self-privation. Treatments on offer included radioactive mud, sweat grottoes, *salles de pulvérisation*, gas injections and percussion douches. Dr Granville sampled the offerings in a number of German spas: 'The modes of applying the water vary greatly; they include baths of all descriptions, lavements, douches, moistened bands, moistened blankets wholly to envelop the patient, frictions with moistened cloths.'[54]

The key treatments were purgative. Bowel afflictions were agonisingly common, as were liver problems, gout, scrofula and corpulence. As Dr Glanville understatedly put it: 'Constipation will occasionally tease a patient at the Spas.' According to *Quacks and Quackery* every hydropathic treatment on offer was in the end simply an emetic, a violent laxative to rid the body of the results of toxic gluttony. The experience of the vapour baths, which were debilitatingly hot, was described by one traveller as producing 'profuse perspiration without inducing subsequent debility',[55] and by another, who spent an hour in the 'sulphurous and repulsive' Bain de l'Empereur in Aix-les-Bains, as 'like bricking up a nun alive in the walls of a convent'.[56] Inhaling noxious brimstone was supposed to help bronchial and pulmonary problems.

Sir Erasmus Wilson thought the health of skin was greatly improved by immersion in bubbles. He relished the 'pearly whiteness' of his skin under the green water at Aix-Les-Bains: 'an eruption of glittering pearls'.[57] At Wildblad, there was an outdoor variation whereby a patient lay on wooden planks over a stream while a 'million tickling, tremulous bubbles came up from the sandy bottom and burst around him'. Dr Granville found this experience rapturous: 'It partakes of tranquillity and exhilaration; of the ecstatic state of a devotee blended with the repose of an opium eater.'[58] Frederick Harrington Brett, however, undergoing his own researches in the bubbly mineral spring spas of Tuscany, found the bubbles produced headaches and warned that 'in nervous subjects may occasion considerable excitement'.[59] A cold cure was just as the name suggests: 'The temperature varied greatly but it was very rarely warm or even tepid' was how the medical journal *The Lancet* circumspectly described the freezing waters at Graeffenberg. Icy douches were either set up in special shower houses (men and women separately of course) or simply involved the patient standing naked in a cabin situated below a fast, gushing mountain torrent.

Cold water was bracing but hot water could be positively terrifying. When, in 1834, Sir Francis Head tried the Koch-Brunnen (boiling spring) at Wiesbaden, he 'stood before this enormous cauldron, with eyes staring at the volume of steam which was arising from it . . . I could not help feeling a sort of unpleasant sensation similar to what I had experienced on the edges of Etna and Vesuvius.'[60] Mary Eyre attempted the slow boiling treatment of a Russian vapour bath in Bagnères-de-Bigorre: 'Now you begin to understand the sensations of a lobster in a pot.'[61] Another patient described a vapour bath as 'close as in a coffin, hot as in an oven, roasting, burning, fuming, I endured it till the luxury of a profuse transpiration changed pain into pleasure'.[62]

At many spas, including Marienbad in Bohemia, there were gas baths where the patient sat in an enclosed tub into which warm or cold gas was piped from below; one or two even had specialist gas baths for eyes and ears where gas was injected via a small quill. Sand and earth cures, known as 'arenation', were popular for the relief of stiff joints and according to Dr Thomas Linn, who tried them out in 1894: 'Covering the body with sand is a very old form of treatment . . . The patient is put in a hollow scooped out of the sand, and has a layer of damp, hot sand thrown over him while he is exposed to the sun. It causes free sudation, and stimulates the skin.' Boiling mud baths, good for the skin, were available at nearby Franzenbad. Dr Linn tried these out too:

> The mud-bath is a variety of this treatment. The mud of rivers (such as the Dax, in France) and of hot springs in other places, is put into baths, and hot steam turned into it. The patient lies in the liquid mud, and after a certain number of minutes steps into a plain water bath, or is douched with clear water to take off the mud. The idea of these baths is that the mud contains the deposit of the waters, which ought to be the strongest part of the mineral constituents.[63]

Full immersion was particularly revolting, what with all the bodies already in there. The communal dipping pools were often described as soupy, resembling chicken broth, mulligatawny or Palestine (thick, milky, made with artichokes) soup; at Wiesbaden, for example, the water looked like a 'thick yellow soup' or 'treacle pot'.[64] At Langen-Schwalbach, the waters were coloured so red with iron oxide that the drying gowns of invalids that festooned the village were stained deep ochre from the waist down; even the local snails were bright orange. An unbroken film on the water's surface was taken in some spas to be happy proof that you were the first one in. Wiesbaden, though fashionable, seems to have inspired some particularly horrible memories in spa-goers. One survivor of immersion there remembered that a 'white, thick, dirty, greasy scum, exactly resembling what would be on broth, covered the top of the bath.'[65] In Aix, Erasmus Wilson saw 'a thin pellicle of calcareous matter which floats on the surface of the water, and the soup-looking colour and fragrance of the water itself as I stepped into it'; a fellow bather 'could hardly be persuaded that one of my patients had not been in before her and left his skin behind him'.[66]

Patients in mineral water establishments were generally enjoined to drink from twelve to thirty glasses of water a day. According to reports, the taste ranged from bearable to disgusting; a Baden patient in 1844 likened it to 'the washings of a gun barrel with a dash of rotten eggs'.[67] The smell was generally due not to sulphur but to 'Badeschleim' (bath slime) – a kind of vegeto-animal matter that covered the base of the hot springs and left a dark sediment in the glass. At Wiesbaden, the thick scum on top of the water was called 'cream' and opinions were divided as to whether it was 'vegeto or animal in origin'. Perhaps to distract from the unpleasantness of these thoughts, the drinking of the waters was often presented as a ritual – sometimes attended by healing nymphs: at Aachen, in Westphalia, the women behind the water counter were given the title of 'water maidens' while in Carlsbad (now Karlovy-Vary), in Bohemia, the daily glass came courtesy of girls dressed in green robes and bearing four-foot sticks with cupholders into which each patient solemnly inserted their beaker. Francis Head found the sight of the morning water queue for the taps and spigots at Wiesbaden 'melancholy beyond endurance. At the rate of about a mile and a half an hour, I observed several hundred quiet people crawling through and fretting away that narrow portion of their existence which lay between one glass of cold iron water and another.'[68]

And no amount of nymphs could conceal the fact that not only did most gassy mineral waters taste horrible but sometimes they actually made the drinker ill. At Carlsbad, drinkers were even advised to wipe their teeth with stale bread or sage leaves to remove mineral encrustation. Dr Granville warned: 'Most of the waters contain a quantity of free carbonic gas. Some patients cannot bear the action of this gas on their nerves, if the quantity be considerable. They become giddy, flush a great deal, have a congestion of blood in the head and feel altogether uncomfortable.' The doctor recommended gulping it down as quickly as possible and adding cream of tartar to make an effective laxative.[69] Then there was the question of how to mitigate the attacks of burps and rumbles that were a common side-effect of the water drinking ritual. Dr Granville thought the water should be gulped down in one shot, Frederick Harrington Brett recommended sipping slowly in stages, with a few minutes between each gulp to let the gases settle – and Dr James Johnson suggested 'cheerful conversation' between glugs – presumably to distract from the taste.[70] Poor Francis Head found that he was even punished for his enjoyment of the local Nassau apricots by the fact that 'whenever raw fruit and mineral water unexpectedly meet each other in the human stomach, a sort of bubble-and-squeak contest invariably takes place'.[71]

When bottles of local mineral water started to be exported abroad the magic spell of regional particularity was broken. At the tiny *brunnen* of Nieder-Selters in Hesse, the locals had in the mid-eighteenth century spotted a commercial opportunity and begun bottling their own fizzy spring water. Known as 'Seltzer water,' it was exported in large quantities (in 1787, reportedly a million bottles a year) to soothe indigestion. When he visited the village in 1840, Francis Head was dazzled by the spectacular efficiency of the bottling plant ('I stood in utter amazement'), which covered eight acres: 'The moment I entered the great gate of the enclosure . . . so strange a scene presented itself suddenly to my view, that my first impression was, I had discovered a new world inhabited by stone bottles.' The bottles were filled at the rate of about seventy per minute from a small well roughly five feet square. They were then left overnight un-stoppered and the next day a water officer from the court of the Duke of Nassau inspected the crates, checking each bottle for holes or cracks.[72]

Purists of course disapproved. Dr Frederick Harrington Brett thought that mineral water was only truly effective as a cure if it was drunk in the landscape from which it originated: 'Artificial mineral waters are not so beneficial when used by patients who never quit their homes.'[73] And Dr Granville, on a visit to a hydropathist in Brighton, was horrified that imported bottled water was drunk there with no regard to the mystical properties of sequence, origin or quantity: 'A lady who had some years before been in my care in London was in the act of drinking the Theresianbrunen of Carlsbad and the Pyrmont together; while a relative of hers applied her glass successively to the spouts of Kissingen, Ems and Pullna.'[74]

A number of towns promoted their treatments as traditional remedies, spas having been sites of health-giving pilgrimage since ancient times. At Aix-les-Bains, one could have one's kidneys massaged under hot sulphur water by masseurs whose skills, according to Thomas Linn, had been passed down to them 'parent to child for generations'. Naturally, wellness gurus, promoted as emerging, like the springs themselves, from primeval founts of local wisdom, abounded in the world of water cures. Among the most celebrated was the parish priest at Bad Wörishoven in Bavaria, Father Sebastian Kneipp. In 1850, Kneipp claimed to have cured his own tuberculosis through a wholefood diet and highly specific applications of cold water. He particularly advocated an early morning barefoot stride through wet grass. The Kneipp method also involved splashing the thighs or the ankles with alternating hot and cold water, footbaths and regular applications of damp hay. Thomas Linn visited Bad Wörishoven in the early 1890s and was impressed by Father Kneipp:

> In this age of neurasthenia and chronic nervous affections, treatment by water is of vast importance . . . and while his methods are of the crudest they meet with the success that

hydrotherapy always does. He has two new ideas – one is to dress after taking a bath without wiping the skin, or else to get into bed so, and the second is to walk barefooted in wet grass, or even snow.[75]

The most celebrated hydropathy guru was Victor Preissnitz, a peasant farmer from Graeffenberg in Austrian Silesia, whose 'Nature Cure' was made famous in Britain by the writings of Captain Richard Claridge. In 1799, when Preissnitz was born, Graeffenberg was a hamlet of thirty houses. Preissnitz claimed to have cured himself of broken ribs that would otherwise have made him a lifetime invalid and he acquired a reputation for apparently miraculous healing through a strict vegetarian diet, fourteen glasses of water a day and a 'friction cure', a regime of hot and cold baths followed by a thorough rub down with scratchy towels. Rheumatic Captain Claridge, who went to Graeffenberg in 1842 to investigate the rumours of Preissnitz's success, reported that the 'Nature Cure' had healed a child with scrofula, a soldier with a hernia and several more patients with rheumatism; an eighty-seven-year-old gout sufferer had thrown away his crutches and was mountaineering like a young man. Claridge asked Preissnitz to help him: 'The first thing he did was to request me to strip and go into the large cold-bath, where I remained two or three minutes.' This was followed, at four in the morning, by being folded into a large blanket under which he sweated for an hour. The servants then brought a pair of straw shoes and helped him into another cold bath for three minutes. Then he dressed and walked till breakfast, which comprised milk, bread, butter and strawberries. The rest of the day was divided between sitz baths and foot baths. He retired to bed with his legs and feet bound in cold wet bandages. After a week of this, Claridge said he was entirely restored to health, having seen 'the total departure of my rheumatism'. On leaving Graeffenberg, he walked a thousand miles without a twinge. 'I enjoyed more robust health than I had ever done before.'[76]

Preissnitz's personal simplicity and frugality, his apparent lack of interest in profit or fame, were key to his appeal. After a society of hydrophiles was formed in Vienna for the purpose of propagating information about Preissnitz's cure, Graeffenberg was overwhelmed with visitors and devotees, and the entire population was soon employed in the service of the Nature Cure. In 1829, forty-five foreigners had made the trek to Graeffenberg; in 1832, it was 118; 1836, 469; and by 1840, when nearly 2,000 foreigners descended, the Preissnitz 'mania' had reached such a height that the local restaurants ran out of wine and were reduced to selling the very water that was available in the spring. Claridge's claims as to the effectiveness of the Nature Cure were responsible for a boom in hydrotherapy among the British, but the journal of the medical profession, *The Lancet*, was sceptical. In 1843, in a review of Claridge's book, the paper took issue with the quasi-religious devotion with which Preissnitz's methods were viewed by his admirers (or 'disciples' as they were known). It scoffed at the 'illustrious' crowned heads all queuing up to be treated by a 'Silesian peasant'. Claridge presented him as an illiterate sage, an 'idiot savant': 'I fancy that if asked where the liver was situated, he would be at a loss to say; but that he can cure the liver complaint there is not the slightest doubt.'[77] But for the author of the *Lancet* article, although conceding that Preissnitz showed a 'rare sagacity, a determined will and an acute judgement', the absence of scientific evidence was damning.

Many health tourists went to spas (then as now) simply to be saved from themselves and their own appetites. Obesity – or corpulence as the Victorians commonly referred to it – was among the commonest reasons a patient might seek a rest or water cure. The corpulent tended to regard their girth as an illness which needed expert treatment, though Francis Head thought it all boiled down to greed and sloth: 'I must say I never see a fashionable physician mysteriously counting the pulse of a plethoric patient . . . but I feel a desire to exclaim, "Why not tell the poor gentleman at once – Sir – you've eaten too much, you've drunk too much, and you've not taken exercise enough".'[78] At Homburg, noted one visitor, 'powerful iron waters were beginning to attract hosts of over-eaten diners-out'.

Weight loss was beginning to be a subject for serious scientific study and in the 1870s, the naturalist and hygienist Gustav Jaeger was among those to advocate for extreme changes in clothing as well as diet. Jaeger swore by undergarments made only from animal fibres such as wool rather than plant fibres like cotton. (Father Kneipp, on the other hand, advised only underwear made of coarse linen.) Jaeger's 'woollen system' was a kind of ever-present form of friction cure, designed to promote 'cutaneous evaporation . . . and gently to titillate and rub the skin' in order to bring the blood up and to 'assist, instead of hindering, the self-cleansing process of the skin which consists in the shedding of the outer cuticle'.[79] Jaeger maintained that wearing only wool, buttoned to the neck and with no tie, had reduced his waist size from 42 inches to 34.

Diets for weight reduction and easing overtaxed digestions were often rigorous, though advice seems to have varied widely, depending on the ideas of the establishment and the range of the patient's other symptoms. The most important aspect of any healthy diet seems to have been to avoid any overstimulation or excitement of the digestive organs. As is so often the case with diets, there seemed to be one for every taste. In Vichy, for example, salad was banned for being too acid-inducing but wine and cheese were encouraged. Although many physicians recommended masses of seasonal vegetables, Father Kneipp thought vegetables were fattening, instead prescribing tisanes of boiled wormwood and St John's wort. A patient who was told by his doctor in London that pickles were good for him, as were claret and lemonade, and two sugar plums every night, was dismayed on arrival at the French spa of Aix-la-Chappelle to be told that all these delicacies were strictly forbidden. In his hydropathy guide, Dr Granville made a list of the foods that patients could freely eat and those they should avoid. Barley water was recommended, as was coffee, milk of almonds, milk, asparagus, white bread, beef, carp and cucumber (but only stewed), eggs, hare, pike, oatmeal, pigeon, peas, strawberries and venison. On the strictly forbidden list were: apples, anchovies, cheese, carrots, herrings, onions, pears, parsley, salmon, sausages, radishes, quinces, turnips and truffles. At Graeffenberg in 1842, Dr James Freeman's encounter with the Preissnitz dietary regime ('At Graeffenberg, the force of hunger suffers no obstacle!') was dispiriting:

> He recommends as wholesome the fare of the poor. At his table is supplied pickled cucumbers, melted butter in its oily form and greasy German gravies. He prohibits tea, coffee, spices and aromatics . . . There were shapeless dumplings, made of scraps of bread left at table and soaked in the skimmings of the pot liquor and squeezed into lumps.[80]

Alcohol was for the most part prohibited for those on a diet but thankfully the rules could usually be bent. Harrington found, for example, that 'mild ale, sherry and water, or porter may be allowed with dinner, or if these prove too exciting, a glass of Rhenish wine, or of pale ale'.[81] Port, widely considered the cause of gout, was not generally encouraged – but sherry was thought to be a suitable alternative.

Specialist diets were available for every kind of ailment. The 'grape diet' was popular for catarrh and haemorrhoids and the 'milk and whey diet' (which according to Thomas Linn had been in use effectively by doctors in Appenzall since 1750) was commonly prescribed for liver, kidney and skin problems, and for the correct function of the mucous glands. Both, of course, acted as laxatives. Poor Dostoevsky, suffering from constipation at Ems in 1875, wrote to his wife: 'I am to eat more acid things and take vinegar with salad . . . and to eat meat with fat. I am also to drink red wine, either from France or the local wine.'[82]

For the lucky spa-goer who was not on a restricted diet, the larger resorts offered culinary temptations on a grand scale. Sir Francis found the food at Wiesbaden so plentiful and delicious that it enhanced the company he kept. 'I own I felt that in the scene around me there existed quite as much refreshment and food for the mind as for the body.'[83]

By 1903, Nathaniel Newnham Davies, author of the first foodies' tourist guide, was sickened by the ostentatious and self-indulgent food faddiness that went with a water cure. What a joyless way it was to spend a holiday. 'Probably ten Englishmen go to Carlsbad for their livers' sakes for every one who goes to Vienna to be amused.' In Carlsbad, he observed:

> In the morning, after the disagreeable necessity of drinking three or more glassfuls of the hot water, every man and every lady spends a half hour deciding where to breakfast and what kind of roll and what kind of ham that they shall eat. The bakers' shops are crowded by people picking over the special rusk or the special roll they prefer – and these are carried off in little pink bags.[84]

Alexander Shand cannot have been alone in finding that food relieved boredom. 'Meals became the milestones of the dragging days and no doubt the effect of the waters was neutralised.'[85]

In these self-contained, enclosed and artificial worlds, the genuinely ill mingled with the bored, the hypochondriacal, gamblers and drifters. 'Nothing seems to me more singular among all the singular tastes and practices of our world than the fashion which brings miserable sufferers, anxious invalids and gay fashionables, or restless pleasure-seekers, congregated together at what is termed a watering place,' wrote one observer.[86] A visitor to the French spa town of Pau called it 'a sort of end of the world'.[87]

To those who were not enamoured of spa-hopping, it was the nervy invalidism of the company that was dispiriting. In the 1830s, in Carlsbad, Dr Granville found only 'despondent, dejected, misanthropic, fidgety, pusillanimous, irritable' types. Descriptions of spa visits are often tinged with a terrible, fly-blown melancholy and an awakening to mortality. Dr James Johnson captured the feeling in his sighting of a group on board the steamer from Folkestone: 'pallid beauties from Portman Square, with their anxious mammas, bound to Ems and Schwalbach in hopes of transmitting their lilies into roses, by exchanging the midnight waltz for the "mittag" meal and fiery port for the sparkling wein-brunnen – faded belles and shattered beaux, of certain and uncertain ages, repairing to Schlangenbad for satin surfaces and renewal of youth'.[88]

But as spa towns and culture expanded, so did a clientele, which formed its own stateless elite. The atmosphere of the fashionable continental spas, with their transient, washed-up, diverse populations, and their reputation for loucheness and for behaviour outside rules and conventions, had a potent appeal for many. At Baden, for example, Shand thought the cure far less interesting than the pleasure of the casino and the exciting freedom from convention: 'I daresay the Baden waters are good for something, though I never came across any friend who drank them . . . but what I liked about Baden was the double life you could lead.'[89] What made the spas attractive to many residents was their feeling of both subversion and transgression: Alexander Shand, looking back in 1903 at the 'harmless vices' of his youth, regretted the passing of a 'golden age of cosmopolitanism' and its replacement by spa-trippers who 'even when dissipated are comparatively dull'. He thrilled in old age, to his recollections of 'gay toilettes and bright faces, rouged or au naturel, illuminated by constellations of coloured lamps'.[90] Shand recalled the occasion in Wiesbaden when a young Dutch officer shot himself after losing at the card table: the body was immediately removed by the manager to the lavatory 'by way of marking his resentment of this ungentlemanly outrage'.[91] Ah . . . 'It was all very wrong,' sighed Shand, 'but we must remember that we owe a debt of gratitude to the gamblers who wantonly and foolishly flung their money away. They bequeathed us the buildings and pleasure-grounds which are now somewhat grudgingly kept up by municipalities.' Baden, so fashionable in its mid-Victorian heyday, was excitingly naughty in a thoroughly socially acceptable way – 'respectability and rascality were inextricably confounded'.[92]

The British hydro never acquired the borderland glamour of its continental counterpart. Even its scandals were of the earnest variety: it had the 'respectability' but not quite the 'rascality'. The British continued to find continental spas enticing but Europeans turned their noses up at the delights of Smedley or Leamington. Erasmus Wilson thought this simply demonstrated the foreigner's corrupted spirit: 'In England a purer taste inclines us to an almost arcadian simplicity of enjoyment, our donkeys, our pic-nics, our broad hats, and our Margate slippers.' But alas the Germans could not be persuaded by the arcadian pleasures of donkeys and picnics, and by 1911, one in every hundred patients taking the waters in Europe was British, while only one in every thousand in Britain was European.[93]

In Britain, hydropathy came gradually to be seen by the medical establishment with scepticism, more in line with the views of the author of *Quacks and Quackery* who thought that hydropaths should be viewed as on a par with 'shampooers, tooth-scrapers, toe-trimmers . . . mesmero-phrenologists and other highly mischievous absurdists'.[94] And the British hydro tended to be more spartan. One traveller returning from a continental spa thought he'd try out a vapour bath on his return to Britain and found the experience disappointing. He was cramped and squeezed into a machine with mackintosh curtains, then steamed and heated. On emergence, he was ignominiously wrapped not in a clean hot sheet but in a 'disgusting' woollen blanket.

But like all places which are destinations but never quite homes, the spa town enjoyed its own community of the homeless, and remained reassuringly familiar. In fact, one spa town is very similar to another, its inhabitants held in parenthesis until the time of their release. Thomas Linn disliked the sameness of it all – 'the inevitable casino with the usual music' – but for others this was the appeal. When the author of the *Hot Water Cure* returned to his favourite spa, Aix-les-Bains, after a year, he was delighted to report that some of his 'old cronies' were still there. As for the rest, the spa sojourn had inevitably lost the shine of either invigoration or dissipation: 'Crutches are cheap,' he noted, and 'more than half the old set are gone home rejoicing'.[95]

'LUNGS AND ANEMONES'

To be 'ordered south' was the standard prescription for almost all sufferers of ailments of the lungs. 'Sensible individuals', wrote William Chambers in 1870 of his preferred wintering destination, the French Riviera, 'leave and return to England with the swallows; by which not unpleasant contrivance they spin out their lives, if not ninety, still to something considerably beyond what, to all appearance, was to be their allotted plan.'[96] Thomas More Madden, author of *Change of Climate*, estimated in 1860 that the number of British by then wintering on the Mediterranean every year (taking into account retinues of nurses, companions and relatives) would have been about 16,000. People rarely travelled alone: Lord Londesborough, heading off for warmer climes in Malta in 1863, took with him a relatively small team of three: 'my impedimenta' he wrote, consisted of a wife, a maid and a valet.[97] Other entourages numbered many more.

The Victorians were not the first to find the curative properties in air – though, as the skies above British cities became darkened with industrial smog, clean air became an obsession. When Tobias Smollett went with his family to the southern Mediterranean in 1763, he kept a personal weather diary, noting that the 'the air, being dry, pure, heavy and elastic must be agreeable to the constitution of those who labour under disorders arising from weak nerves, obstructed perspiration, relaxed fibres, a viscidity of lymph and a languid circulation'.[98] The Smolletts settled for the winter at Nice, which Tobias judged just right for a 'moist, phlegmatic constitution such as mine'.[99] The humid, dense sea air was charged with salts, sulphur and bitumen and several observers of the time had noticed that there seemed to be fewer cases of consumption among those who lived by the sea than inland.

Health-conscious weather-watchers viewed changes of temperature in anxious detail. Climates were graded as to their specific active properties. Tonic climates were exhilarating and uppish; relaxing ones were sedative and calming. Tonic was good for the digestive and nervous systems. The pulmonary tuberculosis, or wasting disease, from which so many Victorians suffered was considered 'essentially a disease of debility and malnutrition': it needed the bracing stimulation of 'tonic climates'. At a time when a diagnosis of tuberculosis meant a painful, early death, the promise of the revitalising effects of warm air was understandably attractive. 'Even at the present day, consumptive invalids are hired away from these islands to the shores of the Mediterranean or elsewhere, with an unbroken faith in, or rather blind credulity, in the talismanic efficacy of foreign climates,' observed Dr Thomas Burgess in 1852.[100] No wonder that the devotion to change of air had about it the feeling of religious observance. Gustav Jaeger, the eccentric health guru, thought there should be institutions, perhaps even churches, to ensure that everyone had the chance to remove from one climate to another every year, 'similar to that which was formerly provided by pilgrimages'.[101]

In the nineteenth century, one of the chief advocates of the effects of tonic climate was Dr James Henry Bennet, whose book *Winter and Spring on the Shores of the Mediterranean* sold widely on its publication in 1861. Dr Bennet had taken up residence in a small fishing village in the south of France called Menton, on the Franco-Italian border, the climate of which he thought ideal for 'uplifting' degenerative diseases. Bennet's book established Menton (in Italian, Mentone) as the pre-eminent destination for those in search of a tonic booster. By 1870, when Bennet updated the introduction to his book, he described a bustling tourist health spot:

> Now it has become a well-known and frequented winter resort, with a score of hotels, three times that number of villas, and a mixed foreign winter population of above fifteen hundred. Many of the winter visitors are invalids in search of health, but by far the larger proportion are mere sun-worshippers, who have left the north to bask in the southern sunshine, or travellers to or from Italy, glad to rest for a time under the lemon and olive clad hills of lovely Mentone.[102]

By the 1880s, Menton had an English church, English shops and English pastimes on tap for winter residents. In his guide to healthy resorts of the Mediterranean, Dr Thomas Linn listed the diseases for which the town's climate would be most beneficial: 'laryngeal disease, bronchitis &c and skin diseases. Scrofula, chronic gouty and rheumatic affections in those who like warmth and a quiet, indolent life.'[103]

The tonic breezes of the southern Mediterranean were a magnet for those escaping cold, wet British winters. The most popular stretch of coast was soon established as the Franco-Italian riviera between Hyères and Genoa, though resorts went in and out of fashion rapidly. Algiers, for example, was known for a while by British visitors as the 'Torquay of Africa'.[104] Egypt was considered more widely appealing than Algiers, though it was not thought as comfortable as Menton. The 'invalid memoirist' R. H. Otter, fretfully searching for uplifting air, stayed for a spell in Egypt but found the dust whipped up by donkeys, walkers and drivers in Cairo 'one of the most irritating and poisonous compounds that can well be imagined'.[105]

Everyone sniffed the air expectantly, and most people concluded that the air was almost always better away from home. Robert and Elizabeth Browning, who lived in Florence, went to hilly Lucca after a 'summer of blots, vexations, anxieties'.[106] Expectations ran high: change of air was not just bracing, it was a stimulant. It could even be mind-altering and mood-enhancing. Margaret Maria Brewster, daughter of the physicist Sir David Brewster, was an air connoisseur. In 1857, she reported that in the Mediterranean resort of Nice, 'the air is the most curious air that ever anybody inhaled, and I should think unfavourable for keeping the peace. It is both exciting and depressing – instead of coming in refreshed and soothed, one has a longing to box the ears of all one's friends, and to cry for an hour after doing it.'[107] Moving on to Cannes, she found that 'the climate seems to me a very strange one – the air is wonderfully strengthening and exhilarating; it seems as if at every inhalation one were drinking champagne! Indeed it is necessary to leave off all the stimulants that in England are considered necessary. As yet I have found it rather too exciting.'[108]

Robert Louis Stevenson spent a winter in Menton that coincided with Dr Bennet's residence there. Sent south in November 1873 for the incipient consumption that would eventually kill him, he wrote to his mother from the Hotel du Pavillon from which he could see newly built villas 'shelf after shelf, behind each other'. 'Nevertheless,' he told her,

the hills, I am glad to say, are unaltered . . . the sea makes the same noise in the shingle; and the lemon and orange gardens

still discharge in the still air their fresh perfume; and the people
have still brown comely faces; and the Pharmacie Gros still
dispenses English medicines; and the invalids (eheu!) still sit
on the promenade and trifle with their fingers in the fringes of
shawls and wrappers; and the shop of Pascal Amarante still, in
its present bright consummate flower of aggrandisement and
new paint, offers everything that it has entered into people's
hearts to wish for in the idleness of a sanatorium.[109]

The search for air coincided with the rise of popular tourism. The
opening of the Suez Canal in 1869 had brought the prospect of
international travel within reach of the ordinary tourist. Thomas
Cook himself took a round-the-world trip in 1872 (finding
unlimited potential for spreading the temperance message) and on
his return the grand circular tour became a mainstay of the Cook's
packaged holiday. Charles Nottage, who in the 1880s suffered from
a persistent chest complaint, went all over the world in search of
the right air – including Australia and the Sandwich Islands. He
pooh-poohed Menton's claims for air pre-eminence:

> Menton, as everyone knows, is the favourite place for invalids.
> I have only stayed there for a short time on two or three occasions,
> and have invariably found it depressing and enervating. There are
> two climates available. That of the East Bay is the warmer, and
> those living on this spot and sheltered from the Mistral. Those
> who choose the west side of the town find a climate some degrees
> colder, but are less tempted to commit suicide.[110]

R. H. Otter was another restless air faddist. Advised to go abroad
by his doctor 'because of threatening mischief in the lungs',[111] Otter
didn't limit his search to Europe: he went to Australia, Algeria and
the Cape of Good Hope. In fact, just about the only place he did
not go to was Palermo in Sicily – but only because he had heard it
was no good for livers.

Disease was a present danger for all travellers, and bad-air
places were thick with disease. Rome, for example, was swirling

with invisible and fatal gases. Before the 1890s, when malaria was discovered to be transmitted by mosquito bites, Richard Colt Hoare wrote that he lost a 'worthy friend and companion' to 'mal'aria', otherwise known as 'bad air'. It is, he writes,

> supposed to originate from the effect of the sun on the wide extent of marshy and uncultivated ground with which the district between Velletri and Terracina abounds. The density of the atmosphere encourages somnolence; and sleep frequently proves fatal. It is therefore highly advisable not to attempt the journey from Rome to Naples until the frost has purified the air; and the precaution in all places liable to mal'aria, of not going out after sunset, is highly prudent.[112]

Mosquitoes had always been viewed with horror. Mrs Beeton, in her 1861 *Book of Household Management*, suggested rubbing the body all over with olive oil or eau de cologne as an insect deterrent. Another travellers' tip was an all-over ointment made from a mixture of butter and turpentine. One of the poor Miss Wilsons wrote: 'flies and fleas which exceed everything one can imagine in Rome'.[113] And Susan Horner reported that in low-lying Pisa in 1861, her parents were so badly bitten by mosquitoes that their faces 'were quite disfigured'. They used rags soaked in rosewater on the bites.[114]

Medical climatology was a serious business and big business, with many health tours undertaken under the strict guidance of a physician. Temperatures graded with minute difference were prescribed by experts, and opinions on the subject are often puzzling. Take the ever-popular town of Pau, in the foothills of the French Pyrenees: the climate guiders couldn't make up their mind on the precise nature of Pau's air, although most seem to have found it calming rather than exciting. Linn thought it

> scarcely a fitting winter resort as it has a tolerably severe winter. On the other hand it has none of the sudden transmissions from cold to heat like Nice, and it is not windy. The climate is sedative and humid. The altitude is 660 feet. The mean temp is 42 F for the

winter. There are 119 wet days. The atmosphere is still, and during the season much more rain falls than on the Mediterranean.[115]

Also writing in the late 1850s, the pseudonymous John Wittiterley found 'a soft climate' there – 'a sort of warm Ventnor or Penzance – a sort of cool Madeira. The heavy soft air common to them all, seems to be very soothing to many consumptive patients.'[116] Pau became, like Menton, a hub of wintering British visitors who were then catered for by the townspeople in all the comforts and accoutrements of home. But air fashions changed and, thirty years later, Isaac Burney Yeo, author of an 1890 climate guide, wrote that Pau was 'cold, variable, damp and dreary'.[117] And R. H. Otter was so seriously disappointed by Pau's air that he said he'd rather have stayed at home.

The writer C. Home Douglas, who, like Nottage, roamed anxiously all over the world feeling for every shade of climate, air and atmosphere, spoke scathingly of the tendency to self-diagnosis among amateur climate curists: 'I remember an invalid lady who had been to morning church one Sunday . . . and had taken a very un-invalid dejeuner thereafter, came home from afternoon church with a headache, and no appetite for dinner; which two facts she accounted for, quite to her own satisfaction, by the presence of "an intoxicating lightness in the air of this place".'[118]

Tuberculosis, known popularly as consumption, was the cause in Britain of over 60,000 deaths a year in the 1840s and 50,000 in the 1850s. Sir James Clark, Queen Victoria's physician, was among many medical advocates of a change of air for lung disease. Clark (who had been the poet Keats's physician) had travelled in 1818 to France and Italy with a consumptive patient and his ensuing observations on the effects of climate had been influential. The restless search for a new air forced a re-examination of the conditions in which tuberculosis had arisen. The chief advantages of the tonic climate cure were due to the rest and recuperation made possible by gentle warmth unavailable in a British winter. But was it the air itself that cured or the rest made possible by the temperature? 'Cold, damp weather is, in short, the great enemy to health,' wrote the physician William Chambers, who had gone to Menton reluctantly.

Without undervaluing the comforts of an English fireside,
when frost dims the window-pane with its beautiful
efflorescence, I am on the whole disposed to think that health
is best secured by a reasonable amount of outdoor exercise in
the sunshine; but that enjoyment is unfortunately denied on
anything like a salutary scale to those who are enfeebled by
pulmonary or bronchial affections or by advancing years, in
any part of the British islands.[119]

Naturally, however, congregations of people made fresh air less
fresh. The railway, constructed between Marseilles and Ventimiglia
between 1858 and 1872, brought more visitors and prosperity to
the Riviera, but put more pressure on the shaky infrastructure of
rapidly expanding small villages. Cannes pioneers who disapproved
of all the new tourists spoiling the air were less than enchanted
at the arrival of the railway in the town in 1863 and even less so
when they found that the line was to go through the grounds of
their villas. (Under pressure from residents, it was later rerouted
at a cost of £20,000.) Resident medic Dr Edward Sparks advised
that people of means taking villas in the Riviera for a long stay
(much more economical than a hotel – 'wine and beer are nearly
always extras, and the prices charged for them are often exorbitant')
should check the drainage, the water supply, the aspect and the
elevation.[120] Stuffy public rooms, noxious fumes and the stench of
sewage were intensified in warm weather; sanitation was inadequate,
draughts were legion and heating erratic. Sparks warned that for
invalids, visiting even the public dining room could be dangerous.
'Especially in the evening, persons must leave their warm rooms
and go through chilly passages, and up and down draughty
staircases to reach the dining room; and on leaving it, matters are
still worse, owing to the excessive heat caused by the gas and the
want of proper ventilation which makes the contrast between the
temp[erature] of the room and of the passages still more marked.'[121]
Tourists expected modern heating and new-fangled devices that
often made the problem worse. The introduction, for example,
of gas heating into hotels 'does more to render the breathing air

hot and unwholesome than all other bad influences put together', wrote Sparks.[122]

New villas proliferated year by year, their inhabitants retreating further into the hills to escape the stink in the town. Dr Bennet suggested that villa-winterers in Menton check first that these rented dwellings had a decent modern cesspool with a manure pump. He noted that before the introduction of pumps, the pits had to be laboriously emptied with ladles, a process that took two days every month; the sludgy contents were put into small casks which were then emptied into the sea or simply poured all over the garden.[123] Yet, a decade later, in 1882, 'an exasperated exile' reported to the *Pall Mall Gazette* that his retirement in Cannes was still ruined by 'defective drainage and the foul smells that overpower the scent of the orange blossom'. The author noted the irony that 'disease is rife in many of the so-called health resorts along this favoured coast'. Visitors, he reported, were still heading for the hills and the main sewer of the town 'still empties itself into the harbour and its contents are still washed back to break in inky waves under the windows of the villas that skirt the bay'.[124]

Drinking water was dangerous, as it was at the time in most of Britain. John Leland Maquay, a banker who had settled in Florence, noted in his journal in June 1839, when the Italian sun was beating down, that a friend had come to stay with them from Britain and hadn't heeded the warnings: 'Poor Barker's wife died of drinking cold water, inflammation and constipation.'[125] The only alternative to unboiled water was generally alcohol. According to Samuel Butler: 'When the water of a place is bad, it is safest to drink none that has not been filtered through either the berry of a grape or else a tub of malt, the safest way to keep hydrated: these are the most reliable filters yet invented.'[126] It wasn't until the invention of sterilising tablets and water purifiers (known as Lyster Bags) for military purposes during the First World War that the problem of drinking water in over-crowded holiday resorts was at least partly overcome.

The popularity of miasma theory – that diseases were spread by odours – made the search for efficient sanitation even more pressing. In Cannes: 'Foul smells pervade the whole atmosphere, and the usual results follow. Typhoid fever is rife in every quarter . . . everyone who travels knows that fever in one form or other is never out of nearly all the hotels on the Riviera.' The residents of the villas, with their stinking cesspools and their inadequate ventilation, were not protected and fever would often run rife through a whole family in the hills.[127] 'Constipation is the great bugbear of the travelling public,' wrote Dr Stewart Tidey in 1899; he put it down to the excessive dryness of continental air combined with the impossibility of drinking the water in sufficient quantities.[128]

The ailing expats exiled in these floating communities led lives of often stultifying boredom. Robert Louis Stevenson was ordered to rest in Menton 'at a distance from all causes of mental agitation', but he found it so agonisingly dull that it made him more agitated. In Cannes, 'all the talk was of lungs and anemones', wrote someone who had wintered there in the 1860s.[129]

Invalids were warned of the dangers of too much confinement and routine but also of too much exertion. Dissipation was an ever-present danger, but then so was lassitude; resting was applauded but indolence was frowned on. Dr Bennet may well have written 'a winter passed at Menton is a drama, a little epitome of life',[130] but many there went quietly mad with the tedium.

Out of season was even worse. Home Douglas spent an unfashionable summer on the French Riviera:

Half closed are the shops; opening only now and then fitfully during the day. You call at the post office, in the hope that letters or papers may force you into action; but the bureau, like things in general, is shut, not to be open till some hour which seems as far off as a month hence in more stirring times. It is impossible to walk or drive in the heat of the sun. sitting in the hotel from the plague of flies seems equally so.[131]

On the island of Madeira, a popular spot for British consumptives, an American visitor was struck with melancholy at the sight of all the 'pale hectic girls, and young men, struggling vainly against decay'. She was assured, she said, that 'consumptive patients at Madeira lose in the charm of the scenery and under the influence of the climate, a sense of their danger, and the preciousness of their existence; that their spirits become raised, and that at the last they quietly sink to eternal rest with their sketch-books in their hands, and hopeful smiles upon their lips – I doubt it.'[132]

As the century progressed and the healthy air of the south came to seem overcrowded, *pulmonaires* began to look to the high-altitude Alps for pristine tonic air. Dr Bennet, advocate-in-chief for the warm winter (though not for the warm fug of an indoor stove in all weathers: a 'pernicious' British habit), noted that from the mid-nineteenth century onwards, the mood was shifting in favour of a cold blast, for 'freezing patients instead of roasting them'.[133]

The first mountain health resorts initially attracted a heartier, less fashionable crowd than the hydro-spas or the wintering resorts. Alexander Shand deplored the lack of glamour in a Swiss resort near Zermatt: 'The matrons knitted and the men smoked; the girls, who mostly wore spectacles, went botanising with green cases strapped to their square shoulders.'[134] Enthusiasts for the effect of mountain air on damaged lungs often spoke in awestruck tones of being close to God and of the toughening effects of forcing the body to work in adverse conditions.

The *Guidebook to Davos*, written in the 1880s when the mountain village had become an established health destination, describes how the resort 'demands qualities the very opposite of the resigned sentimentalism in which too frequently the phthisical [tubercular] youth or maiden was encouraged. Here is no place for weak or despairing resignation; here you are not pusillanimously helped to die, but are required to enter into a hard struggle for life.'[135] When the climate-bibber Isaac Burney Yeo asked the question 'sea or mountain air?' in 1890, he concluded, from his experience of writing about climate both warm and cold, that the revivifying properties of mountain air were too heady, too stimulating, for most consumptives. 'Those who suffer from great muscular debility as well as general exhaustion, and who need absolute or almost absolute repose, are unsuited for mountain climates. Such climates are too rigorous, too changeful, too exciting; and the persons to whom I now allude, when they find themselves in the cold, rarefied, exciting mountain air, feel out of place and become chilled, depressed, and dyspeptic.' Suitable candidates for a cold weather cure included those suffering from nervous exhaustion and overwork, who would thrive in the 'bracing atmosphere and the soothing effect of the quiet and stillness of high mountains, and the absence of the human crowd'.[136]

In the mountains it was nature unmitigated. Humans vanished from these altitudes during winter and there were few 'colourful peasants' and quaint villages to admire: up there in the sharp, white cold of the high Alps many said they felt it was like being with the gods. The influential writer and mountaineer Leslie Stephen said of the Alps that in the winter 'the whole region becomes part of the dreamland . . . the very daylight has an unreal glow . . . the pulse of the mountains is beating low . . . the peaks are in a state of suspended animation'.[137] Most important for some change-of-air seekers was what they sensed was the climate's *energy*: the cold seemed to kick-start recovery in debilitated bodies. In 1870, *Cook's Excursionist* magazine hailed 'the wonderful active influence of Alpine air'. Note the word 'active': for bodies that could barely walk without breathlessness, the air itself seemed to breathe new life.[138]

The idea of actually seeking out cold temperatures would have once seemed perverse; now it was fashionable. But it was the German-Swiss physician Alexander Spengler who promoted the healing properties of mountain air. In 1853, Spengler visited Davos, then a remote and roadless collection of crude wooden chalets, and noticed that the inhabitants, despite a poor diet, seemed surprisingly healthy. There were virtually no cases of scrofula or similar conditions and unusually few of pulmonary tuberculosis. Spengler attributed this to Davos's particular climate, which as well as cold in the winter was also unusually dry in the summer months. Spengler's first 'cure station' was established in 1855 and by the 1860s, British tuberculosis sufferers were making their way to the mountains. Conditions were rugged: in the early days the sick were put up in haylofts in the nearby settlement of St Moritz, which expanded rapidly to accommodate them; in only five years there were several hotels built there. In 1869, the cure station at Davos admitted 150 patients and ten years later 700.

The promotional literature for Davos in this period suggests that the air in the mountains not only cured disease but had a vital quality that its most ardent advocates said felt almost divine. According to the Davos guidebook of 1880, written when the clinic was well established: 'The effect of a residence at Davos cannot be overrated. The hollow chest fills out, narrow shoulders expand, the pale cheek or hectic bloom is replaced by the clear brown and red of robust health, and a year or two in this valley not only rescues the doomed from an early grave, but gives them the strength and vitality necessary for a career in life.'[139] It was this bracing quality which had impressed Dr James Johnson, thirty years before, when he was hiking with a group in Switzerland. He had been amazed by the effect that the combination of hard exercise and cold mountain air had on his companions: 'The descent on the Martigny side was the hardest day's labour I ever endured in my life – yet there were three or four invalids with us, whose lives were scarcely worth a year's purchase when they left England, and who went through this laborious, and somewhat hazardous descent, sliding, tumbling and rolling over rocks and through mud, without the slightest ultimate injury.'[140] Even R. H. Otter conceded that following a spell in St Moritz his 'gastric organs had never been better'.[141]

The writer A. J. Symonds arrived in Davos in the summer of 1877, very weak and not expected to live longer than a few months. He had collapsed with a tubercular haemorrhage and been advised immediately to leave Britain for a more congenial climate. He found that Dr Spengler's cold cure, which he said was 'very simple', seemed to work:

> After a minute personal examination of the ordinary kind, your physician tells you to give up medicines, and to sit warmly clothed in the sun as long as it is shining, to eat as much as possible, to drink a fair quantity of Valtellina wine, and not

to take any exercise. He comes at first to see you every day, and soon forms a more definite opinion of your capacity and constitution, then, little by little, he allows you to walk; at first upon the level, next up-hill, until daily walks begin to occupy four or five hours. The one thing relied upon is air. To inhale the maximum quantity of the pure mountain air, and to imbibe the maximum quantity of the keen mountain sunlight is the sine qua non. Everything else – milk drinking, douches, baths, friction, counter-irritant applications, and so forth, is subsidiary.[142]

Symonds found his health improving so vigorously that he decided to settle permanently in Davos, building a home there.

Symonds's presence in Davos added to its attractions for the British. The doctor in Davos during this period, Dr Carl Rüedi, was a popular figure whose excellent English and experience working in the United States (Dr Rüedi had learned his particularly nasal, colloquial, racy English full of frontier idioms, in Colorado) made him much trusted by British patients.

When, three years later, in 1880, Robert Louis Stevenson arrived in Davos, he too was in a state of exhaustion, nearing collapse. He had tried the warm air of the Riviera, both tonic and relaxing, and the bitter clarity of cold mountain air was now his last chance. He came bearing a letter of introduction to Symonds from the critic Edmund Gosse, and was accompanied by his wife, Frances, his stepson Lloyd, and his Skye terrier. William Lockett, the British consul in Davos, years later recalled Stevenson's stay there: 'One knew at once, recalled a fellow guest, that he was, in Davosian parlance, "lungy" – more "lungy" even than the majority.'[143] In Stevenson's day, wrote Lockett, only the very worst 'lungy' cases tried the open-air rest cure. 'In summer especially they would stroll in the pine woods above the resort and sit up there for hours or swing in hammocks between the trees.'[144] Dr Rüedi put Stevenson on a diet of red meat, lots of wine and milk, no cigarettes, and no more than three hours of work a day; Stevenson, in turn, gave the doctor one of his books, dedicating it to 'the good genius of the English in his frosty mountains'.[145] He left after only six of his prescribed eighteen months at Davos, unable to bear the silence and isolation any longer: the mountains, he found, had a 'prison-like effect on the imagination ... a mountain valley, an Alpine winter and an invalid's weakness make up among them a prison of the most effective kind'. It was not that it was not beautiful but 'that there was always the same narrow-scaled, monotonous, monstrous scenery to look at'.[146]

By 1912, when Lockett was writing his memoir, Davos had expanded to become 'one of the foremost health resorts of the world'. Care, he wrote, was now taken to present an image of cleanliness, order and overall efficiency: it was a thoroughly modern sanitorium. 'There are almost no bath chairs to be met with. Almost everybody in the street looks plump and bronzed – because the bad cases are not allowed out. If it were not for the invalids doing the rest cures on balconies, you would never guess you were in a health resort.'[147]

Behind the scenes, however, the number of visitors and the hasty and unregulated erection of new buildings was putting pressure on drains and resources. A local doctor called for action, pointing out that when a small Alpine village with a small population and few dwellings became a town, unless care was taken to improve basic sanitation, the result would be disastrous. He suggested that while waiting for adequate drainage systems to be put in place, hotels should be encouraged to keep their windows open and their rooms fully aired.

Isaac Burney Yeo was among those who felt that the health-giving white clarity of the mountain air was threatened by its popularity. He warned that Davos's ruin would be as speedy as its rise. 'The breath of many hundreds of consumptive patients aggregated at close quarters' had, he wrote, caused a cloudy and unhealthy haze to hang over the valley.[148]

At the Leaning Tower of Pisa, a tourist captures a moment to take home with her.

III

The Ocean in a Seashell

It would have been almost unthinkable for a nineteenth-century tourist to travel abroad without notebooks, pens and sketching materials. In *Little Dorrit*, Dickens described the highlights of the grand continental tour as humming with thousands of sketchers and scribblers: 'While the waters of Venice and the ruins of Rome were sunning themselves for the pleasure of the Dorrit family, and were daily being sketched out of all earthly proportion, lineament and likeness, by travelling pencils innumerable. . .'.[1]

For many diarists, the observations they jotted down are simply the barest facts, but their lack of adornment is in itself evocative. The anonymous journal-keeper, for example, who went on tour in the Low Countries in 1827, confines himself for the main part to the baldest chronicle of expenses and accommodation, but in pencil on the front page of his book in the almost unreadable, bone-shaken scrawl, are the words 'written a good deal when in the act of travelling on a Diligence'. For a moment, the reader feels acutely the miserable jolting of that vast leviathan, wending its way along unpaved roads at 3 miles per hour.[2]

At the end of the eighteenth century, printed, pocket-sized little almanacks, elegant little repositories of useful factoids, were immensely popular. The *Royal Engagement Pocket Atlas* and *Pocket Remembrancer* were even illustrated with designs by the royal

academician Thomas Stothard and architect Humphrey Repton.
But in 1816, the City of London stationer John 'Honest Jack' Letts
published a series of ruled and dated notebooks specifically for
the purpose of recording daily reflections and observations. Born
in Cornhill, London in 1772, Letts was a bookbinder's apprentice
when, aged only twenty-four, he acquired the business of a stationer
called Walter Mudge, among whose popular imprints was an annual
almanack of useful knowledge. Letts, noting the new rage for
continental travel, had spotted a gap in the market for something
with more mass appeal. A Letts diary was similar to its eighteenth-
century predecessors, but new printing technologies, such as the
steam-powered rotary press introduced in 1814, had vastly expanded
the potential for speedy manufacture and wide distribution.

After 1820, Letts diaries incorporated much of the information
contained in almanacks but aimed their notebooks more towards
the business traveller; they were designed to be less of a journal
than a memory prompter. This marked an entirely new concept
of daily organisation: the diary was now viewed as a project into
the future, rather than a meditation on the past. Its pristine
pages marked with the days of the year unfolded before the user,
forthcoming public holidays already marked in. They recognised a
new appetite for standardisation – of time and work management,
and a life timetabled. Letts also published variations on the daily
diary theme: specialist medical, legal and clerical diaries, ledgers,
logbooks, calendars, registers and housekeeping notebooks. As the
Letts advertisement put it, 'enabling Everybody to secure to himself
a faithful Record of the Past, the Present and the Future'.[3]

By the time of Honest Jack's death in 1826, Letts & Co. were
producing twenty-eight different variations of their basic diary,
from pocket editions to foolscap-sized – all with the name Letts
emblazoned on the cover. Early editions assumed that the user
would account for only a six-day week and excluded Sundays. Most
of them also included a section of ruled columns for payments and
expenses and others with useful information, such as tide tables
for sea travel. By the 1850s, Letts & Co. (now run by John's son
Thomas) had expanded worldwide, into all the nations of the

empire. In 1858, in a canny early example of celebrity endorsement, Letts offered Dr David Livingstone, then just about to embark on his doomed expedition to the source of the Zambezi river, a supply of the firms' diaries to take with him. (By the 1870s, lost in Zambia, Livingstone had run out of ink and the diaries were written using the dark juice of a local berry.)

In 1856, the cost of a Letts 'tourist' pocket diary was one shilling – a price which remained unchanged until 1885, when the company's diary department was sold to Cassell & Co. The name on the diaries was, however, retained under the new ownership because of the pre-eminence of the Letts brand. Other firms joined in the boom in diaries, notebooks, almanacks and journals: they were available in an infinite variety, for every possible kind of purchaser and for every conceivable requirement. Letts's pocket-sized 'Quikref', with its handy information boxes, maps and tables, was its most popular seller for half a century. Victorian diaries came in all sorts, plain and serious, with leather covers tooled in gold, with padlocks, silk ribbon markers and marbled endpapers; they were produced by firms or department stores as advertising vehicles and as promotional gifts. Many of the advertisers in the Letts range were patent medicine suppliers. An 1874 annual, for example, contained advertisements for 'abdominal supports for Ladies before and after confinement', 'Lamplough's Pyretic Saline' for the relief of headaches, and a range of 'artificial Legs, Arms and Eyes'.[4] These printed diaries seemed to anticipate horrors and anxieties at the same time as offering, in advance, their control and containment.

The literary interest in diary-keeping had been boosted by the publication for the first time in 1815 of the complete diaries of Pepys, which were followed by those of John Evelyn in 1818. There is an evangelical appeal to self-improvement in the exhortation in Letts's catalogue to: 'Before you lie down to sleep, or before you leave your dressing room in the morning . . . Read over the Entries of the Past Day to provide against any omission, and then of tomorrow (if there be any) to arrange your time in the most advantageous manner.'[5] Modern life, with its turmoil and stress and movement, must be reflected on to be successfully managed; and without management all is chaos and the day wasted. The traveller in particular had to bear in mind the importance of the experience as related at some future date. 'Every traveller ought to have two objects in mind,' thought Richard Colt Hoare in 1815: 'the one to amuse himself, the other to impart to his friends the information he has gained.'⁶

The Beswick siblings, Mary and Tom, from Gristhorpe in Yorkshire, who travelled through Europe and Egypt between 1839 and 1840, are typical of the early Victorian travel diarists, compelled to dutifully record their experiences but refreshingly disinclined to add any literary or emotional colour. Mary and Tom were both meticulous in maintaining their shared diaries but only occasionally allow themselves to roam beyond the bare events of the day, possibly for reading aloud or perhaps as reminders for later letters. On the road from Calais to Paris, Tom carefully noted: 'The country in some parts is much wooded and the wood in general being planted in Rows makes it look very formal. We had apple trees for about 50 miles on each side of the Road which were loaded with fruit, beggars in abundance, curious looking sheep.'⁷ The Beswicks are curious and observant but on the whole unawed by 'abroad': when their boat docked at Leghorn, they didn't bother to disembark as they had heard there was 'not much to see at the place'.⁸

Sometimes, the Beswicks' diaries capture atmosphere without apparently intending to, such as when Tom notes how they stayed awake listening to the howling of jackals at night from their boat on the Nile. But for the most part, Tom's diary approaches his daily experiences with a firmly held belief in what things should look and seem like. He then records how (or if) they came up to expectation. Foreign sights are thus either pleasingly to order or thoroughly disappointing. Mary Beswick (then aged twenty-seven) seems, according to her diaries, to have done very little but copy music, mend her clothing, occasionally pay calls on expats living in, for example, Valletta, or go to the nearest Anglican church. With her brothers she climbed Mount Vesuvius and goes into some detail about the general discomfort of the expedition and their mangy donkeys. In passing, she noticed one woman coming down the mountain in the other direction: 'poor Miss P' had been so overcome with fatigue that she'd had to be carried down, then forced to take to her bed for three days to get over the ordeal. Mary too is determinedly unimpressed.[9]

Tom, like many diarists, included little watercolour sketches in the pages of his journal. Again, there is a pre-packaged feeling about his responses to what he sees and his pictures show the influence of the commercialised images of Egypt and the Middle East that were popular at the time. One of Tom's drawings, for example, shows two camels and a single palm tree in front of the Great Pyramid of Giza. Visiting during the same period as the Beswicks was the former scenery painter David Roberts, who was to become one of the most prolific and celebrated orientalist image-makers, but Tom's aesthetic owes more to the rules of the picturesque aesthetic laid out fifty years before. This was how tourists imagined the scene would look and how they hoped to record it to bring home: a palm beautifully positioned in front of a pyramid was Egypt in a nutshell.

The Reverend John Mitford, travelling in Europe a few years before the Beswicks, also painted some watercolours on the blank pages of his journal of a tour of France and Italy. Unlike Tom, Mitford is alive to all sorts of interesting details – in his entries he writes of hearing cuckoos and seeing apple trees hung with mistletoe, of fig trees coming into leaf, the large bonnets worn by the women along the Loire valley, an unusual oxen harness in Lombardy. But he is firmly conventional when it comes to his subjects. Mitford searched for views that were familiar from other paintings, adding an overhanging tree or a small human for perspective in the picturesque manner. He painted all the favourites: the wide bay of Naples at Salerno, and Amalfi, and the cascades at Terni. To some of them he even included an ornamental frame, as if the images were already hanging on his wall at home. Later commercial diaries in fact sometimes included printed picture frames into which a painting could be inserted. In 1866, Trollope described in an article the cultivation of holiday sketching – the 'creation of a distinct and new subject of investigation and study' – as a particularly notable feature of mass tourism. Sketching was, he thought, a harmless hobby and 'innocent, pretty and cheap'.

The holiday art show had the added advantage, once the traveller had returned home, of not being as dull to any listeners as that of the amateur naturalist: 'the persecution which you are called on to endure in inspecting cupboards full of pickled snakes or legions of drawers full of empty egg-shells'.[10]

The careful monitoring of expenses was encouraged by diaries, with their pages of columns at the back in which to keep accounts. In 1819, when Robert Hudson travelled to the continent he left almost all the daily pages of his diary blank except for furiously scribbled lists of expenses, starting on the day he set off from Ramsgate (porters' charges were one shilling for a portmanteau, sixpence for hatboxes and small parcels, a trunk was 1/6) and continuing for all the months of his tour – there is a lot of heavy and clearly outraged underlining. The book is crammed with scraps of receipts, tickets and bills.[11]

Private diaries aired complaints that were then smoothed over in published ones. Mary Browne maintained a ferocious loathing of all things French from the moment of departure. Mary's diary was found in a drawer and published fifty years later, when her sister Euphemia recalled: 'Even to admire anything foreign was the blackest treason. Starting in this firm belief, she treasured up everything ugly, eccentric or uncouth that she came across in their travels.' The Brownes had no sooner disembarked than France let Mary down. 'About Calais was the ugliest country without exception I ever beheld.'[12] The paintings in the Louvre were disappointing, the aniseed soap smelt disgusting, the vines in the vineyards were regrettably small, there were too many beggars, the cows were too thin, the pigs too long-legged, the babies over-swaddled, the ladies wore clashing colours, the Seine was filthy, French drivers stopped too often and drank too much; the French people in general always 'seemed to be creeping along and looking like oysters'.[13] In her diary, Mary is outraged by everything she sees but she lets no sight go unrecorded. Her crude pencil sketches are wonderfully vivid and through her disdainful eyes we get a very detailed sense of everyday life in France – in the sight, for example, of workmen outside her hotel eating their breakfasts by dipping a 'very long roll' into a pot of jam and each man (to Mary's fury) drinking his own bottle of *vin ordinaire*.

Diary-keeping spoke to a number of often contradictory Victorian attitudes: the self-improving nature of self-reflection, daily discipline, discretion and time management on the one hand and on the other, something far more transgressive: secrecy, even furtiveness, the expression of inner passions and introspection. It was the opinion of the physician James Johnson that learning to describe what one had seen while travelling, to capture it in words, was a health-giving therapy in itself. It suggested that learning the discipline of careful observation helped cultivate broad-mindedness.

> Pure description is, perhaps, the humblest species of mental
> exercise. It is little more than the notation or record of
> impressions received through the medium of the senses – as
> those resulting from a rugged road, a steep mountain, or
> a rapid river. It requires little more than seeing, hearing,
> and feeling, with moderate knowledge, attention, and
> some command of language, to be able to convey to others'
> descriptions of what we ourselves have seen or felt, as far at
> least as these can be conveyed in words.[14]

But there was also much doubt over whether personal diaries could ever be really private. Increasingly many diaries, in particular travel ones, were destined for publication and written with that in mind. The *English Catalogue of Books* shows that after 1820, the number of published diaries and journals doubled – then further peaked in the decades between the 1830s and 1860s. Diary-keeping (or 'diarising' as it became known) became a ubiquitous feature of Victorian middle-class life, and in particular the lives of women.

Diaries began to appear regularly in novels as fictional devices by which to reveal troubling emotions, in Wilkie Collins's *The Woman in White*, for example, and Anne Brontë's *The Tenant of Wildfell Hall*. In 1857, in Robinson vs Robinson, the first divorce case to be heard after the passing of the Matrimonial Causes Act, Henry

Robinson sued his wife Isabella on the grounds of adultery with their family friend, the married physician Charles Lane. Robinson's only evidence of infidelity was several volumes of diaries (Letts ones, bound in red morocco leather) in which were outlined apparently explicit details of Mrs Robinson's physical relationship with Dr Lane. Lane then counter-sued on the grounds that what was written in the diaries was only a menopausal fantasy. It was even suggested in court that Isabella had intended to publish the diary in the form of a novel, as though women's secret, troubling, uncontrollable desires, poured onto the private page, blurred dangerously the lines between fact, fiction, subjective desire and objective truth.[15]

Diaries, intended to encourage management of the world and the new experiences offered by travel, became associated with the idea of romantic subjectivity – and in fact became its most intense vehicle. Many commentators wondered if the mental capacities of ordinary people could bear the weight of such emotional release. Both published and unpublished diaries show diarists straining to deliver an account of grand feeling that lived up not only to the experience itself but to other, literary renditions of emotional response. Marianne Baillie, whose 1819 diary of her continental tour was clearly intended to be read aloud, worried in advance that her writing failed the test of literature as well as accuracy:

> My friends will not, and readers in general must not, look for fine writing from the pen of such a novice as myself; nor ought they to expect me (labouring under the twofold disadvantage of sex and inexperience) to narrate with the accuracy and precision of a regular tourist, the history (natural, moral, political, literary and commercial) of all the places we visited . . .

Baillie thought it best too to pre-empt any sniggers about her taste for popular gothic novels: 'Among the many fears which assail me, there is one that recurs to my mind with more pertinacity than the rest: that I may be taxed with having bestowed too warm and glowing a colouring upon some objects of natural beauty and sublimity. Formerly indeed, I believe I was in danger of leaning towards romance in describing scenes which had particularly impressed my imagination or interested my feelings, and of attempting to imitate, with too rash and unadvised a pencil, the fervour of a Mrs Radcliffe.'[16]

Tourists' guidebooks seemed even to encourage this kind of dangerous meditation in their readers. The early editions of Murray's handbooks to Switzerland are sprinkled with little snippets of Byron's verse and nuggety anecdotes from the poet's life. Shorn of their context or even of the surrounding verses, these little quotations use the celebrity of Byron, who might represent the absolute antithesis of the group tourist, to add a romantic frisson to the plain and useful information of the guidebook. Four decades before the first Murray handbook, John Haygarth, a charmingly unpretentious commercial traveller who visited Switzerland just after 1815, discovered that his fellow tourists did not like the romantic view of the lake to be spoiled by modern real life. Haygarth himself was more interested in the steamer than the view:

> It is quite the fashion to cry shame upon steamers on lakes –
> & I talk about the utilitarian slant that sets a peaceful lake
> on fire as it even with a great heaving monster that ploughs
> up & dirties its pure waters, & diffiles its scenery with smoke
> and steam – I cannot at all join the cry – There is as much
> poetry in the wonderful advance of art as has triumphed over
> distance and has brought distant races & nations to be near
> neighbours – and has sent the white man with his round hat &
> straight coat over all seas and rivers of the world . . . There is as
> much poetry in these ideas, if pursued, as there ever could be in
> the quiet, unpolluted lake.[17]

Published diaries were often sold on the promise that the diarist had given vent to the expression of an authentic self generally kept under wraps. Anna Jameson's semi-fictional *Diary of an Ennuyée*, published in 1826, a self-conscious study of agonising self-consciousness, was particularly influential. This 'diary' was written when Jameson was a governess, accompanying a consumptive charge to Italy, and it

purports to contain the eager revelations of a young but physically
frail woman encountering the intoxicating romanticism of abroad
for the first time. 'What young lady, travelling for the first time on
the Continent, does not write a "Diary?"', the book begins.

> No sooner have we stept on the shores of France – no sooner are
> we seated in the gay salon at Dessin's, than we call, like Biddy
> Fudge, for "French pens and French ink" and forth steps from it
> case the morocco bound diary, regularly ruled and paged, with
> its patent Bramah lock and key wherein we are to record and
> preserve all the striking, profound and original observations –
> the classical reminiscences – thread-bare raptures – the poetical
> effusions – in short, all the never-sufficiently-to-be-exhausted
> topics of sentiment and enthusiasm, which must necessarily
> suggest themselves while posting from Paris to Naples.[18]

Yet, in her diary, the 'ennuyée' sickens and languishes from a nameless
disease that leaves her listless and unhappy. Like Marianne Baillie,
the weight of literary expectation overpowers her. The accepted *vade
mecum* of the sentimental traveller in Italy was at the time Madame de
Staël's *Corinne*. The ennuyée purchases a copy at Molini's in Florence
to get herself in the mood for writing her diary but baulks at the
prospect of what it might expose her to: 'But when I began to cut
the leaves, a kind of terror seized me, and I threw it down, resolved
not to open it again. I know myself weak – I feel myself unhappy;
and to find my own feelings reflected from the pages of a book, in a
language too deeply and eloquently true, is not good for me.'[19]

On its first publication, *Diary of an Ennuyée* was widely assumed
to be genuine. The actress Fanny Kemble in 1828 was disappointed
to learn that the author was not only still alive but hale and hearty.
She reported: 'The Ennuyée, we are given to understand, dies, and
it was a little vexatious to behold her sitting on a sofa in a very
becoming state of plumptitude.'[20] Jameson's book was not a work
of satire (though it does occasionally seem to skirt very close to
one) but it is an early example of the use of a fictional travel diary
to express what was thought to be a particularly female sensibility.

The art historian and travel writer Elizabeth Eastlake scorned the trend, remarking sarcastically in 1852: 'There are particular powers inherent in ladies' eyes.'[21] Forty years after the ennuyée had expired, the effusions of lady diarists were mercilessly spoofed in 1863 by Lady Helen Dufferin, herself a diariser of great determination. Her fictional tourist, the hopelessly susceptible Impulsia Gushington, after being diagnosed with biliousness, is advised not only to read Alexander Kinglake's *Eothen*, a wildly popular travel book about the Middle East, but to go abroad to Europe immediately. Impulsia pours her romantic fantasies into her private diary: '*Eothen* is indeed a delightful book! I fell asleep over it last night, and dreamt that, mounted on an ostrich, I was careering over the boundless sands of Arabia with the author by my side! . . . I gather from the book he is still unmarried . . . if so – *why*?'[22]

Impulsia's literary pretensions, her addiction to romantic posturing, sent up the mid-Victorian taste for secret longings exposed. 'I have been endeavouring to revive faint recollections of a long-vanished past,' writes Impulsia.

> I know that – when a little child of five summers – I accompanied my honoured parents to some bathing establishment on the coast of France ('twas the first and last time I ever quitted my native land) – I cannot recollect its name of situation – but this broken link in memory's chain adds a tender pleasure to the zest of foreign travel. Dear, dear "Abroad!" your image is henceforth connected with the memory of my sainted parents, whose portraits seem to bend from their frames, and to smile in mild approval of my determination.[23]

The title of Dufferin's book, *Lispings from Low Latitudes*, takes aim too at the torrent of travel books that poured from British presses after 1815. These volumes became so ubiquitous that by the 1840s, travel writer Catherine Gore heaped disdain on single women who came home from their travels to dash off 'little lady-like books of travels'.[24] But men too were at the travel-writing game. Titles often suggest a capricious spontaneity far from the time-tabled plod of the commercial tourist group. There are scampers, rambles (if walking), scrambles (if mountaineering), perambulations, wanders, pilgrimages and peregrinations. As early as 1819, Sir Francis Hall commented: 'The public has banqueted on Travels, Agricultural, Philosophical and Political; on Visits and Visitations, from Six Months to Six Weeks; on Letters and Observations; on "reflections during a Residence," and "Notes during an Abode;" on "walks in, round and about Paris;" on "Sketches of Scenery," and "scenic Delineations;" on Journeys, voluntary and forced; on Excursions on Horseback and on Foot; by Old Routes, and New Routes and Unusual Routes.'[25]

Such works left the ordinary travel diarist often feeling their own reflections inadequate. 'Can anything new be said of Italy?' wondered Catherine Taylor in 1840.[26] Joseph and Mariana Fox, whose diaries were never published, loved their tours through Europe in the 1870s and 1880s. Yet Joseph confides to his diary his modest regret that he can't express himself in the required high romantic manner ('for what word-painting can grapple with such a subject') when it comes to describing a dramatic avalanche in the Alps: 'I would hold my readers for a few minutes in suspense, as I piled up simile upon simile, and made them realise – though even then but imperfectly.' Yet Joseph's diaries, in their simple statements of experience and encounter, are as atmospheric as anything more polished. The Foxes eat roast marmot in the Alps, and 'black bread, cheese, milk and sausages reeking of garlic'. In the fashionable Dutch watering place of Scheveningen in the 1880s, they could hardly see the sand on the beach for the rows of straw chairs sitting there 'like beehives cut in two'. In the zoological gardens in Antwerp, a monkey plucked Joseph's spectacles from his nose and ran off with them.[27] And even bluff John Haygarth sometimes can't help himself and is moved to raptures. Though he admonishes himself for getting over-poetical (not thinking he is up to scratch for a 'prose poem'), here Haygarth is at Lake Maggiore where he is in such raptures that his handwriting becomes almost illegible: 'All this from the lemon & the golden orange, & the myrtle and the soft breeze and the blue heavens . . .'[28]

By the end of the century, keeping a diary had almost become a shorthand for publishing one. In 1895, Oscar Wilde's Cicely Cardew discreetly covers her diary with her hand when Algernon Moncrieff tries to look over her shoulder. 'You see it is simply a young girl's record of her own thoughts and impressions and consequently meant for publication. When it appears in volume form, I hope you will order a copy.'[29]

'SUNSET AT ANY HOUR'

'What is it that we seek for,' wondered Lady Mary Herbert in 1865. 'We Englishmen and Englishwomen who, year by year, about the month of November, are seen crowding in Folkestone and Dover steamboats with that unmistakeable "going abroad" look of travelling – bags and wideawakes, and bundles of wraps and alpaca gowns?"'[30] Perhaps, like thousands of others, Lady Mary was hoping for a view, one perhaps that would rouse in her that pleasurable terror of the romantic traveller.

A 'good' view is mostly one that conforms to prior expectations: it looks pleasingly like a picture of a view. As a woman tourist in Greece in 1885 remarked:

Perhaps the first delightful experience on seizing the natural and acquired features of the scene, is that of finding yourself so at home in them. Pictures, painted and verbal, have for once done their work with due effect, since nothing seems strange or wholly unexpected. Your coming seems rather a return; in any case, you have arrived, you are not parvenu.[31]

With such mighty expectations resting in views, many tourists were inevitably disappointed. As Matthew Todd reported from France: 'I went to the top of the rocks to look out for views, but returned not much gratified.'[32] And in 1854, Augustus Hare was made positively queasy by his first sight of the famous Matterhorn: 'It is a grand view, but I could never care for it . . . I am very glad to have seen it, but if I can help it, nothing shall ever induce me to see it again.'[33] It is difficult to describe a new view without resorting to a comparison with a more manageable one at home. A significant number of Victorian tourists visiting the Alps seem to have been reminded of Box Hill in Surrey, the highest point of the North Downs. Katherine Fry found the countryside between Dunkirk and Calais 'flat and uninteresting, a good deal like the fen country about the Isle of Ely'.[34] And Albert Smith, who knew the power of comic bathos, cut the steeply wooded banks of the Rhine down to size by comparing them to Hoxton: 'My Hoxton home! Whilst on the Rhine/ A thought of thee my bosom fills;/ Its steeps recall the mountain line of Haverstock and Highgate Hills.'[35] Thomas Beswick thought Lago a Aguano 'a pretty lake and it rather reminded me of the Mere at Scarboro'.[36]'Even Dickens fell at the challenge: 'We began, in a perfect fever, to strain our eyes for Rome, and when, after another mile or two, the Eternal City appeared, at length, in the distance, it looked like – I am half afraid to write the word – like LONDON!!!'[37]

The view is the quintessence of the touristic experience. By the early nineteenth century, Edmund Burke's famous distinction between the beautiful and the sublime had produced the dominant and most desirable aesthetic for the Romantic age. Beauty was soothing, harmonious, polished – sunrise over a duomo, for example – and the sublime was elating and terrifying, the spiritually stretching reward of physical effort – sunrise over Mont Blanc, perhaps. The eighteenth-century poet Thomas Gray reflected that the dangerous mountain journey to the Carthusian monastery of the Grande Chartreuse offered the ideal conditions for an encounter with the sublime as 'you have death perpetually before your eyes'.[38] In a letter home, Gray's travelling companion Horace Walpole laid out the elements of their approach and how, in their perfect asymmetry, they were the very embodiment of sublime experience:

> But the road, West, the road winding round a prodigious
> mountain, and surrounded with others, all shagged with
> hanging woods, obscured with pines, or lost in clouds! Below, a
> torrent breaking through cliffs, and tumbling down fragments

of rocks! Sheets of cascades forcing their silver speed down
channelled precipices, and hasting into the roughened river at
the bottom! Now and then an old footbridge, with a broken
rail, a leaning cross, a cottage or the ruin of a hermitage! This
sounds too bombast and too romantic to one that has not seen
it, too cold for one that has. . ..[39]

It had it all: the grandeur of nature made more awful by the little
asymmetrical reminders of man in all his insignificance.

It took an eighteenth-century clergyman to codify the thrill-
inducing elements of Burke's sublime into the portable pleasures of
the excursionists' view: he called it the picturesque. The Reverend
William Gilpin's picturesque is the sublime tamed and framed
and taken home to hang on the wall. Gilpin made the picturesque
view a destination in itself; a reason to visit the Lake District, for
example, to take home the experience and neatly slot it into an
album. The picturesque scene is pleasingly untidy but balanced,
and any signs of human cultivation or order are carefully controlled.
The elements of the scene had to be imagined as if framed – either
by a real frame or by the eye. 'We precisely mean by it that kind of
beauty which would look well in a picture,' wrote Gilpin in 1798. It
was really very simple. The excursionist had to seek out landscapes
which accorded with this pre-ordained ideal: their features would
ideally include a background of soaring peaks, say, or great lakes, or
cascading waters; in the foreground should be a ruin, a tumbledown
cottage or a great tree; perhaps it would include a solitary figure to
give perspective.

The viewer was then encouraged to use imagination to enhance
and then alter the composition of the view to make it even more
pleasing to the eye, enjoying how the rough elements contrasted
with the smooth, adding variety and ruggedness. The picturesque
landscape was human in scale, the addition of a coil of smoke from
a cottage or a peasant figure herding sheep only adding to the sense
of containment. 'The imagination', wrote Gilpin, 'can plant hills;
can form rivers, and lakes in valleys, can build castles and abbeys.'[40]
As the Gothic novelists discovered, by following Gilpin's rules, an

exciting frisson of dread could be achieved merely by adding the description of a ruined tower to an empty hill.

For Gilpin, the paintings of the seventeenth-century landscape artist Claude Lorrain most successfully embodied the picturesque ideal. He therefore encouraged English tourists to take with them on viewing excursions a 'Claude glass' – a plano-convex mirror, which reflected back at them the landscape modified with a tint of Claudian blue and with foreground features pre-darkened. According to Gilpin, the Claude glass 'gave the object of nature a soft, mellow tinge like the colouring of that Master'.[41] As the Claude glass required the user to stand with their back to the view, as if taking a selfie, they need never actually even look at the original, only the new, improved version.

Father John Eustace's *A Classical Tour through Italy* was the standard companion for the tourist following in the footsteps of the Grand Tour ('Everybody was walking about St Peter's . . . Nobody said what anything was, but everybody said what . . . Fr Eustace or somebody else said it was,' observed Dickens in *Little Dorrit*). Father Eustace often exhorted his readers to observe what surrounded them as though creating a painting. Sometimes he even framed it for them, as he does in this description of Lake Albano, near Rome, which has all the elements of which Reverend Gilpin would approve: 'Another umbrageous alley, partly through woods, leads us to Marino, a very pretty town: the approach to it with the rocky dell, the fountain in the midst, the town on the eminence above, the woods below and on the side of the road, might furnish an excellent subject for a landscape.'[42]

To its critics, the picturesque was about neatening and touching up nature: it was twee and reduced the great sights of the world to little bubbles of manufactured feeling. In his *Alpine Journal* of 1816, Byron spotted an English woman at Chamonix gazing out at Mont Blanc and exclaiming to her party: ' "Did you ever see anything more *rural*" – as if it were Highgate or Hampstead – or Brompton – or Hayes. "Rural" quotha! – Rocks – pines – torrents – Glaciers – Clouds – and Summits of eternal snow far above them – and "Rural!" '[43] The sight of tourists stumbling over the Lakes holding up Claude glasses inevitably made Gilpin's prescriptive aesthetics the object of lampoonery, most famously in William Coombe's *The Tour of Dr Syntax in Search of the Picturesque* (1812), in which a poor parson goes off on a tour in the hope of saving his household from penury:

> I'll make a TOUR and then I'll WRITE IT
> You well know what my pen can do,
> And I'll employ my pencil too: –
> I'll ride and write, and sketch and print,
> And thus create a real mint;
> I'll prose it here, I'll verse it there,
> And Picturesque it evr'y where:[44]

Although the Claude-glass enthusiasm was short-lived, the legacy of Gilpin's picturesque was to make the framing of visual experience almost inseparable from tourist experience as a whole. Nearly two hundred years later, the French critic Roland Barthes found the Blue Guides (the cultural guidebooks, in both French and English, that were first published in Britain in 1918) still determinedly favouring the Gilpin ideal over any other. 'The Blue Guide hardly knows the existence of scenery except in the guise of the picturesque,' wrote Barthes, 'The picturesque is found any time the ground is uneven.'[45] It has become what the twentieth-century American historian Daniel Boorstin has described as a 'pseudo-event', in which the traveller is given the illusion that they are admiring nature in all its grandeur but in fact see only a tamed and modified version, made safe for looking at, not living in.

The picturesque view embedded itself firmly in the popular imagination as the gold standard of views. Mountain vistas, accessible only through physical effort, carried additional moral kudos. When, in 1863, the travel agent Henry Gaze escorted his groups to the Swiss Alps, he threw in a view with gothic knobs on, for ten guineas extra. In his guidebook, he wrote that it was not enough for his tourists just to look; they must *feel* 'these rugged mountain walls – these pinnacles like Gothic towers' – and they would produce a 'sensation that will never be obliterated'.[46] In the

1850s, a spectacles manufacturer in Islington produced an item of viewing apparatus of which William Gilpin would have heartily approved. 'Sunset at any Hour' reads his advertisement: 'Scenery, however extensive, viewed through the IMITATION SUNSET GLASSES, appears as if glowing in a beautiful Sunset. Invaluable little boons for viewing Scenery. It is better to use two glasses – one to each eye.'[47]

Sir Francis Head, travelling through the spas of Europe in 1862, carried with him a 'paneidolon' (patented in 1832) – a contraption which appears to have been somewhere between a camera obscura and a camera lucida. Sir Francis used it to create the neatly framed images with which his book, *Bubbles from the Brunnen of Nassau*, was illustrated. 'This exceedingly clever, newly invented instrument, the most silent – the most faithful – and one of the most entertaining *compagnons de voyage* which any traveller can desire, consists of a small box, in which can be packed anything it is capable of holding,' he wrote. 'On being emptied for use, all that is necessary is to put one's head into one side, and then trace with a pencil the objects which are instantly seen most beautifully delineated at the other.' Among the other advantages of the Paneidolon was that the operator's face being hidden in the box, crowds didn't gather to look over the artist's shoulder, and 'laugh outright at the contortion of countenance with which the poor Syntax in search of the picturesque, having one optic closed, squints with the other through a hole scarcely bigger than the head of a pin, standing all the time in the inquisitive attitude of a young magpie looking into a marrow-bone'.[48]

Naturally, however, ubiquity led to the picturesque being viewed by connoisseurs as chocolate-box: a downmarket version of the more sophisticated sublime. When 'Miss W', a governess, travelled to Europe in 1845 with her charge Minnie, she wrote that while crossing the Alps they had climbed to the Col de Balme, a high mountain pass near Chamonix from which they had been assured they would get a view worth their efforts. Miss W reported to her diary that though the vista was 'magnificent', 'the prints will give you a wrong idea of it. All I have seen dress it up to look picturesque which it is not. Consequently, Minnie does not like it. I could gaze upon the scene for hours, but, having only a short time, I looked with hungry eyes to bring away a distinct impression of that amphitheatre of snowy mountains and savage rocks.'[49] Miss W was after a terror only available in the original form – the child Minnie preferred the prettiness of the secondhand version.

By 1845, when Miss W was worrying about her view, the ascent of mountains was no longer a test of masculinity and mental endurance; it could be had by almost anyone who wanted a view that would move the earth for them. Albert Smith had put the Alps in a box; Thomas Cook's tours, and later those of the winter sports pioneer Sir Henry Lunn, were bringing parties of British tourists to the mountains in ever increasing numbers. Geologist Thomas Bonney observed:

> Personally conducted parties, such as those organised by Cook and Lunn, were unknown half a century ago. I remember in 1875, seeing one, gathered by the former walking into Chamonix. It was an irregular procession of incongruities, headed by an elderly clergyman in a top hat who "pegged" the footpath with his alpenstock at every step as if that were a ceremonial observance.[50]

In 1867, in a letter to his sister-in-law, Anny Thackeray, Leslie Stephen expressed his horror at the spectacle of tourists tainting the awesome natural majesty of the mountains:

> Fat sort of commercial travellers who plump into other people's chairs & yell for brandy and water tout de suite, & women with tartan petticoats of blowsy appearance, & a vile parson with a neckcloth like a tall white chimney pot, & a wretched crowd of limp beings with alpenstocks tipped with chamois horn such as I never saw before in real life . . . One creature said he had been driving in a charabanc up and down avalanches . . . I really am disgusted.[51]

Nonetheless, it was still a physical challenge. In 1863, a Rochdale woman on a Cook's tour crossed the St Bernard Pass at Chartreuse and watched the workmen hacking out the road that would eventually lead through the pass (it would take twenty years to complete):

> At every turn during our ascent did we realise the colossal nature of this vast undertaking. The number of bridges constructed for the passage of the road and thrown from one awful chasm to another, numerous galleries bored through the most obstinate and solid granite, immense houses of refuge to shelter travellers and protect the labourers constantly employed upon the road, the savage character of the precipices overhanging the pass, the road jammed in as it were between them, and the mighty torrent boiling in the abyss below – all these combinations testified to the magnitude of the work, and produced upon our minds impressions impossible to describe.[52]

One of the most interesting features of the passion for ascending mountains is how early it engaged the enthusiastic involvement of women. Mary Petherick, the wife and climbing companion of mountaineer Alfred Mummery, scorned the exclusivity of the Men's Alpine Club which opened in 1857 (there was also a women's one). 'The masculine mind is, with rare exceptions, imbued with the idea that a woman is not a fit comrade for steep ice or precipitous rock, and, in consequence, should be satisfied with watching through a telescope some weedy and invertebrate masher being hauled up a steep peak by a couple of burly guides.'[53] But travel was opening up opportunities for women's independence that would have been unthinkable two decades before. 'The only use of a gentleman in travelling is to look after the luggage,' wrote Emily Lowe, exploring alone in Norway in 1857, 'and we care to have no luggage.'[54] The popularity for climbing among women initiated new developments in clothes that helped them move more efficiently and didn't impede movement. Among them was the 'discardable skirt' invented by Mrs Cole, for example, in the 1850s. She recommended sewing small rings inside the seam of the dress, and passing a cord through them, the ends of which should be knotted together in such a way that the whole dress may be drawn up at a moment's notice to the required height. The discardable skirt came with a caution, however. Mrs Aubrey Le Blond, founder in 1907 of the first woman's climbing club in Britain, remembered that she had left her skirt on the far side of the mountain and was forced to retrace most of her day's route to retrieve it.[55]

When, in 1845, Charles Dickens and his party (accompanied by twenty-two guides, six pack horses and an armed guard) ascended Vesuvius, the intention was to spend the night halfway up to see the sunset and then another night at the summit 'where the fire is raging'. Dickens's wife and sister-in-law were conveyed all the way by sedan chair and a 'fat Englishman who was of the party, was hoisted into a third, borne by eight men', while Dickens himself went by foot, using only a stick. The ascent was 'very nearly perpendicular', he noted, and the experience like 'a dry waterfall, with every mass of stone, burnt and charred into enormous cinders and smoke and sulphur bursting out of every chink and crevice'. And the view at the top? 'I never saw anything so awful and terrible.'[56] In 1888, John Mason Cook (son of Thomas) purchased the funicular railway up Mount Vesuvius which had been installed there by a Hungarian tramway promoter. Cook and his companion took the car to the summit and reported that with the railway permanently at an angle of 65 degrees they travelled a thousand yards in twelve and a half minutes, pulled by a wire rope driven by a winding engine. The funicular transported 300 people to the volcano's crater a day and in 1890, Cook commissioned a five-mile-long electric railway which linked Vesuvius directly to Pugliano and Naples (it was completed in 1903). From its twenty-four-seater coaches, the train climbed up from Propriano and stopped at an especially chosen site for tourists to gaze at the famous views of the Bay of Naples, with the islands of Ischia and Capri and the Sorrento headland.[57]

At Mount Vesuvius, 'viewing' was a lucrative local business – and had been since the eighteenth century. When Hester Lynch Piozzi went to Naples in 1789 she asked a local friar: 'Is that the famous volcano?' 'Yes,' he replied, 'that's our mountain which throws up money for us, by calling foreigners to see the extraordinary effects of so surprising a phaenomenon'.[58] Climbing to the volcano's crater was popular but it was also arduous, and poor Mrs Piozzi had to take to her bed for three days after the efforts of her descent from the volcano.

Because the emotions traditionally inspired by a good view are difficult to describe, we are, as always, left with many testaments of the ones that disappoint. Dr James Johnson was unmoved, for example, by the Simplon Pass in the Alps. 'The most professed scene-painting travellers', he lamented,

> have rather magnified unimportant views, and fallen short in their descriptions, if not in their perceptions, of magnificent scenes; thus, the tourist who goes over this celebrated mountain pass, with book in hand, is sometimes agreeably – sometimes disagreeably surprised. No one can be blamed for inability to convey adequate ideas of scenes that are, in truth, often indescribable; but there can be no necessity, unless on the stage or in Paternoster-row, for exaggerating the beauty or sublimity of mediocrity or insignificance. I feel considerable qualms, doubts, and fears, in venturing to give even a very concise sketch of what has been so often described by those who have infinitely greater command of language and fertility of imagination than myself.[59]

In 1860, a young theology student, R. D. Bennett, accompanied by his friend Ramsbotham, went on a walking holiday in Switzerland. They covered thirty-one miles a day, and one of the long-anticipated highlights of the trip was to watch a sunrise near the Alpine village of Arth. Alas, it didn't deliver: Bennett noted in his diary that they had seen the dawn but missed the promised added extras: 'Which we saw, but not the effect supposed to be produced of it, as the sun rose too clearly for any "rose tints" etc.'[60]

The traditional view experience, which relied on large perspectives, was often ruined for visitors by zooming in too close on the human element in the landscape. Horace Walpole, travelling before mass tourism transformed lives in the Swiss villages, was appalled by the 'filthy, diseased' local Alpine people with the goitres that resulted from bad water, and the painter William Brockedon found his experience of the grandeur of Mont Blanc ruined by a 'fat and filthy landlady' with garlic breath who ran a place with 'dirty beds, rickety tables and rotting food'.[61]

The promise of the view seems almost destined never to be fulfilled. Outside Gilpin's Claude glass, nature cannot be bent to the view-seeker's preferred elements. When Olivia Stone visited Tenerife in 1887, she spent a whole day getting to Orotava Valley where she'd heard there was a celebrated vista – the island's only one:

> The usually ugly-flat-rooved houses are here covered, gracefully festooned, and hidden by lovely flowering creepers, straying in what appears a wild, uncared for state, suggestive of a tropical wilderness rather than subtropical civilisation. One misses the stately trees, the growth of some scores of years, the soft green turf, soothing to the mind and welcome to the eye, the running rivulet, dancing in the sunbeams, the crash of the waterfall, or the glide of the deep, still river. There is a feeling of something lacking that prevents one looking at the scene with that perfect sense of satisfaction born of the knowledge that we are gazing at the most beautiful sight we have ever seen. The blood does not tingle and run through frames with that exquisite sense of happiness which is next of kin to pain at sight of something wonderfully lovely. So we were disappointed with the valley of Orotava.[62]

'JUST LIKE A POSTCARD'

During the summer of 1815, there was, according to Lady Caroline Lamb, one unmissable jaunt: 'The great amusement at Bruxelles,' Lady Caroline wrote to her mother, 'indeed the only one except visiting the sick, is to make large parties & go to the field of battle – & pick up a skull or an old shoe or a letter, & bring it home.'[63]

The blood of battle was (literally) barely dry before the fields of Waterloo were crawling with excursionists who came to gaze on a scene of horror or to scavenge a memento. Charlotte Eaton arrived at Waterloo two days after the English victory on 18 June. 'The road, the whole way through the forests of Soignies,' she reported,

> was marked with vestiges of the dreadful scenes which had recently taken place upon it. Bones of unburied horses, and pieces of broken carts and harness were scattered about. At every step we met with the remains of some tattered clothes, which had once been a soldier's. Shoes, belts, and scabbards, infantry caps battered to pieces, broken feathers and Highland bonnets covered with mud, were strewn along the road-side or thrown among the trees . . . The bodies of the wounded who died in the waggons on the way to Brussels had also been thrown out, and hastily interred.[64]

Eaton was amazed by the sight of hundreds of thousands of packs of cards, books and innumerable papers of every description: 'The quantities of letters and of blank sheets of dirty writing paper were so great that they literally whitened the surface of the earth.'[65] Tourists often came across corpses or dismembered limbs in the area, and for decades afterwards all sorts of take-home souvenirs in the shape of bones or teeth or bullets could be foraged as mementos of a visit. In August 1815, Sir Walter Scott and his son John visited the farmhouse at La Belle Alliance, where Wellington and Blücher had met as allies. It was already being used as a hotel and the Scotts purchased there a piece of body armour removed from a French corpse and pierced by a bullet hole, which they took back to their Scottish home, Abbotsford, for display.[66] English tourist Susan Mackenzie, visiting Waterloo at about the same time as the Scotts, was appalled by the commercialisation of La Belle Alliance – 'a most wretched hovel full of people eating and drinking'.[67] John Scott was unembarrassed by the profiteering, in fact noting that everyone in his own party of tourists had pocketed 'shreds of cartridge paper, pieces of leather, and hats, letters, songs, memorandum books'. John called his collection 'my little collection of curiosities'.[68]

Curiosities are the ragbag essence of tourist souvenirs. *Objets trouvés* – shells, bullets, interesting pebbles, artisanal trinkets, flowers for pressing – represented collector's serendipity. However, tourism created a weight of demand that 'genuine' objects could soon no longer satisfy. By 1817, hawkers of fake mementos were swarming over Waterloo, and when Marianne Thornton visited that year she could no longer be sure of the real article: 'Boys were continually offering us bones, pieces of hair, buttons, bullets etc. . . . but I have no faith in them.'[69] Almost fifty years later, in 1863, Finetta Staley encountered a battle veteran, 'old Sergeant Mundy', who was still showing tourists round the battle field, and bought from him some bullets for her children – but she acknowledged they were almost certainly fakes.[70] By 1913, nearly a century after the battle, *Cook's Travellers Handbook to Belgium and Ardennes* warned of the tourist racket at Waterloo: 'It is hardly necessary to say that buttons, spurs, helmets or sword handles can be purchased cheaper in Sheffield or Birmingham, where they are manufactured, than on the field of Waterloo; nor must we forget that the battle was fought in the year 1814 and there the numerous guides of about fifty years of age who declare they were in the engagement are not to be relied upon implicitly.'[71]

John Scott thought of the pieces he picked up at Waterloo as 'relics', and he mused at what he saw as a particularly 'English' pleasure in accumulating them. More than mere fancies from abroad, relics were associated with pilgrimage and devotion: medieval pilgrims to Compostela, for example, took home cockleshells, the emblem of St James, to show that they had been to the cathedral of Santiago. For who would believe your travel stories if you had nothing wondrous to display for them? Between his adventures, Swift's Gulliver has to show the sea captain little mementos from each episode to prove his tales are true: gold sprugs, Lilliputian cattle, mouse-skin breeches, a Brobdingnagian ear of corn. In cabinets of curiosities, quirkiness – the result of artless foraging and inquiry – is more desirable than luxury or splendour. A dodo's egg or an ancient Egyptian shabti is far preferable to the antiquarian taste than a replica of a Roman vase. The antiquary Robert Finch, who lived in Rome from 1814, was given £20 by the Duchess of Leeds to buy her some 'foreign articles that would look odd in England'.[72]

In the mid-eighteenth century, returning grandees brought back souvenirs from the Grand Tour on a massive scale. Entire regional economies in Italy were kept afloat by the sale of paintings, artefacts and sculptures in either the original or reproduction. Richard Boyle, the third Earl of Burlington, shipped home from the tours he made between 1714 and 1719, 868 huge crates of paintings, marbles, vases, musical instruments and books.[73]

The booming trade in souvenirs helped define the parameters of the Grand Tour – and made its booty available in watered-down form for the less wealthy tourist. Souvenirs reduce experience to defining little scenes and moments. Manufactories catered for tourists' appetite for portable knick-knacks by creating ingeniously delicious miniatures that said 'I have been here'. Shopping became an integral experience of the Grand Tour and its popular descendants. In Rome in the 1780s, visitors could pick up biscuitware reproductions of classical sculptures, faithful in every detail but in luggage-friendly dimensions. (Biscuitware was particularly popular because when glazed it took on a faintly off-white tinge which made it appear aged; in a dark room, it could even pass as an archaeological find.) Also delectably pocket-sized were *smalti filati* – or boxes and plaques decorated with colourful micro-mosaic depictions of classical sights: the Colosseum, for example, or a view of the Palatine Hill, or the head of the Apollo Belvedere. The tiny plaques were sometimes strung into a bracelet of views. Then there were popular cork models, precisely detailed renderings in miniature of monuments or ruins – and perfectly light. You could pick up the same Roman views on chicken-skin fans: one flourish displayed the Colosseum, the Pantheon and Trajan's Column. Sometimes you could buy the fan leaves separately, picking out the views you wanted to combine, and take them home to be assembled in an order of your choosing.[74]

The fascination with the archaeological discoveries in Pompeii in the last half of the eighteenth century sparked a popularity in imitation classical objects adapted, not always successfully, for early nineteenth-century British homes. The archaeologist Sir Austen Layard, looking back in 1864, deplored the fashion for making tea services resemble temple ewers. 'Too much was attempted. The true principles of application were misunderstood. The walls were overladen with colour and gilding and comfort and utility were sacrificed to classic forms,' he complained. 'Furniture, fire irons, teapots and the various objects of daily domestic use, made after the manner of the ancients, could scarcely be turned to their legitimate purpose, however well adapted they may have been to the sacrifices and ceremonies of a Greek or roman temple. Chairs and sofas strictly made upon the model of the *sella curulis*, and the bronze *bisellium*, might have been comfortable in the forum but were execrable in the drawing room. We were at last driven out of the classic mood.'[75]

But it was the development of the technologies of mass-production and manufacturing that brought the holiday souvenir into the parlour of the middle-class home. Victorian homes were stuffed with the fruits of visits to the continent. The 'infinite variety of lumber' that Dickens puts on display at the Meagles' house in *Little Dorrit* included: 'antiquities from central Italy, made by the best modern houses in that department of industry; bits of mummy from Egypt (and perhaps Birmingham); model gondolas from Venice . . . morsels of tessellated pavement from Herculaneum and Pompeii, like petrified minced veal . . . Spanish fans. Spezzian straw hats, Moorish slippers, Tuscan hair pins, Cararra sculpture . . . Rosaries blessed all round by the Pope himself.'[76]

It was no wonder that yet more inventive forms of luggage were required to contain the souvenirs for the journey home. Trunks and suitcases became lighter and storage more ingenious. The *Railway Travellers' Handy Book* of 1862 listed a wide range of useful forms of equipage, pointing out that the 'clumsy and cumbrous' trunks of previous generations with their heavy iron bands and brass nails were a thing of the past. The popularity of railway travel had brought all sorts of inventive ideas for trunks with lots of compartments or ones which could be converted into chests of drawers. Lighter portmanteaux (large travelling bags) had 'collapsing propensities' which meant they could be squeezed or extended, depending on requirements.[77]

Albert Smith, with his showman's genius for distilling a place to its essence, collected souvenirs on a frenzied scale. His friend Edmund Yates once visited him at home in London: 'I found him as usual, in his foreign blue blouse, pottering about in his sanctum in Percy Street, in which there never was such another room for the collection of extraordinary and quasi-artistic rubbish of every possible description, thickly overlaid with dust.' Smith had an appetite for the odd and particularly for those kinds of souvenirs that happily yoke two disparate ideas together; his home was a riot of joyful kitsch, a *reductio ad absurdum* of all the places he had visited on his great adventures. On his mantelpiece, Yates saw 'a figure of a Swiss peasant with a clock-face in his waistcoat; all kinds of small Swiss carved toys, Turkish slippers; Egyptian small idols, Danton's statuettes of Rubini and lablache, Venetian glasses, goblets and flagons – rare then, in the pre-Salviati period – a lady's black silk mask with a lace fall, an Italian stiletto, and an old roman lamp.'[78] The writer Henry Vizetelly was amazed by Smith's overstuffed parlour: 'trumpery and bizarre knick-knacks, picked up by him on his travels abroad. Soap from Vienna moulded in the shape of fruit, iron jewellery from Berlin, a working model of a guillotine, miniature Swiss chalets, porcelain and meerschaum pipes and a model of a diligence.'[79]

There was a craze for knick-knacks. While abroad, local markets became the popular hunting ground for bits and pieces that were 'authentically' of the place. They also gave tourists the opportunity for that enduringly popular activity: haggling. The Wilson sisters, Mary and Anne, travelling in Europe in 1847, wrote in their shared journal of how they went shopping in a local Dresden market 'full of merchandise of every description, quantities of stuff for gowns, shawls, toys, cakes tapes and bread, woodenware such as butcher's trays and shovels, metal pots, an earthenware pans in loads, jewellery which seemed to be very attractive as all the men, rich and poor, wear rings and sometimes earrings, you may always know a German by his wearing a seal ring nearly as large as his face on his forefinger'.[80] Back home in Britain, arbiters of taste like Mrs Florence Caddy, author of *Household Organisation* (1877), suggested snapping up humble domestic objects for artful display: 'Souvenirs of travel, such as the quaint wooden pails seen at Antwerp or the brass frying-pan-shaped candlesticks at Ghent, should be eagerly sought, as they add much to the picturesqueness and piquant liveliness which are so desirable.'[81]

As in all things, the choice of souvenir was a marker of class. The further removed the object was from its origins then the more vulgar it was considered by arbiters of taste: a wooden pail is one thing but a paperweight shaped like a wooden pail is another. The souvenir hunters pursued their quarry energetically, even if it meant vandalism – such as picking up bits of masonry from a ruin or (in a reverse impulse) graffitiing their initials on an ancient monument. In 1817, Marianne Todd snipped some gold fringing off a curtain in the bedroom at Napoleon's palace at Saint-Cloud 'as a remembrance of the Emperor'.[82] Many seemed quite impervious to embarrassment. In the 1840s, John Mayne visited the Baths of Titus in Rome, where he was undeterred by locals' disapproval: 'Our guide seemed to watch us pretty closely, but I carried away a piece of the painted stucco.'[83]

In Egypt, tourists seem to have plundered almost at will. In 1861, Eddie Huth wrote from Cairo to his mother that he had been to see the Sphinx and had 'broke[n] a bit off its neck to take home with us, as everyone else does'.[84] In 1847, Lady Harriet Kavanagh watched the British consul unwrap for the first time a newly discovered mummy, thought to be of a Roman soldier: 'There was nothing found on him but some gilt tinsel and endless bandages of linen which was divided among the spectators,' she reported.[85] Lady Harriet picked up all sorts of curiosities from the Valley of the Kings, mementos of looted tombs. Her young son Arthur wrote home in jubilation to describe their trophies to the rest of the family:

Tom has got a Turkish dress all embroidered with gold for £13. Hoddy has got a lady's dress and I have got a Bedouin's costume. Tom has also got the carpet Mehemet Ali Pasha used to say his prayers on. It is white satin, all covered with gold. It cost £10. He has also bought an Arab gun, nearly sixteen feet in the barrel, all inlaid with silver. He and I have joined together

and bought a brace of Arab horse-pistols all inlaid with silver,
besides sabres, scimitars, daggers, and knives innumerable.
I also bought a beautiful little horse-piece inlaid with silk –
what the Mamlouks use. We have also got shields made of
giraffe and crocodile skin, along with spears and Nubian
knives.[86]

Geological fragments were popular and mostly free. In 1840 Mary
Beswick was among thousands of tourists who picked up some
pieces of sulphur ('quite hot') while climbing Mount Etna; she
stowed them away to bring back to the East Riding. For tourists
who wanted something not so much 'in the raw', then they might
do as Captain Jousiffe recommended in his 1839 guide to Naples
and visit a shop which specialised in artworks carved from volcanic
lava or Mediterranean coral. He particularly recommended a shop
kept by an Englishwoman who had a 'repository' of 'objects of great
curiosity and interest' made of Vesuvian minerals. In 1863, Robert
Louis Stevenson's nanny, Alison Cunningham ('Cummy'), on her
first year of travelling with the Stevensons, noted that in Pompeii,
Robert's cousin 'Miss Bessie' bought some sleeve links made of lava.[87]

Miniaturism makes sense in a souvenir. Portability is key but
so is the comforting message that your object captures the beating
heart of a place, its singularity and distinctiveness. Albert Smith's
mantelpiece-sized model of a French guillotine, for example. But
does the souvenir come to dictate the experience? Do we long for
the Swiss chalet because the chalet on the keyring is the distillation
of Swissness? The Eiffel Tower, though one of the city's most recent
landmarks, is now more 'Paris' in the rankings of the souvenir
market than the cathedral of Notre Dame. In 1889, when the
tower was finally finished for the Paris Exhibition, it was the tallest
structure in the world at just over one thousand feet. Not only did
its appearance coincide with a surge in mass-produced souvenirs
but it also became emblematic of the appetite for cheap, humorous
kitsch, its distinctive shape appearing on keyrings, candlesticks,
napkins, watchchains and, later, T-shirts. It represents the kind of
souvenir that doesn't take itself too seriously.

The catalogue of the 1889 Paris Exhibition lists a miniature Eiffel Tower held within a snow globe (*boule à neige*), the first time that these two icons of the souvenir industry were brought together in a single object. The invention of the snow globe brought miniaturism to new heights of wild imagination. These glass balls, which shaking covers a tiny scene with a falling snow, have their own particular kind of enchantment; there are elements of the folkloric in snow globes, a hint of melancholy and nostalgia. And they are tiny. The first ever reference to the globes seems to have appeared in a report from the United States Commissioners to the Paris Universal Exposition in 1878, where they are given the category definition of 'paper weights' and described as 'hollow balls filled with water, containing a man with an umbrella. These balls also contain a white powder, which, when the paper weight is turned upside down, falls in imitation of a snowstorm.' The first snow globe patent was issued in 1900 to the Viennese surgical instrument maker Edwin Perzy who, working on improved illumination for operating theatres, put ground glass into a glass globe to enhance reflectivity. The glass didn't work so he tried semolina – which as it sank created the appearance of a snowstorm. A friend, in an inspired stroke of creative genius, asked Perzy to make a miniature of the basilica in Mariazell, Austria, and put it in a semolina globe. The snow globe was born.[88]

The mass industrialisation of tourist souvenir manufacture runs parallel to the evolution in techniques of photography. The travel writers and aesthetes Charles and Elizabeth Eastlake, who pioneered photography in Britain, saw it as a means of purveying accurate data to the uneducated classes, who were assumed to be unmoved by art but could be helpfully stimulated by facts. The Eastlakes now seem unlikely figureheads for the expansion of photography. They viewed the technology very firmly as inferior to the traditional arts (a view shared by many photography pioneers: Charles Eastman inventor of the Box Brownie saw the photograph merely as a useful aid for drawing and painting). But they perceived that it had an educative function. Photography was made, wrote Elizabeth Eastlake, for the mid-Victorian moment, 'in which the desire for art resides in a small minority, but the craving for cheap, prompt and correct facts resides in the public at large. Photography is a purveyor of such knowledge to the world.'[89] Charles Eastlake, in his *Hints on Household Taste*, even regarded too much accuracy of representation as vulgar: for example, a pattern in wallpaper of a fruit that looked too much like a real fruit was less pleasing aesthetically than a stylised fruit.[90]

The earliest popular form of photograph was the daguerreotype, of which John Ruskin, despite his dislike of new technology, was an early advocate. In 1845 Ruskin wrote to his father: 'Daguerreotypes taken by this vivid sunlight are glorious things.'[91] While John and Effie Ruskin were touring Europe on their honeymoon in 1848, George, his manservant, made daguerreotypes for Ruskin, as well as rubbings of brasses and sculptures, and copied out his manuscripts: Ruskin recalled George 'indefatigably carrying his little daguerreotype box up everywhere and taking the first image of the Matterhorn, as also of the Aiguilles of Chamonix, drawn by the sun, a thing to be proud of still'.[92] It was a slow process: daguerreotype exposures could take between fifteen and thirty minutes to complete. In 1839, according to photography pioneer Fox Talbot, 'Lord Brougham assured me once that he sat for his Daguerreotype portrait half an hour in the sun and never suffered so much in his life.'[93]

Yet the speed of photographic technological progress and popularity was dazzling. The accessibility of photography and the development of cameras took hold with astonishing rapidity, manufacturers producing ever lighter and more convenient equipment. In the 1840s, a complete daguerreotype outfit, including lens, cost between eight guineas and £26 but by 1851, the price had halved. The arrival of the first Kodak cameras from North America in 1888 revolutionised photography further with the Kodak promise that they would see the process through from click to development: 'You press the button, we do the rest.'

Suddenly, photographs were the new memories, accurate proof (of the sort that the Eastlakes had found vulgar) of your presence in a place: a landscape with you in it. In 1864, a student staying in the Riffelberg Hotel, Zermatt, wrote in the hotel visitors' book that he and his group had climbed the Pollux and as proof of their achievement had left a box of photographs of themselves under a flag at the top.[94] Tourists could later relive their experiences in the images they brought home. A painting caught the long view but a photograph captured the moment. They represent a characteristically Victorian paradox: the establishment of order and control by means of the exciting but often fearful forces of technology; the huge, new, expanding potential of travel framed and brought back into the safety of the domestic sphere. In 1855, Ernest Lacan wrote in Paris: 'You dream that you are there instead of here, you dream of dark forests, dappled plains, picturesque valleys posed like rests along your route, majestic mountains and frothing seas, the Alps, the Mediterranean, Italy, Spain, the Orient. Wait, open that album!'[95]

The sale of ready-made photographs for personal consumption was popular at tourist sites before the word 'postcard' was commonly in usage. 'Hill', a diarist on a continental tour in 1867, observed in Naples that:

> at several parts of the city there are boards set up announcing in different languages that the guides [to Pompeii] are not allowed to take any fee or gratuity from visitors on pain of instant dismissal. The guides, to evade this restriction, sell photographic views of Pompeii, taken from different situations of the casts of the bodies in the glass cases; of Vesuvius as seen from Pompeii; and other scenery in the neighbourhood. So after we had finished our view of the city the guide took us into an apartment, brought out his box of photographs and spread them out before us for inspection. They are all well done; of considerable size, and very cheap – about fifteen pence each.[96]

The origins of what we now think of as postcards come with the introduction of pre-paid postage stamps in 1840; this was then followed by pre-paid cards (with envelopes) for shorter communications. In 1869, the Austrian mail service issued the first card which could be posted without an envelope; it had a space on one side for a short message and the address. Souvenir-sellers saw an opportunity. The growth of the postcard industry is so closely allied with the expansion in popular tourism that it is often hard to work out whether the postcard makes the place or the place makes the postcard.

By the 1880s, postcards were popular throughout Europe and America. With the development of new colour-printing techniques it became common for cards to be decorated on the front with illustrations of the places from which they had been sent. By 1900, about 10,000 different views of Paris were on sale in postcard form.[97] Cards showed images that covered every aspect of Parisian life beyond the canonical sights: as well as markets, monuments and slaughterhouses, they showed rag-pickers, umbrella salesmen, dog-shavers, mattress-makers, shoe-shiners, rat-catchers and purveyors of other small crafts and trades. Inevitably the popularity of postcards came to signal one of the salient features of popular tourist culture: its speed and disposability. According to the *Evening Standard* in 1899:

> The illustrated postcard craze, like the influenza, has spread
> to these islands from the Continent, where it has been raging
> with considerable severity. Sporadic cases have even occurred in
> Britain. Young ladies who have escaped the philatelic inflection
> or wearied of collecting Christmas cards, have been known to fill
> albums with missives of this kind received from friends abroad.[98]

In 1902, the first dividing line (between message and address) appeared and became the standard format. By 1903, the *Glasgow Evening News* worried that: 'In ten years Europe will be buried beneath picture postcards.'[99] Those hours of correspondence that once took up long hotel afternoons were now replaced by a dashed-off, cheery and not always sincere 'wish you were here'. Being chatty, non-confidential and fundamentally unserious, postcards were also naturally assumed to be a woman's preserve. In 1907, James Douglas wrote: 'The postcard has always been a feminine vice. Men do not write postcards to each other. When a woman has time to waste, she writes a letter, when she has no time to waste, she writes a postcard.'[100]

Postcards appealed to every conceivable taste and interest and therefore form an interesting barometer of the preoccupations of an era. The most successful producers of picture postcards in Britain were the London firm of Raphael Tuck & Sons whose 'Wide, Wide World' series ran into hundreds of thousands of images. The postcard industry also gave work to vast numbers of local photographers who printed their own pictures on ready-made postcard backs.[101]

By the end of the nineteenth century, however, the postcard had already become an easy shorthand for the artificial, mass-market experience. 'Real travellers' most certainly did not send postcards. In E. M. Forster's 1908 novel *A Room with a View*, the crucial moment of Lucy Honeychurch's awakening occurs as she drops her recently purchased cards outside the Duomo in Florence after falling in a dead faint, the result of witnessing a murder. The postcards are here of course symbolic (is anything more symbolic of popular tourism than a postcard?) of the disengaged observer suddenly startled into an encounter with real life.

Even illustrated luggage labels acted as little trophies of abroad; manufacturers rushed in to make what a comic poem, 'To My Luggage Labels', in an 1892 issue of *Punch*, called 'visiting cards, so to speak, of hotels'. In 1890, *Cassell's Magazine* carried an advertisement for innovative self-adhesive labels: 'At this season, when all the world and his wife are travelling, new luggage labels have more than usual interest. One of the most recent novelties in this direction is a book of well-named "Savetime" labels, which are ready gummed and show on each a large and distinctive letter or figure on a boldly coloured background.'[102] There would be no mistaking the destination of a label which showed a pyramid or a silhouette of the Matterhorn. 'A little orange flag of ostentation,' Vita Sackville-West called the label marked 'Persia', which she left dangling from her suitcase on the train rack to arouse envy in fellow passengers going to humdrum places like Cannes.[103]

Inevitably, the mass-produced souvenir became viewed as one of the most egregious examples of both tourist tat and consumer capitalism. In the mid-twentieth century, Walter Benjamin thought souvenirs 'an assault on memory', as if the object had become itself a replacement for experience. In this line of thinking, the souvenir is an object without a function: a tea towel, for example, that never gets to dry a dish. Mass leisure, mass tourism, mass taste – it was all horror to the discerning consumer of experience with an eye for oddity, quiddity and quirkiness. 'The world, as it appears to the tourist, vomits kitsch all over itself,' wrote the French art historian Gillo Dorfles in the 1960s. For Dorfles, the consumption of cheap souvenirs, products of industrial capitalism, corrupted our appreciation even of natural landscape, creating a way of looking at the world that makes even the real seem artificial: 'this is where kitsch, that iconoclast of authentic values, that corrupter of our most treasured experiences, intrudes'.[104] Clocks in the shape of the Parthenon, for example, or little Dutch dolls with clogs on, were viewed as ghastly invitations to sentimentality and false feeling, like wiping away a pretend tear at the sight of the Matterhorn or a local dance.

The economies of tourist destinations would become increasingly dependent on the manufacture and sale of souvenirs. Take Venice, for example, where writer Warren Hall spent some weeks at the end of the Second World War. 'For centuries Venice has been filled with tourists. She came to rely on tourists for her very existence. Every industry in the town was diverted to making "knick-knacks" for tourists. But the war came for Venice and there were no more tourists. Surely it isn't surprising that Venice, in a valiant attempt to raise herself out of the slough of war depression, now uses every means in her power to exploit the tourists. Without a tight hand on the "purse strings" it's possible to spend more money in Venice than even Paris or London.'[105] Hall reported that shops in Venice were almost entirely given over to the sale of trinkets and bibelots, objects that served no use:

> Modern shop fronts in the *calli* slice across the mediaeval
> architecture overhead. They are filled with endless piles
> of *bric a brac*. Cartloads of cheap dolls, chromium-plated
> ornaments, glass ornaments, postcards, pipe racks, fans, beads,

cheap reproductions of paintings from the Doges' palace and
souvenirs of all descriptions. They stare out from stall and show
windows in all directions, and all at fabulous prices. They are
one and all pointless, functionless and devoid of artistic value
. . . In the backs of the shops you will find old ladies busily
making lampshades or cutting out colour prints of the canals
and mounting them with *passe-partout*. Glass is made at the
famous Murano glass works . . . hundreds of twisted curious
but functionless ornaments are churned out daily – mostly in
coloured glass. Tourists carry them fondly away as priceless
examples of Venetian glasswork.[106]

Although many souvenirs were - and still are - cunningly created
by industrial processes to imitate ancient skills, in some regions, the
market in souvenirs also preserved artisanal crafts that would otherwise
have disappeared. 'Handicrafts' remain of course a mainstay of the
souvenir industry: an object that is 'made' is a valuable commodity
in a world where most things are 'produced'. Shopping, for tourists,
is elegaic. When William Chambers wintered in Menton in 1870,
he was delighted to find a representation of the regional costume
immortalised in a piece of locally crafted woodwork: 'The dresses
of the women are picturesque, and their favourite mode of carrying
things is to poise them on the top of the head. The peculiar costumes
of the district are well represented in the wooden mosaics which form
a remarkable local manufacture. I have never returned home from
Nice without purchasing specimens of these beautiful *mosaiques en
bois* at the shop of the brothers Mignon in the Rue Paradis.'[107]

At the end of the nineteenth century, the Catholic Church
in Italy promoted the idea that regionally based, small-scale
manufacture was a way of maintaining the family unit. It was
supported by successive regimes who feared the political militancy
of the urban proletariat and supported small artisanal firms with tax
exemptions.[108] After the Second World War, for example, the revival
of basket-weaving became a major feature of Italian design. Among
the new scooters, cars and sleek modern furniture exhibited in the
promotional exhibition 'Italy at Work', which toured the United

States in the early 1950s, was a little straw donkey. Basketware reminds the traveller of markets, artisanal craftsmanship, slow living: the straw donkey can't help but be a memory of another world, one only just disappeared. As Susan Stewart puts it: 'It is an object arising out of the necessarily insatiable demands of nostalgia.'[109] Other Italian designs in straw included ornamental hats, turkeys, palm trees and goats, but it is the straw donkey that is still the most popular reminder, in toy form, of a rural, working life now almost completely disappeared.

Romantic decay: two tourists contemplate the ruins of the past.

IV

Valedictions

'UNTAINTED BY KNOWINGNESS'[1]

'Tut tut! Miss Lucy!' says Miss Lavish to Lucy Honeychurch in *A Room with a View*. 'I hope we shall soon emancipate you from your Baedeker. He does but touch the surface of things. As to the true Italy – he does not dream of it. The true Italy is only to be found by patient observation.'[2] But where and what is the true Italy, the true France, the true anywhere? Where can the diligent tourist find the truth of a place? Nowadays, we call it 'authenticity' and, like Miss Lavish, it fuels a common touristic conviction that the realness of a place is to be found far from people like oneself. For these tourists, there must be something to look at (Miss Lavish's 'patient observation' perhaps) that is particular, unique to that place – and more importantly, inaccessible to the less sophisticated viewer.

Increasingly, it was local people who provided the something to look at, especially if they could be observed practising regional traditions that satisfied a visitor's idea of the spirit of place. The display of many traditions in this way long outlived their functional practice. The nineteenth-century tourist began to look beyond the classical canon of the Grand Tour towards new experiences that said in retrospect, to an audience back home: *I have travelled.*

A popular tourist occupation was visiting manufactories, particularly ones which made porcelain, lace and, especially, the complicated, often gruesome, business of silk-making. Jane Austen's brother Edward Austen Knight, travelling through Europe in 1790, recorded in his journal a fascinating trip to silkworm breeders in the Veneto, where he noted that a few worms could support the economy of an entire village: 'We watched the eggs and worms being boiled and the silk skimmed off the surface.'[3] Making pasta (known among the British as macaroni-making) was already a popular visitors' attraction near Naples in the early nineteenth century. Locals pulled out all the stops for a spectacle – particularly popular was the sight of Neapolitan beggars, *lazzarone*, making a few lire by swallowing as much of a long string of spaghetti as possible without gagging. From the 1830s onward, many of the mechanical presses, the kneaders, extruders and cutters, that were used in Neapolitan pasta factories were made and installed by British engineers.[4] Yet locals maintained the traditional method, the dough swarming with flies and trodden with bare feet, for the tourists. The honeymooner Emily Birchall went to look at some pasta-making near Naples in the 1860s: 'We watched the making of macaroni – which involved meal being poured into a large trough then threaded by being vigorously stamped on by a barefooted dirty vagabond, then rolled hard between rollers . . . it was pressed through an iron press and the pasta emerged through whatever holes had been put on the press according to type. Then hung on long sticks and baked in the sun.'[5] Industrial pasta driers had in fact been common since 1800 – but the sun-dried version was more appealing to the British visitor.

Rural communities had to make do with what they had in the way of tourist offerings. The Wilson sisters, having in 1844 crossed the Alps into Italy, stopped in the town of Civita Vecchia, near Rome. Here they heard of an infamous brigand imprisoned there for murdering more than 230 people; 'silly' American tourists were being invited to visit him in prison, where he would dress up for them in exchange for five francs.[6] In Arezzo in 1840, Captain Jousiffe, in his road book, recommended a jaunt to see the body of a walled-up monk – 'perfectly dry and when touched, like leather'.[7] Among the high-minded there was enthusiasm for visiting orphanages, schools and prisons, some of which offered ideas for the running of similar institutions in Britain. Mary Browne went on a tour of a girls' school in provincial France where the pupils put on a spirited performance: they 'jumped over the stools, spirted ink at one another, tossed about the books, and danced upon the tables'.[8]

Then there were the religious festivals and ceremonials. The encounter with Roman Catholicism never failed to ruffle the equilibrium of the Anglican tourist. The Reverend J. A. Cunningham, author of *Cautions to Continental Travellers*, reserves very special caution, over a very large number of pages, for the iniquitous religious practices the unwary traveller to the continent might find in 1818: 'vanity and unbridled sensuality', 'mock homage', 'mummery', 'the Sabbath is not a day of rest but of increased dissipation', the 'curse of Popery', 'gross indecency', 'the lurid glare of superstition' and Roman Catholic Europe 'a marsh land in morals, where everything noxious is generated'.[9] Many visitors were confirmed in their prejudices by the spectacles of, for example, local religious processions – many of which compounded the conviction that the rituals of Roman Catholicism were mere ornament, reeking of artifice and decay. Anglican churches in European cities were listed right at the beginning of every Murray's handbook. 'Protestantism means cleanliness, education and domestic morality, and Catholicism the reverse,' pronounced Mrs Edwards in her 1879 *Holidays in Eastern France*. Though the reviewer of her book in the *Spectator* quoted the line as an example of Mrs Edwards's own narrow-mindedness – 'the worst of this style of writing is the injury which it inflicts upon the author's own credibility' – many British tourists on the continent in the mid-nineteenth century would have agreed with her.[10] Roman Catholicism was everywhere too lurid, too obvious, too violent in its representations for the British visitor.

In 1874, the Quaker Katherine Fry reflected on a Cook's excursion to Paris where she was shocked by the sight of crucifixes with graphically painted blood and 'painted to imitate flesh'. And fifty years earlier, Miss A. W. Power visited Italy and found everywhere similar evidence of 'primitive and popular piety', of saints, miracles and relics that trapped Catholicism's adherents in poverty and superstition. 'With few exceptions I believe the priests are very ignorant,' she told her journal.[11] Miss Power had the good fortune to meet one priest, a former superior of the Augustines, at Santo Spirito in Florence; she was pleased to find that he agreed with her that 'monkish establishments' were 'nurseries of vice and at best tended to destroy the best affections of the heart'. Miss Power, who engaged in vigorous conversation with those she met, wondered how it was that they had never heard of Luther or Calvin, noting with bewilderment that during a discussion on prayer, they had even asked how it might be possible to pray without a crucifix.[12]

The Baptist Thomas Cook made no secret of his hostility to Catholicism, deploring 'the power of the Papacy' and pitying the victims of 'priestly domination and besotted superstition'.[13] By 1861, three Anglican churches had been established in Florence and English resident Susan Power noted with approval in her diary that they were having an effect on the local population: 'The people have lost faith in their priests the last two years. Bibles are hawked about in the cafes and read by the intelligent, who at least perceive there are two sides to a question.'[14] It was often the lax attitude to Sunday shopping and commercial activities generally that disturbed British tourists: it was not uncommon for shops to open on the Sabbath on the continent, a situation many British found deplorable. In the more established wintering resorts, such as Pau or Menton, Anglican churches were rapidly established to protect the moral sensitivities of the English winterers. St John's in Menton, built in 1867, is the very model of a small Victorian Gothic, English parish church – under the blazing blue of a Côte d'Azur sky.

Many British tourists felt unable to subdue their desire to put Roman Catholics right. Several guidebooks advised that the visitor should always be polite when visiting a Catholic church: Baedeker in 1913 warned the tourist in Spain to 'refrain from expressing an opinion on religious or political questions'. Although the governess 'Miss W' and her charge Minnie, in Rome in the 1840s, joined a small English audience before Pope Gregory XVI (and found the pontiff, then aged eighty, very spry), they found others in the group were less broadminded: 'I am sorry to say many of our party were most uncourtly, neglecting to curtsy when introduced, and turning their backs upon the Pope in going out. One German not only did that but, when especially presented, took it upon herself to speak first.'[15] Fanny Kemble in the 1820s saw a party of fashionably dressed British concealed behind a pillar in St Peters, unpacking a picnic hamper and popping champagne corks during the celebration of Mass.[16] But many tourists were perplexed by what they saw as a combination of brutish irreverence and idolatry. The Reverend Cooper was appalled to find that in Parma cathedral in 1887, the priest spat into his handkerchief. It turned out although no smoking was allowed in the church anyone could take snuff. 'On all sides of me men were spitting on the marble pavements and even women . . . expectorated as they sat at their prayers.'[17]

Encountering people (or as much as was possible without the language) was naturally limited for groups, and tourists often struggled to describe the people they saw. 'Even the houses and dogs here have a Frenchy look,' wrote governess Henrietta Thornhill in her diary of a trip to the continent with her employers in 1873.[18] Working locals were, in most accounts of travelling, represented as either innocently honest and industrious, or sly and devious. Often they are found amusing; sometimes they are menacing; they very often have photogenic children. But what tends to be most enjoyable for the tourist about the rural poor is that they have retained the local singularity that the visitor looks for; they have not been made bland and uniform by industrialisation and urbanisation. They are a glimpse into what went before, and they add to what William Empson once called 'the pastoralisation of experience': washing their laundry in rivers, having quaint folkloric customs and, particularly, wearing regional costume. The nineteenth-century tourist tended to see the peasants of Europe as the last survivors of a pastoral culture that had vanished in Britain under smokestacks, slums and tenements. They added to the view, and were seen to be in touch with a non-specific ancient wisdom long forgotten by their urban counterparts. 'Are these peasants wiser, better, happier than the sallow, squalid inhabitants of Glasgow and Leeds?' asked Elizabeth Carne in Pau.[19] It was a question to which the answer was usually 'yes'.

Mariana Starke gave the subject of 'peasantry' its own separate sections in her 1818 guidebook. On the Tuscan variety, she writes that the females 'besides working in the vineyards, almost equally hard with the men, often earn money by keeping poultry, and sometimes one or two lambs, whose fleecy coats the children decorate on the Festa di San Giovanni, with scarlet ribbons tied in fantastic knots'. Starke noted coyly that for men and women, 'shoes and stockings are deemed superfluous, and merely ornamental' and only worn on marketing expeditions to town. For Starke, the women in particular, with their 'Arcadian dresses and lovely countenances', were examples of a rustic sexuality untainted by modern knowingness or sophistication.[20]

Richard Ford, eccentric and opinionated author of Murray's handbook to Spain, introduced the people of the Spanish south as 'impressionable as children, heedless of results, un-calculating of contingencies, passive victims to violent impulse, gay, clever, good humoured and light-hearted, and the most subservient dupes of plausible nonsense. Tell them that their country is the most beautiful, themselves the finest, handsomest, bravest, the most civilised of mortals, and they may be led forthwith by the nose.'[21] The Valencians, Ford offers later on, are 'perfidious, vindictive, sullen and mistrustful, fickle and treacherous', while the Catalans are 'strong, sinewy and active, patient under fatigue and privation, brave, daring and obstinate'. Starke summed up the Carinthian peasants of Upper Austria in a couple of sentences: 'The peasantry have fine complexions, with a great appearance of health an strength, but their countenances seldom express good-humour, or quickness of apprehension; they dress neatly and wear high shoes like those of our English farmers. The women are said to be depraved in their morals.'[22]

Decorative local dress aroused particular excitement among tourists, especially as, from the mid-nineteenth century, it was so increasingly rare in Britain. Costume was an important component of the Romantic traveller – and following Lord Byron, whose most celebrated portrait, by Thomas Phillips, showed him wearing Albanian dress, clothing of a Levantine type was considered particularly dashing. Emily Birchall and her husband, taking a steamer down the Danube in 1873, were delighted to observe, in steerage, 'a most picturesque crowd of natives, the wildest-looking set we ever saw'. On display were 'long fair moustaches, huge pipes, garments of undressed sheep skin, boots of cowhide, or bare feet, below the wide Turkish trousers, and language the strangest in Europe'. There was 'a nobleman, the greatest swell on board, clad in the national dress, tight coat covered with rich embroidery, tassels and bows, with scores of cornelian buttons, soft hat with bright feathers, tight blue trousers, and huge boots up to the knee, his enormously long meerschaum in his mouth'.[23]

What most tourists relished was a serendipitous encounter with peasants, straw-hatted and full-skirted, engaging in pleasingly pre-industrial activities: washing clothes in a river, playing instruments or dancing spontaneously in a village square. Susan Horner was delighted in 1847, for example, to watch old men and women in a 'perfect garden of old olive trees' harvesting the fruit.[24] The line between staring and participating was often a delicate one, as Jemima Morrell, in Switzerland in 1863, found when she visited some public baths:

> Accordingly in the morning we rose at 5 o'clock and already saw the bathers, in semi-toilette, crossing to the baths, to commence their day's soak. We followed them not as bathers, but as observers. It was difficult to shake off the feeling that we were indulging in an excess of curiosity, and still more difficult to maintain a sobriety consistent with good manners . . . In one bath we recognised a lady who was our vis-à-vis at table d'hôte the day before. She was taking her next meal up to her shoulders in water; on a wooden tray was placed a tiny coffee-pot, a pat of butter and slices of bread. We could discern the seat or benches running round the bath on which were seated persons in dark blue or dark red gowns. A moustached gentleman, who would consider himself in the prime of life, was cutting leather work on his floating table, while bathers were preparing for a game of draughts, whilst one portly

round-shouldered party of some sixty summers was executing
a roving commission across the water to salute some ladies in
the opposite corner . . . Judging from the array of work-baskets
on the ledge of the bath, the ladies dry their hands for knitting
and crotchet. . .[25]

The Reverend Greatorex, on holiday in 1878 from his East End
parish, had the good fortune to see a boatload of genuine Moroccan
tobacco smugglers when his boat was berthed in Gibraltar. 'One
of the women undid her dress which was only a loose robe tied
around the waist, and then take flat parcels of tobacco – probably
weighing about 2lbs – and place them under each breast and then
tie three around her body by means of a cord. She then took an
oblong parcel of about equal weight and deliberately lifted up her
garment and tied it in the hollow of each thigh – she appeared
to have no sense of delicacy in the performance, rather, on the
contrary seemed to think she was only doing what everyone did.'[26]

The business of tourism itself, with its inevitable commercialisation
and standardisation, destroys the essence of what it seeks even
as it appears to encourage its survival. Looking for the 'real' or
the 'hidden' is a constant refrain – as early as 1818 Mrs Starke was
mourning the loss of that distinctive something. 'I am sorry to say
that the ancient costume of the Tuscan peasants is less frequently
worn than it used to be twenty years since.'[27]

Tourist accounts often express disappointment that local people
appear too well-off or have abandoned their old customs for modern
conveniences or wear clothing that makes them indistinguishable
from the visitor. It is a theme which is more urgently felt than
ever. Historian David Wills, in a 2007 monograph on travel
writing on Greece after 1945, noted how even twentieth-century
visitors to Greece often strained to find in the faces of modern
Greeks the imagined (and superior) lineaments of the ancient
world. In a fascinating trawl through postwar travel accounts,
Wills found that in 83 per cent of texts, Greeks were referred to as
'friendly' or 'curious'. He notes the prevalence of the assumption
that men sitting at cafe tables in Greek villages must be talking

of politics ('being the heirs of the first democracy'). Orthodox Christianity, Wills writes, is often described as being superior to Roman Catholicism – being more 'passionate' – and that religion was found not to be disturbingly heartfelt but an 'expression of an ancient joie de vivre' – therefore sitting more comfortably with secular western European presumptions. An enjoyable possibility of paganism is hinted at, with ordinary Greeks routinely compared to 'gods'. In 1970, the writer Duncan Forbes, sitting opposite some Greeks on a train, thought their 'sharp noses, bright eyes and half kindly, half cynical smiles reflected with remarkable faithfulness the features that lie in profile on the old vases and stand out full face on the old statues'.[28]

'A LIVING POMPEII'

By the mid-nineteenth century, the more adventurous tourist began to look north – towards the inhospitable cold regions of Scandinavia. Sweden and, in particular, Norway were viewed as being on the very periphery of Europe, and became popular destinations for the off-the-beaten track tour or the sporting fishing trip. There was no train (and has never been) running from Oslo to the far Norwegian north so a journey to view the northern lights in Tromsø had to be made slowly up the coast by ship, an undertaking that, from a tourist's point of view, was pleasingly old-fashioned.

The strange and mineral-rich landscape of Iceland was particularly fascinating to Victorian geologists. There was a burgeoning interest in new translations of its ancient sagas, and for establishing a northern mythology for those who, like Ruskin, did not regard the Norman invasion as the origin of English civilisation: the English and Scots were heirs to the Norsemen, and Iceland was therefore the living source of their lost culture. Norse imagery flourished in the Arts and Crafts movement from the mid-nineteenth century and into the twentieth. The author and antiquary W. G. Collingwood, whose novel *Thorstein of the Mere* was a seminal text for Norse enthusiasts, rehabilitated the Viking invasion of Cumbria as the spark for a burgeoning of the arts in the English Lakeland, founding in 1904 the Lake Artists' Society. For Collingwood, the Vikings were artistic pioneers, lovers of liberty and upholders of law. Arts-and-Crafts types filled their homes with embroidery, decorative woodwork and rushlight holders. The introduction to the first Murray's handbook to Iceland in 1853 flagged up the island's ancient affinities to Britain:

> Prior to the 10th century Scandinavia was the region of romance – of the wildest legends; but even the earliest periods of her history are intimately connected with England, and abound in interest. The conquests and discoveries accomplished by the energy and heroic bravery of the ancient Scandinavians during the 10th and 11th centuries were not only most extensive, but have left a permanent impress upon the character and institutions of great part of central Europe, and particularly in the British Islands.[29]

As Collingwood's friend, the Icelandic scholar Jón Stefánsson, remarked: 'Iceland is today a living Pompeii where the Northmen races can read their past.'[30]

Spending time in Iceland was not for the fastidious tourist. As a destination, it was characterised less by what it offered in terms of cultural attractions than by what it did not have – and that was the degeneracy, moral and ecological, brought about by industrial capitalism. The Icelandic writer Matthías Jochumsson, who frequently visited Britain, wrote in the 1870s:

> Iceland has no army, no apples . . . no atheists, no bridges, no banks, no beggars, no Baptists . . . no corn . . . no clubs, no cathedrals, no dukes, no diplomats, no dynamite, no electricity, no ambassadors, no elephants, no exchequer, no fabrics, no gas, no gamblers, no gibbets, no gallows, no generals, no hospitals (except one), no hydrophobia, no hogs, no heterodoxy, no inns, no infirmary, no locomotives, . . . no laureate, no magazines, no manufactures, no museum, no monks, no monkeys, no Magna Charta, no nihilists, . . . no nobility, no night in May, June and July.[31]

Icelanders, mostly unaccustomed to foreign visitors, were gratifyingly, authentically, rough and ready; in them the tourist was encouraged to glimpse the spiritual echoes of a shared ancestry. According to Murray's handbook, 'The people generally are most primitive and independent in their manners; but they are honest, hospitable, intelligent, and desirous to oblige. The costume of the women is very picturesque. They wear high white caps, like the women in Normandy. Perhaps the Normandy women have retained the custom handed down to them by their Northmen ancestors.'[32]

The tourist could watch the Icelanders at their labours all year round. As Murray's put it: 'During winter time the men are employed in tending cattle, picking wool, manufacturing ropes, bridles, saddles and building boats. In the summer . . . turf-cutting and hay-making. Fishing in the spring.' In the autumn months, the handbook continued, 'they are principally devoted to the repairing of their houses, manuring the grass lands, and killing and curing of sheep for exportation . . . the womankind of a family occupy themselves throughout the year in washing, carding, and spinning wool, in knitting gloves and stockings, and in weaving frieze and flanner for their own wear.'[33]

Early on, the Icelanders seized the chance to profit from the traveller's enthusiasm for gazing on their hard labour. Even in 1853, when tourist numbers were few, Icelandic locals were offering the opportunity, for a small remuneration, of watching them boil mutton in a hot geyser in under six minutes. More conventional tourist comforts were slower to arrive. The cuisine was interesting rather than enticing, according to Murray's: 'The ordinary food of a well-to-do Icelandic family consists of dried fish, butter, sour whey kept till fermentation takes place, curds and skier – a very peculiar cheese – a little mutton and rye bread'. Life was brutish and short: 'Scurvy, leprosy, elephantiasis and cutaneous disorders were common while the custom of feeding babies cows' milk after 3 days led to high infant mortality.'[34]

Getting to Iceland was a challenge. Most tourists went to Copenhagen and then travelled on north via the Orkney, Shetland and Faroe Islands. In 1853, the voyage could only be done on a merchant vessel: 'accommodations are often very bad and dirty', warned the handbook – and this took ten or eleven days, including stopovers. Once in Iceland, there were no roads and in order to get about, it was necessary to hire shaggy little local ponies (Murray recommended the purchase of an India-rubber cushion to ease 'jolting'). The capital Reykjavik, the only large settlement, had about 800 inhabitants and 'consists of a collection of wooden sheds, one storey high – rising here and there into a gable end of greater pretensions – built along the lava beach, and flanked at either end by a suburb of turf huts'.[35] However, the landscape was magnificent, apocalyptic in its bleak splendour. Nothing quite matched the sense of fearsome awe its unique volcanic geology inspired. 'On every side of it extends a desolate plain of lava, that once must have boiled up red hot from some distant gateway of hell, and fallen hissing into the sea.'[36]

The intrepid tourist might have taken with them one of the books that had helped cement the land of sagas and saga-steads in the imaginations of British readers. Iceland, with its lack of amenities, postcards and monuments, lends itself even today, wrote Jan Morris in 1969, to 'a literary rather than a living beauty', and in the first years of the 1860s, a cluster of important publications tried to capture the spirit of the place. These included Sir George Webbe Dasent's *Iceland Grammar*, the first in English and, in 1861, the publication of Dasent's translation of Njál's saga, the longest of the heroic sagas. In 1860, the Reverend Metcalfe's *Oxonian in Iceland* stamped the wild Icelandic landscape and its 'primitive' people into the consciousness of the English tourist. In the same year, Charles Forbes's *Iceland: Its Volcanoes, Geysers and Glaciers* explicitly linked the storytelling traditions of the saga-age (from the ninth to eleventh centuries) with the age of the electric telegraph. Instantaneous communications between Europe and Canada, via Britain, the Faroe Islands, Iceland and Norway, Forbes thought, were a modern symbol of the ancient kinship between northern peoples.[37]

Among the most readable of Icelandic travel writers was the Reverend Sabine Baring-Gould, a polymath of inexhaustible energy and engaging credulity. When Baring-Gould visited Iceland in 1859 he was about to be ordained a clergyman; he went on to write 248 books, including *Iceland: Its Scenes and Sagas* and a 'saga novel', *Grettir the Outlaw*, based on his own lengthy translations of the Norse sagas of Grettir the hero. Before he set out on his tour, Baring-Gould taught himself not only to read Old Norse but to speak some modern Icelandic. He filled his notebooks with every conceivable detail of his experiences, from the sublime to the mundane. What he ate there was of particular fascination: it was generally Icelandic moss stewed in milk, or whimbrel stew.

The Icelanders fascinated Baring-Gould, though, like so many tourists, his interest was generally in types rather than individuals, preferring people to conform to the national characteristics with which he had already endowed them. (In letters home to his mother he had to admit that the 'dissolute Icelander' he had described to her previously on the boat was in fact French and the 'young Consumptive Dane' turned out to be an Icelander.[38]) He nonetheless eschewed the whimsy and romanticism of many contemporary accounts of the rural poor; Baring-Gould may be credulous but he is never sentimental. He reported that Icelanders lived in extreme, not picturesque, poverty: in huts usually without a fire, keeping warm by piling on their bodies stinking sealskins over layers of protective grime. The stench of whale fat and old fish was overpowering. Lamps were made of oily ptarmigans with wicks threaded through their innards. On the advice of his travellers' handbook (which must have been Murray's), Baring-Gould took with him pewter rings decorated with artificial diamonds to use as barter but was embarrassed to find that the locals interpreted them as an offer of marriage.

During his Icelandic travels Baring-Gould encountered a selection of other English tourists, most of them visiting the island for the fishing. He also met, however, a tourist archetype perhaps nearer to Baring-Gould in spirit than he would have liked: a 'Mr Briggs', in search of the ineffable, the spiritual, the 'real' – of whom he affectionately made fun. A group including an American journalist, J. Ross Browne, arrived in Reykjavik at the same time as Baring-Gould (whom Browne later lightly mocked in a magazine article as a 'dandy tourist') but Browne disdained to spend more than six days on the island. It proved enough time, however, to send up a group of British tourists setting off for the interior for eight weeks:

My English friends were so well provided with funds and equipments that they found it impossible to get ready. They had patent tents, sheets, bedsteads, mattresses, and medicine boxes. They had guns too, in handsome gun-cases; and compasses, and chronometers, and pocket editions of the poets. They had portable kitchens packed in tin boxes, which they emptied out but never could get in again, comprising a general assortment of pots, pans, kettles, skillets, frying pans, knives and forks, and pepper castors. They had demijohns of brandy and kegs of Port wine; baskets of bottled porter and a dozen of champagne; vinegar by the gallon and French mustard in patent pots; likewise, collodium for healing bruises, and mosquito-nets for keeping out snakes. They had improved oil-lamps to assist the daylight which prevails in this latitude during the twenty-four hours; and shaving apparatus and nail brushes, and cold cream for cracked lips and dentifrice for the teeth, and patent preparations for the removal of dandruff from the hair; likewise, lint and splints for mending broken legs. One of them carried a theodolite for drawing inaccessible mountains within a reasonable distance another a photographic apparatus for taking likenesses of the natives and securing facsimiles of the wild beasts; while a third was provided with a brass thief-defender for running under doors and keeping them shut against persons of evil character. They had bags, boxes and bales of crackers, preserved meats, vegetables, and pickles; jellies and sweet cake; concentrated coffee and a small apparatus for the manufacture of ice cream. in addition to all these, they had patent overcoats and undercoats, patent hats and patent boots, gum-elastic bed covers, and portable gutta-percha floors for tents; ropes, cords, horse-shoes, bits, saddles and bridles, bags of oats, fancy packs for horses, and locomotive pegs for hanging guns on; besides many other articles commonly deemed useful in foreign countries by gentlemen of the British Islands who go abroad to rough it.[39]

No matter what sneering journalists might think, roughing it paid off for Baring-Gould, and his later descriptions of the eerie landscape he found in Iceland are extraordinarily vivid for his having really tried to live, even for a short time, within it. The isolated region of the Jökulls, for example, he captures with particular power:

> The scene of desolation is quite indescribable: a vast trench between walls of rock and heaps of snow; the crags of great height and flat-topped, with bare precipices of green ice and snow resting on them, ready to topple over in avalanches with the least disturbing cause, and bury us under their ruins; here and there a cone of snow which has thus shot to the bottom and has not yet begun to melt; now a smooth sweep of undinted whiteness, rising to the Jökull top, or barred with black steps of rock glazed with frozen streams. Not a bird, nor insect, not a sound.[40]

Ten years after Baring-Gould's return from Iceland, the polymathic William Morris – socialist, designer, painter, poet, novelist and campaigner – also aflame with the old sagas, arrived to soak up some Norse spirit. He found Reykjavik disappointing but, characteristically, compared it favourably to an English industrial town: 'not a very attractive place, yet not very bad, better than a north country town in England'. Later he conceded, damningly, that 'the town itself might be in Canada and is quite commonplace'.

Morris, like Baring-Gould (and Mr Briggs), was in search of awe-inspiring landscape and 'untouched' inhabitants. It was the first of two visits by Morris – and though he was undoubtedly inspired he found himself often ambivalent about the lives of the Icelanders themselves. In the dramatic scenery in western Iceland that is the setting of the Laxdaela saga, he seems to have come to a realisation that epic stories are often solace for a hard life of everyday survival rather than a reflection of continuing human heroism:

But lord! What littleness and helplessness has taken the place
of the old passion and violence that had place here once –
and all is unforgotten; so that one has no power to pass it by
unnoticed: yet that must be something of a reward for the
old life of the land, and I don't think their life now is more
unworthy than most people's elsewhere, and they are happy
enough by seeming. Yet it is an awful place; set aside the hope
that the unseen sea gives you here, and the strange threatening
change of the blue spiky mountains beyond the firth, and the
rest seems emptiness and nothing else: a piece of turf under
your feet, and the sky over head, that's all; whatever solace
your life is to have here must come out of yourself or these old
stories, not over hopeful themselves.[41]

Morris came home, reported his friend Edward Burne-Jones,
'smelling of raw fish and talking of Iceland more than ever'. But
what had he found? In a letter in 1883, Morris referred to Iceland
as the place where he learned that 'the most grinding poverty is a
trifling evil compared to the inequality of classes'.[42]

As usual, the 'real' is elusive, the search for 'authenticity' nothing
but romantic hubris destined for failure. Reading Baring-Gould one
gets the impression that Iceland was in the 1850s swarming with
tourists who wanted to be thought of as travellers. On one occasion
he saw a lonely figure staggering towards him across a remote lava
flow: it turned out to be the young grandson of Lord Byron, his
heart broken after an 'Icelandic maiden' refused to marry him. In
fact, Icelandic maidens seem to have quickly got the measure of the
romantic English visitor; Baring-Gould's 'portly friend' Mr Briggs,
a-thirst for authenticity, goes into raptures: 'A houri! A tinted Venus!
A Valkyri!' Baring-Gould slyly noted Briggs's horror when the vision
started chewing on a dried stockfish. And as for what the Icelanders
thought of the tourists – when W. G. Collingwood visited Iceland
in 1897, he found that William Morris was chiefly (admiringly)
remembered there for his strong views on probate and income tax.[43]

By the end of the nineteenth century, it was still excitingly
dangerous to get to Iceland (Rider Haggard was lucky to survive

the journey when his ship sank off the Orkneys in 1888) but it had nonetheless become an established tourist destination. This of course brought all sorts of changes to the life of the island. In the sixth edition of the Murray's handbook to Iceland, published in 1888, thirty years after the first, there are reports for the first time of something approximating tourist infrastructure.

Guidebook writers and gazetteers had piled in over the preceding thirty years, and Cook's tours even included Iceland in an Arctic cruise in 1880. Though his emphasis is on sportsmen and geology enthusiasts, William Lock's 1882 *Guide to Iceland* claimed to be as authoritative as Baedeker or Murray but far more up to date. Lock's guide is interested in the Icelandic people, but even more in the comforts of the modern holiday experience. He extols the luxuries of the state room on the steamship *Camoens*, the newly opened billiard room in Hótel Ísland in Reykjavik, and the 'odourless leggings' from Leith now happily available to buy in the Icelandic capital.

Lock noted that the air of Reykjavik was no longer 'offensive to the olfactory senses': the streets were now paved, broad, airy and clean and 'the drying codfish is mainly confined to the shore'.[44] He mentioned an antiquarian museum now located in the jail. There were two booksellers, several photographers, a druggist, a hatter and a post office; the cathedral was in a very sorry state of repair. Accommodation was once scarce (in 1888, Murray's handbook reported that churches had been used until recently throughout Iceland as sleeping quarters for travellers, 'but owing to the behaviour of some people a few years ago in Thingvellir Church, permission to use them has been withdrawn by the Bishop'[45]) but now there were new hotels, one – Smith's – run by an Englishman. Three decades after Baring-Gould and Morris visited Reykjavik, the capital boasted several general stores which sold whisky and American corned beef, as well as Peek Frean's biscuits. There was even an English consul in residence.

The locals had risen to the challenge of tourism and tourism had brought with it its tide of change. The author of the 1888 handbook, torn between regret and approval, reported that while staying in a rural inland farmstead he was offered a bottle of Italian wine with breakfast.

'GOD BE THANKED: A RUIN!'

When, at the end of 1918, the writer Sir John Hammerton visited the battlefields of France he found that they 'abound in evidence of this struggle between the forces of beauty and of ugliness. Here and there, by some odd freak, the utter devilishness of modern destructive ingenuity has been thwarted, and the ruin wrought has proved more beautiful than the completeness destroyed.'[46] The First World War was over but already the real experience of mud and carnage was being translated into the tourists' experience of gazing on ruination.

A great deal of tourism culture revolves around the contemplation of death. Most sightseeing feels in some way valedictory, a glimpse from behind the visitor's rope barrier at a world long gone or vanishing fast. It is a common conviction of all travellers that they are in a race to see the great sights of the world in their authentic, untouched state before they disappear. As early as 1850, the Reverend Henry Christmas advised: 'Those who wish to see Spain while it is worth seeing must go soon.'[47] The atmospheric melancholy evoked by this sense of impending change is all the more pleasurable for being on the whole undefinable. 'I find one of the effects of Rome is to set one longing: I don't know for what exactly,' wrote Thackeray's daughter Anne.[48]

Ruins, by their nature uneven, untidy, unsymmetrical, are an important component of the Romantic view (and even more so of its more macabre subset, the Gothic). For the tourist, ruins present the clear opposite to the soulless standardisation of mass production. Straight lines were anathema to the eighteenth-century picturesque hunter; William Gilpin even suggested that the too-regular contours of Tintern Abbey could be improved by a 'mallet judiciously used (but who durst use it?)'.[49] The classical lines of Palladian architecture, conceded Gilpin, were elegant, but to be properly emotionally affecting required the addition of crumbling masonry. 'We must use the mallet, instead of the chisel: we must beat down one half of it, deface the other and throw the mutilated members around in heaps. In short, from a smooth building we must turn it into a rough ruin'.[50]

The wonderfully atmospheric etchings of ruins by Piranesi were the key visual texts of the idealisation of romantic decay. Piranesi's dramatic perspectives, juxtaposed with tiny figures and the feathery encroachment of flowers and tree roots into ancient masonry, set the template for ruinous grandeur. Tourists were often surprised to find that the real thing was less ruinous than expected and that, as Smollett observed, Piranesi was 'apt to run riot in his conjectures'. The artist John Flaxman's first impression of Rome in 1787 was disappointing: the ancient Roman remains were 'less striking than he had been accustomed to suppose them after having seen the prints of Piranesi'.[51]

Yet Piranesi's depiction of the interior of the Colosseum, its fallen stones mossy and sprouting with foliage, was surprisingly accurate. The six acres covered by the remains of the Roman amphitheatre were filled with an astonishing array of plants and flowers. In 1832, the American artist Thomas Cole described the Colosseum not as a ruined building but as the setting for the natural wonders which had reclaimed it and broken up its man-made angles with curves and abundance: 'From the broad arena within, it rises around, arch above arch, broken and desolate, and mantled in many parts with the laurustinus, the acanthus and numerous other plants and flowers . . . It looks more like a work of nature than of man . . . The regularity of art is lost . . . in dilapidation . . .Crag rises over crag; green and breezy summits mount into the sky.'[52] In 1855, the English botanist Richard Deakin listed all the flora he found there, 420 species of plants in all. These included fifty-six varieties of grass and forty-one legumes. Fig, cherry, pear and elm trees grew on the highest tiers of the ruin; the walls were smothered with vines, ivy, clematis and wild roses. Some of the wild flowers were so rare in Europe that they could only have been introduced into the Colosseum by animals from Africa or the Middle East, imported for gladiatorial games.

These plants were literally the living past, having taking root at the time of ancient Rome.

In the centre of the auditorium a black cross marked the spot where, as Nathaniel Hawthorne, who visited in 1858, put it, 'more of human agony has been endured for the mere pastime of the multitude than on the breadth of many battlefields'. It was, reflected Hawthorne, who watched the parties of Italians picnicking and singing in the ruins, 'a strange place for song and mirth'. He reflected that the Italians moved easily between prayer and irreverence: 'People are accustomed to kneel down and pray or see others praying, between two fits of merriment or between two sins.'[53]

When Dickens visited Rome in 1846, he thrilled to see the Colosseum: 'To climb into its upper halls, and look down on ruin, ruin, ruin all about it,' and 'its awful beauty, and its utter desolation . . . the ghost of old Rome, wicked, wonderful old city . . . never in its bloodiest prime, can the sight of the gigantic Coliseum, full and running over with the lustiest life, have moved one heart, as it must move all who look upon it now, a ruin. GOD be thanked: a ruin!'[54]

But renovation and restoration are always round the corner for the ruin. Are they to be left to sink into the ground and disappear, or should their state of decay be arrested in perpetuity? By 1870 every single tree and plant in the Colosseum had been removed on the grounds not only that they were untidy but that they were pulling the remaining walls down. Under the instruction of the new government of King Victor Emmanuel II's reunified Italy, the walls were scraped clean and the fallen masonry was tidied up. By the time the restorers had finished, the Colosseum looked like a ruin erected only yesterday.

It wasn't long before much of old Rome vanished under new stucco apartment blocks and boulevards. 'Avenues, tramcars, electric lighting and miles of American hotels,' groaned Frederic Harrison in 1893. 'Big vulgar, overgrown, Frenchified and syndicate-ridden.'[55] Hawthorne's observations about the living Italians moving easily among the remains of their city's past were shared by many visitors with both approval and disapproval. The Italians were seen by many British as degenerate, superstitious and unworthy inheritors of their magnificent classical past – and it was believed that their 'casual' attitude towards their cities indicated that they did not know how to honour it. The novelist Maurice Hewlett, visiting Florence in 1900, thought the city had been turned into 'a botched parody of a new one'.[56] The horror felt at the sight of degradation of the classical past was extended to the Italians themselves. One Victorian traveller wondered if any encounter with an Italian could leave an Englishwoman untainted: 'I never could learn from any man I knew that, in the range of his society or information, or interrogation, he ever met or heard of an individual that did not loathingly recoil from the idea of matching himself with any girl who had gone the round of Italy.'[57]

As always, the contemplation of ruins, the sweet sadness they evoked, was compromised by the presence of other people. Or more particularly the wrong sort of other people. Other tourists brought vulgar and invasive noise to places which some tourists thought should be contemplated in silence. Wilfrid Scawen Blunt loathed the Americans he encountered wandering round the ruins of Baalbek in Lebanon: 'Being quite insensible to beauty or decorum and with the manners of shop-boys, who ramble through the gardens of the ancient world was little knowledge of their values as beasts have, defiling all and trampling all . . . They should be kept at home,' he declared, 'for they have no business in these ancient lands.'[58]

Sometimes tourists sought out other kinds of reminders of death. Visitors who at home would never have watched a public hanging might join the mob when abroad as a point of 'local interest and colour', in much the way that a tourist to Spain who disliked blood sports might visit a bullfight when in Spain. The political radical 'W.E.F', visiting Paris in 1816, made a point of going to a guillotining, remarking approvingly that one sees 'none of that horrible struggling that takes place in the operation of hanging'.[59]

Guidebooks were ready with macabre recommendations. The 1853 edition of Murray's handbook to Naples suggested tourists

might attend a pauper's burial in one of 366 deep pits in the Campo
Santo Nuovo:

> The pits are covered with large stones; their number, of course,
> gives one for every day of the year and one over. One of them
> is opened every evening, and cleared out to make room for the
> dead of the day. A priest resides upon the spot, and towards
> evening the miscellaneous funeral takes place. By this time, a
> large pile of bodies is generally accumulated. They are brought
> by their relatives or by the hospital servants, stripped of every
> particle of clothing upon the spot, and left to be disposed of at
> the appointed time, unattended in most instances [by family
> or friend] . . . the bodies are thrown into the pit, with as much
> unconcern as if they were the plague patients of Florence
> whom Boccaccio has described; quick lime is then thrown in,
> and the stone covering is replaced for another year. As many as
> forty bodies are thus disposed of in a single evening. The pits
> when first opened are generally so full of carbonic acid gas that
> a light is extinguished at its mouth; and it is said that whenever
> they have been examined the day after a burial, the bodies have
> been overrun with rats and enormous cockroaches, which clear
> the bones more expeditiously than the lime.[60]

Prisons, charnel houses and burial places were all on the itinerary.
They were often viewed not as exercises in memento mori but
more prosaically as of sociological interest. In 1733, the tradesman
John Mucklowe noted in his diary that he had gone to a prison in
The Hague where the 'whores were decked out' to amuse visitors.[61]
Catacombs were particularly popular and so were corpses, embalmed
or otherwise. In 1836 in Kreutsberg, Mary Ann Nicols had only just
got over a visit to a silk manufactory, where she had seen silkworms
being boiled alive, when her friend Miss Buxton suggested they
visit the bodies in the catacombs: apparently she'd been before and
was keen to go again. 'Oh it was frightful indeed. I shall never
forget it,' Nicols reported. 'An old man of 90 with a candle in his

hand opened the vaults. He went down first I followed. There were 25 dead bodies, some they said had been dead 400 and some 200 years. Some had their shoes on, he touched them and wanted me to, but I dared not. They did look so horrible. The skin was on many of them. It was quite a narrow space between them where we had to walk so their feet did touch our clothes.'[62] In the 1860s, from Paris, Robert Louis Stevenson's nanny, 'Cummy', wrote to her friend: 'I must tell you one other thing we saw, it was a place where persons who are murdered or commit suicide are put. Mr S took me as Bessie would not go, and Lew was not allowed. I saw two men through a glass door, who, I suppose had been murdered. They just appeared as if asleep. The clothes of all the murdered people were hanging along the ceiling. the dirty looking clothes blowing in the wind, and the dead men lying below made it an awful dreary sight.'[63]

The battlefield at Waterloo drew British tourists within days of the battle, undeterred by what Walter Scott recalled as 'the smell of the charnel house [which] tainted the air to a sickening degree'. According to a piece in the *Observer* of 1822, so much human and animal waste was left strewn all over the battlefields of the Napoleonic wars that it was imported back to Britain in vast quantities to be used as bonemeal fertiliser. 'It is estimated that more than a million bushels of human and inhuman bones were imported last year from the continent of Europe into the port of Hull,' the report stated.

> The neighbourhoods of Leipsig, Austerlitz, Waterloo and all the places where, during the late bloody war, the principal battles were fought, have been swept alike of the bones of the hero and the horse which he rode. Thus collected from every quarter, they have been shipped to the port of Hull and thence forwarded to the Yorkshire bone grinders who have erected steam-engines and powerful machinery for the purpose of reducing them to a granulary state. In this condition they are sold to the farmers to manure their lands.[64]

Over thirty years after the battle, in 1844, Adam Blenkinsop found the famous Sergeant Cotton still taking tourists round the battlefield, where he kept a little museum of relics. Blenkinsop was keen to visit the village of Waterloo and the shrine which had been raised over the burial place of Lord Anglesea's leg – complete with the boot which it had been wearing. 'I went to laugh,' he confessed guiltily, but he ended up feeling moved by this strange relic, even though most of the boot had disappeared: souvenir collectors had snipped so much off that only a bit of sole remained. Sergeant Cotton had taken the toe of the boot for his own museum.

Blenkinsop could not work out quite why he was so interested in these objects associated with violent death: 'I was anxious to see the boot. A boot of the time of George the fourth and Beau Brummell is interesting.'[65] He could not come up with an answer but was moved by the remains of the boot despite himself. F. C. Amherst, paying a passing visit to Waterloo at around the same time, tried to put a laboured humorous spin on it. He was disappointed to find Lord Anglesea's leg had not been buried, 'with any witticism [by] way of [an] epitaph such as "Here lies the Marquis of Anglesea's leg, Pray for the rest of his body I beg".' However, as further entries in his diary indicate, he felt guilty about his levity and was keen to note the seriousness of what the boot represented.[66]

Some tourists were attracted to wars actually in progress, hanging about battlefields in sight of the fighting. The day-excursionists who in 1870 followed the action of the Franco-Prussian War in their carriages were criticised in a leading article in the *Observer*, which pointed out that those attracted to this kind of jaunt were creepily, even sadistically, voyeuristic: 'It seems to us that nothing can be worse than for tourists to follow the track of armies, gratifying a mere lust for excitement which is not free from cruelty.'[67]

By the turn of the twentieth century, views had begun to change about war tourism. When, during the Boer War, Cook's announced they would be taking guided tours (at 150 guineas a head) of the South African battlefields before fighting had even ceased, it was widely viewed as poor taste. In *The Times*, Sir Alfred Milner, the British high commissioner in South Africa, called on tourists to stop interfering with the business of war.[68] The debate even inspired a poem in *Punch*:

> In myriads behold they come,
> And almost ere the guns are dumb,
> The picnickers' champagne will pop
> Upon the plains of Spion Kop
> O flag! O Tourist! Powers twain
> That all the world resists in vain
> Where 'neath the one the other picks
> The wings and legs of festive chicks,
> And strews the battlefield with bones,
> Newspapers, orange peel, plum stones –
> There is the reign of darkness done
> And freedom's fight is fought and won.[69]

Although in 1914, Cook's evacuated 6,000 tourists who were stranded in Europe, they continued sending tour groups to unaffected parts of France, particularly the Côte d'Azur, which was advertised as being fashionably 'uncrowded due to world events'. The poet A. E. Housman paid his first ever visit to the Riviera in 1915, 'when the worst classes who infest it are away'.[70]

There is an awkward mix of embarrassed fascination and religious veneration in these visits to the scene of death. The tourist feels it is a duty to go there and yet the more years that roll between the action commemorated and the tourist's visit the more it is permissible also to have a bit of a laugh – to pose for a photograph in a dungeon, or try out some medieval stocks. But by 1920, the unprecedented death tally of the First World War had changed views forever on battlefield tourism: at least on those sites where battles had been fought within living memory. As a new age of mass tourism arrived there came with it a sense that, in the aftermath of such a defining event, there were some places that simply could not be gawped at. When it came to the battlefield or the cemetery, the idea of the tourist visit needed refining – perhaps a better idea would be to return the definition of the tour to its medieval origins. *The*

Times addressed the matter in an editorial, pointing out that: 'The French have a better term for what are described in this country as battlefield tours, they call them pilgrimages.'[71]

Thomas Cook and Sons, whose employees had suffered huge losses in the Great War (153 of the 1,000 members of Cook's staff who served in the armed forces were killed), offered two six-day motorcoach tours to European battlefields. One, conducted in maximum luxury, cost 35 guineas and another, cheaper and therefore more popular, was 9½ guineas. Many charities such as St Barnabas, the Salvation Army and the Church Army gave assistance to poorer bereaved families to go on pilgrimages. Cook's advertising made clear that these were not jaunting excursions. So the visitors became referred to as pilgrims and the tours as pilgrimages. Rudyard Kipling was quoted in the Cook's brochure of 1925: 'It rests with the individual tourist to have respect for the spirit that lies upon all that land of desolation and to walk through it with reverence.' The 1919 guide *Muirhead's Belgium and the Western Front* reminded the pilgrim 'that the ground he is visiting is holy ground, consecrated by the heroism and the grief of nations'.[72]

Among the most moving sites for pilgrims in the town of Poperinghe, 8 miles west of Ypres, was Talbot House. Set up by the Reverend Philip 'Tubby' Clayton and fellow chaplain Neville Talbot as a 'soldiers' club for all', a place of rest and contemplation, Talbot House (named after Neville Talbot's brother Gilbert, killed in 1915) was left exactly as it was, and became a place of pilgrimage. Above the door was a lamp with a continually burning flame to remember the 25,000 soldiers who attended services at Talbot House and had gone to their deaths.

The 1935 guidebook *Over There: A Little Guide for Pilgrims to Ypres, the Salient and Talbot House, Poperinghe*, welcomed: 'Many a man, perplexed and burdened by the confusing issues of everyday, enters here to find his solutions in the simplest secret of the Old House.' Visitors to Talbot House could read the original inscription, painted on the wall: 'This board is intended for the use of men who wish to get in touch with friends, who may possibly see a message left for them. Please use cards provided or put communications in an envelope before placing in the rack.' A long, stained and faded list of men who made use of 'friendship's corner' was still hanging there in 1935. Cameras were forbidden. On the library wall, the sign remained: 'All Rank Abandon, ye who enter here.'

Not everyone, however, went to the battlefields in the spirit of respect. In 1919, H. J. Greenwell of the *Daily Express* reported that the Belgian town of Ypres was thronged with visitors trying to catch the thrill of a terror they had not experienced: 'morbid seekers after sensation. Vandals. Ghouls of the battlefield.'[73] Just a year after the Armistice, visitors were invited to watch what were known as 'devastated areas' being worked over by a 'clearing up army' that continued to bring up bodies, shells and barbed wire.

Eventually, inevitably, little material sign of battle remained. Graham Seton Hutchison, who had fought in the trenches, returned to Ypres as a battlefield pilgrim twenty years later. 'Except in their topographical outline, the battlefields have changed. The rebuilt towns and villages and the resown fields, yielding their crops, bear no resemblance to the crumbling ruins, shattered woods and shell-pitted wastes which marked the war years,' he reported.

> For the pilgrim, revisiting the scene, it may even be difficult to rediscover villages and scenes whose every stone and contour in former years were as familiar as the palm of the hand. But the pilgrim will find that by night the old instinct will reassert itself, and blind in the darkness, he will be able to walk with certainty to any one of the old familiar spots. But the pilgrim goes to see and re-experience and not to grope in darkness.[74]

'Tubby' Clayton, another veteran of Ypres, returned in 1935 and found: 'Not a single building eventually escaped, and within two years the city provided that picture of desolation, crowned by the nobly tragic silhouette of the Cloth Hall tower, which remains so real in the minds of countless ex-servicemen.' For Clayton, the sight of tourists, even designated 'pilgrims', was disturbing.

It is difficult indeed for a visitor of the younger generation which knew not "Wipers" to stand in the Square, where the Ostend charabancs are parked between gay cafes and the brand-new Cathedral of St Martin, and picture the time when his predecessors, halting (but not too long) on the same spot, could look across the breast-high shattered houses and almost survey the city from end to end. At no time in its long, unhappy history was Ypres so desolate and yet so glorious.[75]

"VANNING": A HOLIDAY ON WHEELS
GIPSYING UNDER IDEAL CONDITIONS

GIPSIES BY AN IRISH LOUGH

A CAMP ON THE KERRY COAST

A CAMP IN ESSEX

AN EARLY MORNING SNACK

SPORT BY THE WAY: A NICE GRILSE

BREAD-MAKING

WITH A CAMP CART IN SUSSEX

CAMPING WITH A MOTOR-CAR
Pictures by E. Horsey Jarvis.

WITH A CAMP CART IN MOROCCO

'Lights out very early and a spirit of goodwill'. An advertisement for caravan and camping holidays.

V

'Wholesome and Excellent'

'A CAREFULLY SELECTED MOB'

The cover of the 1865 annual guide to Cook's tours was illustrated by a solitary figure looking out over a landscape untouched by train or road. The challenge of advertising popular tourism by the mid-nineteenth century was how to maintain the desirable illusion of individual adventure and personal restoration without removing the camaraderie of the like-minded group holiday on which Cook's reputation rested. All holiday advertising since has tried to sell the promise of the uplifting personal journey with the reassuring image of companionship in what the *Tourist* magazine of 1898 larkily called 'furrin parts'.

Holidays, as we define them now, are a by-product of the Industrial Revolution. With the value of labour increasingly measured by hours and production, what had once been informal breaks from work centred round religious holy days became increasingly viewed as unproductive idleness. Referring to the introduction in 1871 of the Bank Holiday Act, *The Times* noted that there had been 'an increasing tendency of late years among all classes to find excuses for Holy Days'.[1] Yet before the introduction of these statutory paid holidays, it was employers who controlled all times off work – and increasingly, many of them had whittled back the holy days.

So the mid-Victorian British worker would not easily have understood the idea of 'leisure': it was an entitlement which the rich and aristocratic took for granted but which in anyone else was thought to be an absence of purposeful activity. As Charles Hall put it in 1805: 'Leisure in a poor man is thought quite a different thing from what it is to a rich man, and goes by a different name. In the poor it is called idleness, the cause of all mischief.'[2]

The working-class travel clubs which proliferated in the second half of the nineteenth century were often both politically radical and socially conservative. Many emerged from their founders' anxiety that, left to their own devices, the working classes would fritter their parcels of free time on 'hobbies', and become 'pigeon-fanciers, Canary-breeders and Tulip-growers',[3] or worse. There was a paternalism about the clubs, certainly, but also a free-spirited, democratic camaraderie. It is not coincidental that members of the Toynbee Travellers' Club, emerging from the East End settlement founded by Reverend Samuel Barnett in 1884, called themselves 'pilgrims', in a foreshadowing of the battlefield tourism after the Great War. Their first expedition was in fact a 'pilgrimage' to the tomb of the Italian republican Mazzini. In the spring of 1888, the first Toynbee pilgrims, a group of eighty, went to Florence. They set off from Liverpool Street station, where they recognised each other by their Baedekers and the air-pillows dangling around their necks.[4]

The anonymous Toynbeeite who wrote up the holiday expresses arch regret that the 'romance' of travel has been erased by Cook's coupons, but gives a picture of beneficent leadership – with some mannered (and sometimes improbable) descriptions of the grateful, poor and 'timorous landlubber pilgrims'. One small boy apparently described the trip as 'Petticoat Lane off to the Continent'. Their time was tightly organised: Canon Barnett did not subscribe to sitting about. 'On Monday there were the usual four morning excursions. Miss Paget lecturing on art at the Uffizi, Miss Burke at the Pitti, the Dean of Windsor again acting as Guide to Santa Maria Novella and Mr Key to the Palazzo Vecchio.'[5] All the inconveniences – the late breakfasts, the misleading guidebooks, lost luggage and late trains – were made palatable by the conviviality of the pilgrim gang, or at least in the retrospective retelling. Among many anecdotes, not perhaps so hilarious at the time, is the one about the pilgrim who ruptured a blood vessel in his eye during a snowball fight in Brughaser.

Despite the guidance of their leaders, the group was refreshingly disinclined to fall in with received opinions: 'The first impression of Florence was one of disappointment. Rome was universally voted à fraud and a first visit to Venice we are often told is a great disillusionment,' wrote the anonymous chronicler. The baptistery gates in Florence were so dusty that they all agreed it would be preferable to see them as electrotype replicas in the South Kensington Museum. The pilgrims also took issue with the guidebook's suggestion about seeing Milan cathedral by moonlight, finding the electricity installed there far preferable. When the log-book keeper asked the party to send in impressions, one, signing himself Phil S. Tyne, wrote: 'I find that when people begin talking or writing about Italy they naturally and necessarily talk or write a heap of transcendent nonsense about art and that sort of thing.'[6] Poor Canon Barnett.

All nineteenth- and early twentieth-century working-class holiday organisations followed in spirit the self-improving model that had been established by Thomas Cook. But where a Cook's holiday had become chiefly the preserve of the middle classes, these new organisations tell different stories – of real hardship but also sometimes of an engaging recalcitrance when demanded to respond appropriately to high culture.

In 1905, the Co-operative Society started to run tours for its members. This letter from an unmarried schoolmistress who had joined a group gives a small background vignette of loneliness and cultural dispossession: 'I came here on spec. I knew nothing of these Co-operative holidays,' she wrote, 'but I had bad luck last year with seaside lodgings. The people were not my sort and I had to go on my lone all the time. I have precious little society in the country village where I teach. The vicarage people are good; they sometimes ask me to tea. But if the Squire's carriage happens to drive up, I am bundled off into a sort of butler's pantry for fear I should be seen.'[7]

Naturally, the Co-operative holiday, with its emphasis on healthy outdoor activities interspersed with some improving sightseeing, had become bathed in nostalgia by the time its founder, the Congregationalist minister and social reformer Thomas Arthur Leonard, wrote his autobiography in old age. But after the Great War (in which Leonard had been, like many of his colleagues in the Co-operative movement, a 'convinced pacifist') there was a renewed sense among organisations like the Co-op that organised leisure was a way of bridging economic and national divisions. It seemed unlikely that the kind of person accustomed to going to the Riviera would join a Co-operative hiking trip to, say, the Dolomites, but nonetheless, the Co-op idealists felt that their group tours emphasised the value of common ground.

The point of the group, morally speaking, to Leonard and his partners, was that having to get on with other people of all types and opinions built 'character' (or as Leonard puts it: Character); and the presence of 'responsible' group leaders put a brake on 'silliness'. Echoing Thomas Cook nearly a century earlier, Leonard's view was that the way we spend our leisure is really a test of our education. More than half our trouble comes from not having learnt to enjoy the right things – the things that are 'Wholesome and Excellent.'[8] If people were to use free time wisely, it was better that it should be planned and budgeted for in advance. Just setting off on holiday, unguided, was fraught with moral hazards: it led to thoughtless spending of money, falling into inane and unwholesome amusements, and unhealthy overcrowding in lodging houses; moreover, it promoted vitiated ideas about life, resulting in permanent bad effects on Character. 'Clearly the great majority of our young people did not know how to get the best out of their holidays.'[9] T. A. Leonard himself was viewed affectionately by a less deferential generation of tourists as a ridiculous old bossy-boots:

> TAL of course had his blind spots like the rest of us. They
> appear funny today and indeed were comical to we younger
> folk then. There was the struggle to get the General Committee
> to permit a gramophone in the Common or Games

room: arguments as to whether the Fellowship should admit dancing to those horrible noises known as jazz; the air of conspiracy after TAL had done his frequent 11 p.m. round the huts . . . the conspirators issuing forth darkly to have pop and biscuits in the centre secretary's residence.[10]

These travel groups were run on idealistic principles of equality and aspiration. Travellers on the Quaker-run Holiday Fellowship (also founded by Leonard in 1912: two years later he became a Quaker), for example, insisted that all domestic staff in their accommodations were to be assured of a position of 'social equality and mutual service'. No tipping was permitted and pay for the domestics was therefore much more generous: 'The old servant system with its obsequiousness and "tips" is far cheaper to the employer, but is part of a bad social system that we determined to get rid of,' wrote Leonard[11] The Polytechnic, which ran small tour groups abroad from the 1880s, sold itself as offering an experience beyond material pleasure. Fifty years later, the Poly's director Commander Studd (whose father, champion cricketer Sir Kynaston Studd, had been a founding director of the travel club) introduced the 1935 brochure of tours with the promise: 'I always like to think that we set out to give you for your money something that money cannot buy.'[12] (Money was not totally overlooked by the Poly: in 1896, Thomas Cook Travel had complained that the Polytechnic was running as a commercial travel agency but was subsidised by government grants.)

For modern tastes, there is an infantilising quality to the way these holidays are presented, a suggestion of *in loco parentis*, of being there to save the members from their own disorganisation. The Polytechnic Touring Association (PTA) encouraged participation in vigorous group jollies, based at least in part on similar activities in the public schools that its directors had attended. The Poly took its first trip abroad in 1888, when a group of sixty schoolboys was taken to Belgium and Switzerland to see the landscape they were learning about in geography classes. Later, Commander Studd claimed it (not quite accurately) as a first for working-class organised travel; for tours not for the modestly comfortable-but-genteel, the retired solicitors and lady watercolourists to be found on a Cook's tour, but for those for whom travel beyond Britain had once been unthinkable unless they joined up. 'The tour was more than an experiment in travel. It was a social experiment. Until then Europe had been the prerogative of the well-to-do Britisher. But these youngsters, teenagers, came from the lower middle classes; a few in fact in ragged pants.'[13]

Just how muscular were the activities required of the boys is evident in the instruction given for the tour by the Poly's director of education, Robert Mitchell: 'You will be expected to walk from 20 to 25 miles each day and should any member knock up he will have to cover all expenses that may be incurred for the hire of a conveyance or a mule.'[14] Fortunately, the four accompanying adults in the group included a doctor. The tour was a great success and became an annual event. In 1906 a gentleman climber staying with friends in a mountainside hut in Switzerland was dismayed to find a group of young polytechnic students from London in the mountain hut where he was staying the night. 'We were disposed to resent their intrusion', he recalled. Yet he was delighted not only by their courtesy and their evident pleasure in their surroundings, but also by the fact that 'after dinner they sat outside on the rocks and sang part-songs divinely'.[15]

In 1887, several Polytechnic parties had crossed the Channel to visit the Paris Exhibition. These outings were so successful that the Polytechnic branched out, offering tours to people not affiliated with the institute. The Poly tours expanded rapidly: by 1894 the organisation had acquired the chalets on Lake Lucerne which were to become its centre of operations; and in 1896 it bought a steam yacht, the *Ceylon*, for tours of the Norwegian fjords.

A family from Laurels, Clifton, went on a winter PTA cruise (or 'Viking Tour') to Norway in 1908, and they saved a copy of the daily menu from their trip. From it we learn that on offer for the travellers' dinner was: consommé followed by boiled cod, lamb cutlets, braised York ham, beef à la mode, with potatoes and cauliflower, plum pudding, sweet sauce, Italian pastries, cheese and biscuits. Breakfast included porridge, fried fish, kippers, calves' liver and bacon and mashed potatoes, fried eggs, lambs' tongues, chops and steaks – as well as quantities of toast and rolls. On the back of the menu, there is a handwritten, waggish poem, clearly part of some impromptu group activity to celebrate New Year (other festivities included fancy dress dances, concerts and various deck sports tournaments):

> I've composed a wee song, which I'll now sing to you
> And if you don't like it, you know what to do.
> My rhymes, they are not very brilliant I fear,
> To put it rudely, they're rotten, so happy New Year.
>
> Our hands have all by an old gent been shaken
> Who dances at concerts in a way that is taking.
> And a lady I know, you all must have seen her
> She's jolly hot stuff on the coy concertina.
>
> There's a gentleman I think a lot of you see
> He's standing right there and he's grinning at me.
> With his smiles and his jokes, he's not at all tardy,
> And we all hope that he will keep well and 'Hardie'.[16]

The emphasis on throwing yourself into to all the activities was almost evangelical. After all, as Studd put it: 'You didn't go alone but with a party, a mob, a carefully selected mob.'[17] Mucking in, volunteering, owning up, chumminess and taking it on the chin are all ideas (or rather firm exhortations) that come up in the official descriptions of PTA and Co-operative holidays. Instructions (prescriptive rather than advisory) on what to pack for the trip suggested that there would be no slacking: 'For a vigorous holiday with plenty of exercise' you required 'one suit of strong cloth (medium weight); an extra pair of knickerbockers or trousers; two flannel shirts (well shrunk) three pairs of strong stockings or socks; one pair of strong boots; one pair of thin shoes; four pocket handkerchiefs; one night-shirt; one comb; one toothbrush; one towel; a mackintosh; blue spectacles (sunglasses to you!), or a piece of green crepe.'[18]

Throughout the 1914–18 war, the Polytechnic Institute in Regent Street displayed monthly the roll of honour of those of its members who had been killed. In 1914, the PTA had been setting out on another tour of Switzerland with the Scouts ('Poly boys') when war broke out. At Dover, some of the young men had taken cinematograph pictures of warships gathered in the port and reported 'harangues' with German police. Undaunted, they had continued to Switzerland and been subjected to the usual exhausting timetable of walking and mountain climbing, or 'pushing resolutely forward' as the tour leader described it.[19]

The image of hiking was altered by the inclusion of single women after the the First World War. The 'girl in the office' was everywhere, observed the Poly's Commander Studd approvingly. For financially independent women, a group ethos which laid a stress on decent behaviour would have been attractive. The groups were also forward-looking, even radical, in their treatment of the sexes. Among the claims made by the Holiday Fellowship – which like all the heartier knapsack organisations had tended to be aimed at young men – was that they were instrumental in the eventual 'rationalising' of dress for women: 'There was no comfortable tramping and climbing in the absurd garments that women were supposed to wear,' wrote Leonard.[20]

In 1927, the Holiday Fellowship opened a hostel in Sydenham – 'Hitherwood' – specifically to promote peace by bringing together young people from across the world. Hitherwood entertained guests from the United States (both black and white, it was noted), Canada, Australia, Denmark, Iceland, Sweden, Germany, France, Switzerland, Poland, Russia, Bulgaria, Czechoslovakia, Turkey, Egypt, India, Ceylon, China, Japan, Holland, Hungary, Norway, Austria and Belgium. The Youth Hostel Movement, inspired by the Fellowship, opened its first hostel in Germany in 1912, and in 1930 the Youth Hostel Association was founded to provide cheap country inns where young people on walking and cycling holidays could stay for a shilling a night, with breakfast another shilling.

By 1933, there were more than 3,000 hostels in Europe. 'Its tremendous growth since the War has impressed all who have visited Germany recently,' wrote Leonard. 'In all parts of the country, in the lovely Rhine and among the hills of the Black Forest and Taunus, and in Bavaria, we have met groups of these youths, rucksacks and cooking apparatus on their backs and a wonderful look of joy in their eyes, bound for some "herberg" or other . . . Life is Spartan. No smoking or drinking; lights out very early, and a general spirit of goodwill.'[21]

The idea of holidaying as having a moral purpose apart from one's own diversion was shared by Cecil Rogerson, the founder of the Workers Travel Association (WTA), set up in 1921 explicitly to support the work of the League of Nations. A disorganised socialist visionary, Rogerson was, a former colleague remembered, 'fanatical, dedicated, idealistic, but strikingly unbusinesslike'. Trained as a social worker, he was 'fruitful of ideas, active in promoting good causes: he was a pioneer, but like many such, wholly incapable of carrying his ideas to a successful conclusion'.[22] Rogerson ran the WTA from a bedroom in Toynbee Hall: 'His papers littered all over the sheets, the accounts, such as they were, jotted down on the backs of envelopes and other odd scraps of paper and stored for safety in a brown paper parcel under the bed.'[23] A year after the WTA took its first tour in 1921, Rogerson started another travel group called 'Friendship Travel'. He died within months, on a group holiday to Switzerland, after a fall in the mountains near Lake Lucerne where he'd been gathering flowers.

The first committee of the WTA was composed, among others, of prominent union leaders, including the leaders of the Shop Assistants and the Railway Clerks, as well as Margaret Llewelyn Smith of the Women's Co-operative Guild. Harry Gosling, a shop steward with the Transport Workers union, was in Geneva and remembered the moment: 'We were talking about the need for a closer contact between the working classes of the nations, and saying what a boon it would be if our own people could only travel on the Continent,' he wrote. 'We felt it would be a great thing if we could do something, however small, to break down the prejudice against "foreigners", so readily encouraged by the Press of all countries. If only the ordinary people of one country could meet the ordinary people of other countries and get to know their ways and their movements, what a powerful factor it would be in securing real and lasting peace.'[24]

In 1921, the year it was founded, the WTA took nearly a thousand people abroad, helped by Harry Gosling's expertise in transporting people and freight over long distances. A figure known as 'auld docker' from Grangemouth was among those who took his first holiday abroad with the WTA: 'When I told my cousin Jenny I was going for a holiday to Holland this year she nearly fainted. If I had told her I was going to be hanged the news could not have caused more consternation. She tried every wile she could think of to get me to change my mind but it was useless.' Among the many perplexing aspects of his experience were the way that Dutch waiters approached from the 'wrong side' and that the natives of Edam had flappers 'just like ours – silk stockings, fancy shoes, bobbed hair, powder, paint, lipstick etc.' This implausible auto-didactic Scotsman has form in PTA literature. A similar type to the 'auld docker' appears in the 1897 PTA brochure in which the *People's Journal Dundee* again runs an account of a Poly trip – this time to Switzerland – by an author merrily agog for learning but amusingly embarrassed by the superior learning of his fellow travellers:

> Baillie Brewster told us that up in London there was a Society called "The Polytechnic": that did a wonderful lot in the way of spreading scientific knowledge and encouraging moderately well-off bodies like myself to visit the Continent . . . I got books from the town library, and read about glaciers and crevasses and avalanches and edelweisses, and goitres, goats and gorges, chamoises and mountain railroads, till my head was chokeful of a mighty store of indigestible information.[25]

The Holiday Fellowship renewed its tours to Germany after 1918 but many were deeply affected by the sight of a nation and a people so reduced and desperate. Leonard for the Co-operative and the leading members of the Fellowship saw the opportunity to bring together their idealism and their travel management experience. They were looking for 'young, forward-looking people strongly influenced by the international outlook', Leonard wrote, and Germany – still one of the most popular destinations for English holidaymakers to Europe, despite postwar chaos - was the place to begin. 'In 1922 came the "inflation Zeit" in Germany,' he continued, 'when marks were chasing each other up to giddy heights week after week and losing half their purchasing power. Staying as some of us were in the very sumptuous Schloss Hotel at Braunfels on the Lahn, we felt ashamed to be able to buy so much with so little of our English money. It was a painful experience amid a population on the verge of starvation; it destroyed much of the beauty of the holiday.'[26] The tourists at Braunfels were reminded how difficult it was for Germans to buy books and were asked to leave any they had with them for the local library. Setting off, they were asked to: 'Bring a pound of good English tea; you can make it a present to a German "Hausfrau".'[27]

A group from Carr's Biscuit Factory in Carlisle visited Germany and Austria and were warned by the organiser in advance that they were not to expect any luxuries: 'Milk conditions are worse in Austria. White bread can only be made from "Relief" flour: we shall, therefore, use brown bread and tinned milk. Butter is scarce.'[28] In fact, Germany was so keen to encourage foreign visitors in the twenties that cow's milk was only available for children aged 1–6 and for tourists. A group from the WTA took a trip to Berlin and group member Dr Alex Dessin from Bradford (perhaps more representative of the type as a whole than the auld docker) later wrote about it for the *Yorkshire Post*. He reported that he'd returned home with a souvenir thousand-mark note which was worth less than 'a fraction of a farthing'. The value of the mark had fluctuated during his one-week trip from 2.5 million to 25 million to the pound. 'With a little English money to throw about, it is certainly easy to play the big over there.' Dr Dessin, 'an outspoken socialist', was able to treat six of his companions to a six-course dinner with wine and cigars for 12,889,000 marks (less than 15 shillings).[29]

The 'German people are starving in silence', wrote Dessin. 'If England is mentioned they say to us time after time "Why doesn't England help us?" meaning that we should intervene in the Ruhr. It is absolutely inconceivable that they can live on the money; they steal and break into shops. No wonder! There is absolute hopelessness in the people's expression.' Dessin reported that some on his WTA tour had intervened when they saw acts of police brutality and had got into trouble.[30]

By 1924, the WTA was so prominently established that the prime minister, Ramsay MacDonald, was the guest of honour at their annual conference. He spoke on how tourism, especially manifested in groups of young people, could foster peace in the future. 'When we have been in Germany, Germany means the German people. The difference between the two conceptions – of a nation as something abstract and of a nation composed of individual people, a large number of whom we may have known personally – is fundamental and revolutionary.'[31] By 1929, 22,500 young people had travelled abroad through the WTA – most of them never having been abroad before.

To the modern eye, some of the chumminess of these groups looks perilously like well-meaning coercion. Singing – mostly English folk songs – appears to have been obligatory. In the 1920s and 1930s, *Over the Hills*, the Holiday Fellowship magazine, contained long lists of English folk songs suitable for hiking groups – 'Dashing Away with the Smoothing Iron', 'Widdecombe Fair' and 'Green Grow the Rushes O' among them. Books on recommended holiday reading lists included *Careers and Openings for Women* by the feminist writer Ray Strachey, *The Years* by Virginia Woolf, and *A Calendar of Old English Customs* by Major Hogg. The Co-operative Travel Association in turn called their songbook *Songs of Faith: Nature and Comradeship*. Leaders were on call, like scout masters, to make sure everything was jolly and everyone participating. The minutes of the WTA in 1928 indicate that a shortage of leaders was causing concern because without them the group quickly descended to 'grumbling' about food and amenities.

The minutes also tell us that sometimes group members were not so easily drilled into night-time curfews and ping-pong tournaments. They note that on the WTA's very first trip to Berlin in 1921, the leader was 'so busy doing his accounts' that he wasn't there to deal with one of the party who 'went on a drunken rampage and abused Germans'.[32] The Holiday Fellowship also found that when they were forced, for financial reasons, into charging rather more to attract older holidaymakers on their trips, they had to relax the 'compulsory' nature of the expeditions because the new members wouldn't have it.

Naturally there were many who viewed the groups with suspicion. In 1932, at one of their UK hostels, in the seaside town of Bonchurch on the Isle of Wight, some local residents were outraged. 'Such a hostel would destroy all that Bonchurch means,' they told a reporter from the *Daily Herald*. 'We and other residents would have to leave' and the 'whole tone and value of property' in the town would 'be seriously lowered'.[33] The residents won the battle of Bonchurch but it turned out, as many commentators had observed, they had misread the runes on the knapsack brigade with its rules of conduct and codes of behaviour. As the *Morning Star* noted:

> They have entirely misconceived the outlook of the new type
> of holiday maker who prefers the anonymity of a guest house
> and a fresh-air holiday to the life of a crowded seaside resort.
> Bonchurch is now saved from invasion by a responsible group
> of people under a fine organisation, but it will still be subject
> to visitation by trippers whose sense of responsibility too often
> ends when they catch their departing bus.[34]

The face of tourism, the very idea of a tourist, was changing. More and more people were on the move and more and more of them were going to the same place. It was disconcerting for those who preferred their holidays to be insulated from lower-class compatriots. In 1934, a correspondent to *The Times* objected to the sight of some merry young hikers setting off to the continent in their unisex washable shorts. 'The spectacle of the country's youths and maidens in hideous uniforms' is how the writer put it, before going on to fulminate against the exposure of fat or knobbly knees and the dreary 'potato-colour' of their hiking gear.[35] But many others welcomed the way that the new holidays smoothed out visible class differences. A traveller on a 1933 WTA cruise to Spain wrote: 'One could write an essay on the influence of clothes in maintaining class distinctions and a frightful amount of senseless snobbery. The thing about cruising is that nearly everybody is clad in much the same sort of light and bright clothing, and so you cannot tell the Dukes from the dustmen.'[36]

A sense of disappointment in tourist travel is prevalent in the 1930s, perhaps because of that familiar feeling common in the experience of travellers that everywhere seems to be full up. One WTA diarist went to Majorca and felt a bit let down by its apparently prosperous tourist economy.

> If asked for our previous impressions, we would probably
> have sketched a rocky island with a population of peasants
> or fishermen winning a meagre livelihood from the land or
> the more generous sea. We go ashore in a launch and find a
> Modern Utopia. A beautiful country, a fine town, striking
> builds, a better "Avenue" than Cheltenham, a prosperous-
> looking and independent people – who would rather not have
> English money – what a blow![37]

By 1928 the Holiday Fellowship was taking groups from Bolton to the Riviera: ten days in Nice, Menton, Monte Carlo, San Remo, Cannes and Grasse, for £15. According to Commander Studd of the Poly, foreign food, long viewed as one of the final frontiers to full enjoyment of abroad, was finally becoming more palatable to the British tourist. 'Continental food was still more of an experience than an enjoyment to the conservative palates of Britishers, but we ate it and boasted that we liked it; we were becoming a more sophisticated people . . . and there was something appallingly pedestrian about admitting that you preferred boiled-beef and carrots to cheese tart.'[38]

What Rogerson had in 1921 called 'the lineaments of a social revolution' had stretched across the continent. But a more confident, less deferential generation of young travellers no longer bowed to authority as they had once done. There were indications that group members didn't want to be protected from the unwholesome values of the outside world. In fact, they wanted to embrace them. In the 1937 summer issue of *Over the Hills* 'a comrade' wrote, not entirely in jest: 'As the season is approaching I want to utter a friendly remonstrance regarding the growing custom – especially at our more strenuous centres – of our young stalwarts (of both sexes) disregarding the ways of decent society by coming to the evening meal not merely in their shirts and shorts, but with unwashed bodies and in the sweat-laden garments they have worn all day. I know the Fellowship is not conventional in its ways, but surely there are sanitary limits!' It got worse. 'A few of our girls have taken to the nasty habit of lipstick. Some of them say they do so because the boys like it . . . But the girls of the Fellowship are as nice as they are because they do not "make up" and adopt the ways of decadent society.'[39]

'What would happen now?' Commander Studd wondered as war seemed imminent. Getting tourists out of Europe was the priority for all the travel agencies after Britain declared war on Germany on 3 September: 'Transportation on the continent in the first week of the war was confused. There were troop trains going up to the Maginot Line; trains converging on the Channel ports full of stranded holiday-makers. Compartments were jammed, spilling over into the corridors with travellers.'[40] The Britisher abroad found it hard not to panic, remembered Studd: 'His French, like his father's and his grandfather's before him, was still abominable, and he could not read the newspapers; he just sat on his luggage, determined never to bring as much as a paper bag with a sandwich on another holiday . . . and German propaganda discouraged him.'[41] The PTA, like every travel agency in the country, had to swing into action:

In London, we worked feverishly to bring him home; to get him on that train, into that corridor, on to that channel steamer that sailed, not by itself any more, but accompanied by destroyers, like a child with two heavily armed parents. We took holidaymakers out of remote passes and desolate valleys, and hamlets and big cities and off lakes and beaches, and put them on trains; fast trains, slow trains, and trains that ran, it seemed to sensitive sleepers, on square wheels. But we got them home . . .we got them home from every corner of Europe, intact, without a single casualty. The tourist industry worked as a team, well knowing that its only reward was the satisfaction of having been loyal to its customers in their hour of need. We worked day and night to do it.[42]

British holiday camps and chalet complexes were wrapped in dustsheets – their furniture put into storage – and stayed like that for the duration of the war. Thomas Cook & Son just about stayed solvent, although its office in Berkeley Street lost 2,000 employees to the war effort, maintaining a skeleton staff of 200. The company put its knowledge of taking people all over the world into transporting British children to North America (the London office was requisitioned by the Children's Overseas Reception Board), rescuing British tourists stranded on the continent and to moving supplies and then mail across occupied Europe.

'PROPER GYPSY STYLE'[43]

The solitary figure of the 'tramp' has an unexpected role to play in the story of British popular tourism. The life on the road came to represent the opposite of that of the spiritless factotum of the factory and the office. The early visionaries of the holiday business understood, if unconsciously, the strong appeal of the idea, however romanticised, of 'tramping' to people whose days were bound by clocks and timetables. Henry Gaze's system of tourists' cheques and coupons was based explicitly on the eighteenth-century practice of giving travelling artisans cheques which would entitle them to relief, food or hospitality.

In the figure of the tramp resided the dreams of the trapped: he became the literary embodiment of the little man set free. In E. M. Forster's 1910 novel *Howards End*, the clerk Leonard Bast walks all night through the gimcrack new suburbs of London until he reaches the open fields at dawn. In Victor Canning's popular novels of the 1930s, the eponymous Mr Finchley is a put-upon middle-aged man who dreams of freedom in a canary-coloured caravan. The idea of tramping offered the deep pleasure of anonymity. When D. H. Lawrence was walking the Tirol and given shelter by two sisters, he told them his father was a doctor in Graz, 'because I did not want to be myself, an Englishman, to these two old ladies. I wanted to be something else.'[44]

Yet later in his wanderings, Lawrence encountered a tired young clerk spending his annual fortnight's holiday walking and walking – over a hundred miles in four days. Lawrence, whose desire to escape stemmed from similar sources of anxiety and longing, characterises him as a pitiable figure ('amazing, pathetic courage') doomed only to existential disappointment. 'Under the inflamed redness of his sun- and wind- and snow-burned face he was sick with fatigue . . . he hung his head forward when he had to write a post card as if he felt his way.'[45] For Lawrence, his own bohemian freedoms secure, the clerk is a slave not only of a dreary office but of the shallow promise of popular tourism, of trinkety souvenirs, postcards and small economies.

> I could feel so well the machine that had him in its grip. He slaved for a year, mechanically, in London, riding in the Tube, working in the office. Then for a fortnight he was let free. So he rushed to Switzerland, with a tour planned out, and with just enough money to see him through, and to buy presents at Interlaken: bits of the edelweiss pottery: I could see him going home with them.[46]

Because of course the poor man, unlike the tramp, must eventually go home.

Lawrence disdained the idea that he and the clerk are actually very similar. They share a desire to be 'something else' and both seek it on the open road, in the encounters they hope to have with unchanging traditions and rural peoples, in simplicity, in open-air living and (slight) discomfort.

The language and customs of gypsies, and other itinerant peoples, had become popular subjects of a new study called 'gypsiology'. Romani gypsies also represented these longings for freedom, fellowship and life on the move. What was called 'gypsy living' was given the bohemian seal of approval by the artist Augustus John, whose family holidayed in Romani *vardo* (caravans) and wore their own handmade versions of 'gypsy' clothes. It was an ideal then made thoroughly safe by being taken up by middle-class holidaymakers, who rented horse-drawn covered caravans for group holidays. Elizabeth von Arnim's comic novel of 1909, *The Caravaners*, is narrated by a preposterous Prussian aristocrat who completely fails to get the point that the English group he is travelling with, with their taste for foraging and old clothes, are in fact liberal intellectuals who wouldn't dream of showing off how grand they are. It was a minefield of complicated social signifiers.

Leisure caravanners like Von Arnim's were known as 'gentlemen gypsies'. A caravan holiday had all the elements of an adventure into the past: with a pot over a fire, a kindly farmer to supply eggs and milk and a horse grazing peacefully in a paddock. Caravanning was swiftly untethered from both its gypsy and its bohemian associations, and became one of the most respectable forms of family holidaymaking. Three years after the founding of the Caravan Club in 1907, women constituted nearly a third of the membership, and 'experienced lady caravanners' dispensed advice to novices such as: 'If you are following a route which includes many towns and have any intention of attending evening entertainments, then an evening dress of non-spoilable, non-crushable description is necessary. Let your skirts be short . . . clear of the ground all round and one or two of just above ankle length for wet or muddy days.'[47]

Since the appearance in 1867 of the first bicycle, the 'velocipede', cycling had opened up the roads. Bicycles, many of them inexpensive, were the perfect means of transport for the camp-fire and road trip. They unlocked a national urge to roam, embodied in

Toad of Toad Hall in Kenneth Grahame's 1908 novel *Wind in the Willows* (itself an eloquent paean to the wandering dream). Toad is a show-off whose brand-new gypsy caravan will soon be replaced by a brand-new motor car ('Parp! Parp!'). But his delusions are touchingly universal: 'There's real life for you, embodied in a little cart,' he cries. 'The open road, the dusty highway, the heath, the common, the hedgerows, the rolling downs! Camps, villages, towns cities! Here to-day, up and off somewhere else to-morrow! Travel, change, interest, excitement! The whole world before you, and a horizon that's always changing!'[48]

Naturally – irresistibly – in no time, clubs, groups and organisations proliferated in Britain. In 1878 there was the Cyclists' Touring Club and in 1895, the Clarion Cycling Club (taking its motto from William Morris: 'Fellowship is life'). There was an arch taste for olden-days heartiness in the language of the cycle, caravan and camping clubs. In his 1893 diary of a camping trip to the Wye Valley, not completely tongue-in-cheek, S. K. Baker's foolish fellow camper Dr Goring rhapsodises about 'country maidens' and 'unctuous feasts'. For Dr Goring, a field is never a mere field but a 'demesne'.[49] Genuine 'tramps' were met with a great deal of this kind of pipe-sucking jocularity: an article in *The Camper* in 1910 described a group of campers in Hampstead once found themselves sharing a hedge with a 'knight of the road': 'Waking at daybreak, we shook the clinging hay from our garments and made for the leafy lanes, leaving our professional friend still curled beneath the hedge.'[50]

Religious nonconformism and radical politics were key ingredients of the camp-fire holiday culture. Like so many leisure movements in the early twentieth century, it emerged from the dissenting, teetotalling, self-improving tradition of Thomas Cook sixty-five years earlier. The pioneers of the independence of travel with the comradeship of the collective experience were 'nonconformist philanthropists, evangelising socialists, trade unionists and co-operative societies who simply aspired to comradeship in the fresh air and togetherness in tents'.[51] The muscular Christianity of this movement was of course epitomised by Baden-Powell, the spiritual father of campsite fellowship. The scouting movement took the idea of the camp worldwide, and extolled the resourcefulness and self-denial required by life under canvas that would be useful for young men about to be posted to the colonies.

Other figures (even fanatics) emerge from the early years of the cycling and camping crazes. John Fletcher Dodds, for example, was founder of the Clarion Cycle Club and also, in 1906, the Caister Socialist Holiday Camp. Thomas Holding founded the Cyclists Touring Association (CTA) and the Camping Club in 1901. There are many shared characteristics among the exponents of 'holiday outdoorsmanship' – but the most common seems to be a tireless interest in useful kit. Both cycling and camping spawn an almost interminable range of ingenious solutions to the problems of weight, weather and storage. Holding was a master of kit ingenuity. He was a tailor and passionate cyclist whose Mormon parents had journeyed from Britain to America, then trekked 1,200 miles across the Rockies to Salt Lake City by wagon train. By the time he was thirteen, he was back in Britain, a tailor's apprentice whose hobby was working out innovative ways to transport large amounts of camping equipment on the back of a bicycle. Using his tailoring skills, he also designed his own useful fuss-free costumes for changing on the hoof, adaptable for any social or practical situation. Holding was accustomed to taking at least a tent with him on cycling trips: on one, he and his three companions managed to transport a canoe, a small sailing yawl, two tents and cooking equipment on four bicycles. On a solo cycling tour of Donegal, he listed the following provisions, itemised to the last detail:

> Tent, poles, pegs, ground sheet, ground blanket, cooking apparatus of three or four parts to fold one in the other, five little bags for tea, coffee, sugar, oatmeal and bread, marmalade or jam tin, combined knife and fork, one spoon, half-pint spirit tin, bit of soap ¼ inch thick by 2ins square, small toilet tackle and razor, spare under-vest, gossamer pillow to stuff with hay, etc., pair of spare thin stockings, leg overalls, special cycling cover coat, candelabra, candles, matches, two spare flannel

collars, a pair of knit slippers with thin leather soles, maps, bathing drawers, towel.[52]

Camping was, Holding thought, 'incontestably jollier' than staying in a hotel. It was also a great deal cheaper, opening up the holiday spirit to the poorer family – or 'the poorer cycle man from his rightful feast of fresh air and the grandest scenery his country affords', as Holding put it. 'All the horrors which outsiders fear and with which they threaten us, we neither meet nor find. But it is not a lazy life – far from it. The camp affords exercise without fatigue; fresh air night and day, and sufficient excitement to create interest.'[53] The members of the CTA and the Camping Club exchanged lively banter on their personal experiences with waterproofs and cycle capes (Holding didn't approve of capes on the grounds of flapping). Camping offered endless pleasure for those men and women who relished the arts of tinkering, of fitting things into small spaces and making a little go a long way. In 1890, for example, Manchester man Harold Cox described in his local paper a bicycle tour in France, during which he and his friends had rustled up a delicious soup made from 'nothing' but sorrel with an egg whipped in.

Before long, cyclists and campers had joined forces in yet a new organisation, the Association of Cycle Campers, which held its first camp in Berkshire, just outside Wantage, on the Whitsun bank holiday of 1901. By 1902, the association had 100 members – all of them seemingly agog for practical tips from Holding and other veterans. How to make your own 'gypsy tent', a compact but billowing affair, was a particular favourite; Holding himself had one in an uncharacteristically showy crimson silk. 'Wigwams', inspired by the 'Wild West' shows that had toured London in the 1880s and 1890s, were popular with children. A year later, in 1903, the Cycle Campers association had 143 members, of whom thirteen were women; AGMs were held in Holding's tailor's premises in London. Camp Fires (capitalised) were staged two or three times a year with demonstrations of, for example, how to properly use a billycan or light a Primus stove. There were sing-songs, team games, tent-pitching competitions, and lantern-slide lectures and presentations on yet more camping adventures.

As the popularity of camping grew, strides were made in the development of new technologies to counter the most basic problem of sleeping outdoors: damp. A new 'waterproof paint' that could be applied directly to cotton to make it like rubber won approval in the *Campers' Quarterly*, the first edition of which was published in 1901. Invention rapidly followed necessity. In 1900, the camper would have expected to have to gather some nearby hay to put under his groundsheet. It did not take long before someone invented the 'sleeping bag', a kind of padded garment with a hood and sleeves which enveloped the sleeper; by the 1920s, the first down-filled bag as we know it was on sale. There were mugs with retractable handles, and knapsacks which rapidly became adapted for different uses or distances.[54] In 1906, the Camping Club's handbook suggested a homemade recipe for mosquito repellent that was one-part neat creosote. A Miss Wallace won the competition to make a complete cooking kit for two people, including utensils, that weighed under 23 pounds. Food was sustaining rather than delicious. 'One of the finest pick-me-ups for cyclists, and one that is little known, is the sustaining power of the tomato,' advised the handbook. 'No matter how tired and how exhausted the rider may feel, if only a small piece of tomato is eaten, it acts like magic, taking all the depressed feeling away, and making one feel quite fresh.'[55] Ladies were urged not to cycle immediately after a meal as it shook up the digestion and stopped it working as smoothly as it should.

Acronyms sprouted like the spokes on a cycle wheel. Associations, constitutions, sub-committees and AGMS were devoted to instilling the deep freedom of the primitive outside life. There was the association of campers and the association of lightweight campers; there were boat camping clubs, cycle camping clubs and, a bit later, caravan camping clubs, all of them eventually spawning district associations ('Das'). Offshoots were the Folk Dance Group and the Canoe Club. The CTC became the CCC and the Cycle Camp Club spawned the Camping Club which was later incorporated into the Amateur Camping Club, finally emerging in amalgamation with the Caravan Club to become the Camping Union. In 1909, Captain Scott – extreme camper – became president of the Camping Union, a post he still held when he perished in Antarctica in 1912.

In both camping and caravanning, the speed of technology was combined with the deep contentment of primitive resourcefulness. The cover of the 1909 edition of *Campers' Quarterly* is illustrated by a woodcut of a pot on a fire, a smoke plume wafting into a starlit sky. This is the tramping, camping Gypsiologist's dream. However, the secretary's report in that edition also shows how a once eccentric holiday was swiftly going mainstream. 'Camping made great strides during 1908,' it declared. 'Although only emerging from its infancy, and often sneered at as the impracticable amusement of a few playful crowds, it has rapidly gained a recognised place in the world of sport.'[56]

Although the culture of camping ostensibly appealed to lovers of the solitary and the open road, in reality it quickly became characterised by a communality often enforced by rules, exclusivity and regulations. Camp life shared more than campers would have liked to admit with the humdrum suburban sprawl that was replacing the wild country of their desires. Camp regulations feature strongly in the pages of *The Camper*, with an emphasis on what awaits those who disobey them. There are stern exhortations about 'promiscuous pitching', the importance of 'quietness' and, of course, 'litter removal'. Play was strictly compulsory for all ages. A lady member wrote of her experiences when she and her sister took their three children camping. 'The vagabond idea appealed to the pre-historic man within us,' she wrote. Their tent 'flew a union jack and was decorated with red Indians and bears'. They took with them a small pocket revolver (though that seems to have been mainly for the children to play with). Their new-fangled sleeping bags provoked amazement in the local farmer, who supplied them with milk and other supplies ('Baked a bread-and-butter pudding in a hole in the ground.') Lighting their fire under the stars, 'we refresh ourselves at the very source'.[57]

The Whitsuntide Camp of 1906 advertised in *The Camper* invited members to pitch up, with a call to communal mucking in: 'Camp fires will be lit about 8.45, around which, weather permitting, we hope to pass a communal hour. Members are earnestly requested to bring music, sacred and secular songs, and non-singers to be prepared with recitations or stories.' A contributor called 'Merry Camper' described a group cycling/camping outing from Hampstead and took the opportunity to pass some reproving comments on 'Annoying Types': 'He whose panniers have a happy knack of playing tunes on the spokes of his wheels' – or the 'Don't Care sort of man who has one out of his front forks, brakes out of order, badly packed machine.'[58] Thirty years later, the Annoying Type was so established that a 1938 film about the Camping Club, *With Tent and Rucksack*, showed what disapproval awaited the camper who simply ineptly wandered about looking for someone to pitch his tent. The club pitched battles against restrictive local authority legislation for properly recognised and maintained campsites with properly maintained sanitation facilities. They campaigned for rights of way, countryside access and footpaths.

Caravans meanwhile rapidly expanded in technological efficiency and cosy homeliness. Although horse-drawn vehicles remained popular, a horse was not always practical. The first motorised caravan in 1906 was 21 feet long and included a living room/bedroom, kitchen and washroom with lavatory, an oil stove and 50-gallon water tank: it cost £1,000. In 1928, the Eccles had mullioned windows, carriage lamps and a gently puffing chimney: it was the pre-industrial country cottage of the British holidaymakers' deepest dreams.

The promise of sun: holidaymakers at Benidorm in the 1960s.

VI

'I Want a Holiday More Than Ever'

When Britain came off the gold standard in 1931, it sparked a crisis that the *Illustrated London News* compared to that of 1914. Thousands of tourists were, writes Piers Brendon in his life of Thomas Cook, 'scattered all over Europe . . . needing immediate help in order to save them from an awkward and often ignominious situation. It is in emergencies like these that the national as well as the individual value of such a world-wide travel and banking organisation as that of Thomas Cook & Son becomes apparent.'[1] The rate of exchange soared and holidays abroad became 50 per cent more expensive. The travel agencies produced knock-down offers to induce prospective holidaymakers to venture overseas again. 'Beating the rate of exchange' was the slogan of Polytechnic Tours in 1933: 'Away with Depression! All the pleasure and romance of travel abroad is open to you again in spite of the rate of exchange! The greatest and most carefully planned campaign we have ever conducted to keep the prices of holidays within reach of our clients has been crowned with a greater success than we had dared hope.'[2]

The very thought of taking a holiday in the early 1930s seemed, recalled Commander Studd of the Poly, 'an idle indulgence of better days'. Yet people were still travelling. Thomas Cook & Son, the behemoth of all travel agencies, continued to dominate the travel market in the decade; in 1937, the firm made a record-breaking profit of £270,000.[3] But the field had expanded and there were now many smaller specialist agencies offering new kinds of travel experiences: at the higher end they were bespoke and expensive; at the lower end they were cheap, all-inclusive and communal. They were pinning Cook's in on both sides, undercutting and whittling their prices to persuade customers to go abroad, flourishing more all-in deals and inducements. Poly travellers to Menton were offered subsidised meals and cash discounts in shops and restaurants. 'As well as 3 meals a day, the price covered two-shilling picnic meal-boxes (2 ham sandwiches and cress, 1 meat pie, biscuits, cheese, 1 apple, quarter pound of chocolate and a paper serviette) provided for the train journey – to avoid the soaring cost of eating in the dining car.'[4] As it turned out, the economic depression ushered in 'the golden era of the inexpensive holiday'.[5]

The Polytechnic Touring Association (and its clients) was moving away from the companionable frugality of the early 1900s. Holiday chalets had been widely in use since before the First World War (at the Caister Socialist Holiday Camp, which opened in 1906, they were made of old tramcar bodies) but they became increasingly popular in the 1930s. 'Comradeship in the fresh air and togetherness in tents' began to look less appealing than a chalet and a breakfast buffet. Billy Butlin opened his first holiday camp in Skegness in 1936 with an all-inclusive three meals a day and entertainment (which was generally not folk singing) for £3 a week or less.

Then there was the rapid expansion of air travel. Poly Tours enthusiastically embraced the potential of the aeroplane, decorating their brochures of the early 1930s with flocks of Art Deco stylised birds. 'Many hundreds of Polytechnic travellers have expressed their enthusiastic appreciation of this deluxe method of travel, which is gaining popularity each year,' noted Commander Studd. In 1932 they began escorted air tours in conjunction with Imperial Airways. The Poly brochure for 1933 shows a woman sitting in a plane designed like a train – with large, curtained windows (that could be opened!), a luggage compartment below her seat, a bowl of flowers on the table in front of her and a man seated opposite comfortably smoking a pipe.[6] Within the year, one thousand passengers had flown with the Poly. In 1936, they offered an 'All-British tour to Switzerland', responding to the call to buy

British and give holiday travel a patriotic quality that would make it feel permissible: 'Travel will be by the British machines of the Imperial Airways, piloted by British personnel from London to Basle. Accommodation will be at the Polytechnic Chalets, Lucerne, which are owned and managed by the Poly Tour Assoc, an All-British enterprise.'[7] The constant advertising of holidays abroad, of sun-filled illustrations of beaches, and trains passing along the bright primary colours of Mediterranean coastlines, made stark the contrast between those suffering in economic depression and those weathering it.

The luxury holiday abroad, indeed the luxury *of* a holiday, came to represent a deep economic inequality. This was partly due not to the elitism of the holiday culture but to its expansion. When addressing the British Youth Peace Assembly in 1937, Vincent Duncan Jones, secretary of the Youth Charter Group, called for a forty-hour maximum working week, a minimum wage scale for young workers and two weeks' annual holiday with pay. To prove his point he drew symbolic attention to the holidaymaking classes: 'Young men, told that industry would collapse if they were given two weeks' annual paid holiday, see everyday plans and pictures of "southern cruises" undertaken by sons of the rich.'[8]

Germany was still a favoured destination for the British, and Hitler's Reich was keen to encourage tourism and the concomitant flow of foreign currency. The Nazis also understood the importance of using foreign visitors as a tool of 'enlightenment': the Reich Committee for Tourism, which established a national tourist board within the Ministry of Propaganda, was established almost immediately by the new regime in 1933. Among the 'tourist attractions' it promoted was the concentration camp at Dachau. Robert Dummett, a young Englishman on a cycling holiday with a friend, was among those who took a tour of Dachau (which often included lunching in the same room as the prisoners). In a letter, he described to his friend, approvingly, that it was where the Nazis put 'wasters, idlers, social undesirables, Jewish profiteers and riff-raff'.[9]

The Reich Committee for Tourism displayed 'life in Germany' as a crucial component of the tourists' sightseeing schedule. It was a policy that seemed to have worked with many British visitors. A single woman, travelling on a Cook's tour to Europe in the early 1930s, reported in her diary that she returned to Britain 'singing Hitler's praises': Germany and Italy 'were quite the pleasantest places on the continent; and quite the most exciting Brave New Worlds in the making and well worth emulating'.[10] The international political landscape threw up new reasons to travel abroad, entirely unrelated to anything in the classical sightseeing canon. As Commander Studd remembered: 'Germany, Italy, Russia! You could take your pick of doctrines. Soviet ships took more than a thousand tourists to Russia in 1930; a year later twice that; and in 1932, more than five thousand.'[11] When the civil war stopped holidays to mainland Spain in 1936, the Workers Travel Association put Majorca on the itinerary instead, which 'will attract those who ask for insights into Spanish social and industrial life'. Tourism also proved useful for intelligence-gathering. Major James Lammin, owner of Lammin's Travel Agency of St John's Wood, was recruited in 1937 by Claude Dansey of SIS (MI6) into his secret 'Z' network. Lammin's genteel motor-coach tours of the continent proved excellent cover for espionage work.[12]

Unwilling to relinquish the idea of international fellowship, even for a regime as entirely antithetical to its ideals as the Nazis, the Poly continued to take tours to Germany until the outbreak of the Second World War. In 1937 the frontispiece of a Poly tours programme showed a coloured photograph of the Rhine overlooked by a turreted castle wrapped in a swastika flag, and above it the words: 'The Land of Dreams Come True'. In 1939 the PTA programme contained no section for Austria but instead included Innsbruck, St Anton and Vienna under the heading 'Germany'; at the border, the trains were boarded by SS officers demanding 'Passports please! Passports!' In August of that year, wrote Studd, all over Europe British tourists were on holiday. At the beginning of that year Co-operative Tours were still advertising their Rhineland and Bavarian walking tours, scheduled for August and September, and promoting trips which 'lead to the formation of friendships which break through barriers of race, creed and class, and make for understanding and peace'. These included youth hostel tours in Poland and Czechoslovakia. 'Everyone knew that war would come,' Studd reflected, 'yet most people deluded themselves into a frame of mind that let them believe only what they wanted to believe. And they wanted to believe that Hitler would give them time to have a holiday.'[13]

Cook's found that trips to Soviet Russia were in fact the only tour that actually increased in popularity. But by then smaller agencies were finding that not being Thomas Cook & Son had become a selling point, a marker of superiority and discernment. During the 1930s, small travel agencies offered the middle-class tourist carefully tailored experiences, often incorporating air travel, to suit a client's particular interests and personality. Emmeline, a character in Elizabeth Bowen's 1933 novel *To the North*, runs an agency in London of this type. It is, Emmeline says adamantly, '*not like Cook's*' – although it of course operated on the same all-inclusive model – but prides itself on going off the beaten track. 'Move dangerously' – a variant of 'Live dangerously' – is Emmeline's agency's flattering slogan. 'But surely your clients are always only too safe?' asks her friend. To which Emmeline's response is part Cook's agent and part D. H. Lawrence, both these aspects of the travel experience having been, by then, co-opted into the package tour. ' "Oh yes, physically," she said with some contempt. "But what everyone feels is that life, even travel, is losing its element of uncertainty; we try to supply that. We give clients their data; they have to use their own wits. 'Of course' – we always say to them – 'you may not enjoy yourselves.' " '[14]

Emmeline has in fact cannily commercialised the old snobberies of traveller versus tourist. What her agency offers is a quality-controlled little adventure, an experience flatteringly tailored to the individual who favours the quirky and the out-of-season. Her clients enjoy the sensation that they are venturing to parts that other, less intrepid types would avoid, but they do so without the inconvenience and discomfort of going it alone.

After the Second World War, attitudes to holidays changed again. 'I feel I want a holiday more than ever before – never to come back again,' wrote a correspondent to Mass Observation, the project that recorded everyday life.[15] In 1946, the famous Golden Arrow Train departed platform 8 of London's Victoria station for Basle in Switzerland – the first continental passenger train to leave since 1939. But would there be a postwar appetite for travel in Europe?

The economist William Beveridge's questionnaire on holidays (commissioned by Mass Observation) surveyed attitudes to leisure, aspiration, culture and hobbies. In 1946, a shortage of goods to buy had resulted in an abundance of spare cash: war workers had savings and overtime to dip into, and Beveridge's team were looking for ideas to kickstart the postwar economy. But although a surprisingly high number of Britons (250,000) went across the Channel for their holidays in 1946, the results of the questionnaire, published in 1947, also showed a distinct ambivalence to the idea of 'abroad'.[16] Perhaps unsurprisingly, the most resistance came from middle-aged or older people. 'I don't want to go abroad, never have,' said a fifty-year-old hairdresser, while a 45-year-old man took an equally firm line: 'No I wouldn't like that – I wouldn't stand the strain and the racket.' One respondent took the view that spending money in Britain was the patriotic option: 'I'd rather go to London. Good old England. Keep your money in this country I say.' Some who had been posted abroad during the war reported that homesickness had put them off ever leaving England again: one 63-year-old man wrote: 'I've been many years in the Navy and I don't require it.'[17]

The middle classes were, by and large, more enthusiastic about the idea of foreign travel for pleasure. As Beveridge's report put it: 'Service with the Forces has certainly affected opinion on this matter; but it seems that it affects people in opposite ways in almost equal proportion.' Those who had served abroad sometimes wanted to share the experience or to go to where their husbands had been posted. 'I'd like to go to Italy to see what my husband liked so much.' One 25-year-old woman said she had a 'fancy for

Switzerland': 'The scenery is supposed to be very nice and there's not as much restrictions there as we have.' Among the more unexpected items thrown up by the report was that among those who did express a cautious interest in holidaying overseas after the Second World War, Germany was the second most wished-for destination, only beaten by France.[18]

The report noted that 'the expressed resistances: to leaving England, to travelling; to language difficulties; fear of homesickness; of the effort and trouble involved; mistrust of foreigners, etc. – no doubt represent resistances latent in others, which would make themselves felt if travel abroad became cheaper and simpler'. It went on: 'Over a third of the working class expressed themselves positively against the idea of going abroad, a high proportion of immediate resistance considering the slight extent to which most people would have given the matter personal consideration before it was raised in the interview.' It concluded: 'There is clearly a large potential opening up for simplified and cheap holidays in other countries. But this is not in the nature of an unsatisfied demand, since for the majority the idea has not seemed sufficiently practical to reach the stage of any personal consideration.'[19]

For most British people the question of travelling abroad was entirely academic, as during the decade after 1945 it was extortionately expensive. 'The golden age of inexpensive travel was over,' wrote Commander Studd, noting that in 1939 a six-day holiday in Switzerland would cost £6 9s. 6d.; a holiday for two might cost £15, 'including pocket money'. In 1950, he noted, when the average wage was just over £7 a week, 'you skimped' on £50.[20] Furthermore the passenger had to contend with a vast heap of befuddling paperwork, complicated currency forms and visa applications.

Lines of communication across shattered Europe were restored with astonishing speed. From 6 May 1946 a daily service ran from Victoria Station to Brussels. On 28 June motor cars were being ferried from Newhaven to Dieppe on a new vessel, the *Nantes*. The Orient Express began running to Warsaw on 12 July; the Arlberg Express to Budapest on 6 August. Through-trains ran daily from

Ostend to Basle and back from 7 October, while the Anglo-Swiss Express, Calais to Switzerland, via Lyon, ran daily from 9 December. By 15 December 1946, the railway viaduct over the river Marne at Nogent was reopened and the next day the first overland sleeper, the Engadine Express, left Calais.

The high-minded origins of travel companies such as the PTA and the Co-operative were challenged by the popularity at home of a different kind of group experience – the holiday camp. The all-in nature of a camp like Butlins in Skegness appealed to people on limited holiday time and budgets. Among the commonest gripes found in the respondents to Beveridge's questionnaire was all the unexpected added extras that a holiday could throw at one. However, the idea of an inclusive deal of some kind, in the sun, seemed to have broad appeal. When asked what her ideal holiday would look like, one woman summed up: 'Well I don't like that you pay and then you pay again. For little things like sandwiches, and coffee and cakes. Like to have a high tea or a cup of tea if you want. Everything is supposed to be free and we spend a lot of time queueing for cups of coffee and cakes.'[21]

By 1956 the Co-operative Travel Service was offering coach holidays to holiday camps such as one in Douglas, the Isle of Man, which offered 'projected television, large sports fields and a licensed bar'. It could not have been less like the knot-tying, campfire singing of the early part of the century, let alone the temperance holidays of Thomas Cook.

There were other considerations in postwar travel to take into account. Members at the 1950 AGM of the Camping and Caravanning Club had a fierce debate about whether they would promote tours to Germany: it was a pre-war refugee from Nazism, who had lost his relatives in the camps, who turned the majority in favour of the idea, saying: 'It is the only way to show them how democracy works.'[22] With the end of petrol rationing in 1950, members planned two group trips abroad; the first was to Belgium, the second was a characteristically adventurous one: a tour of Finnish Lapland.

Caravanning boomed during the 1950s, aided by the increase in car ownership. In the early 1960s, there were 75,000 touring caravans in British ownership; another 250,000 were permanently on site as holiday homes. The Caravan Club doubled its membership in this period and there was a flourishing of inventive and ingenious designs for caravans and their kit. The most popular model was the Sprite, a magical, wood-panelled box on wheels which was only eleven feet long – a compact beauty.

New innovations appeared regularly in the eager pages of Camping and Caravanning Club publications, which remained in essence the same chronicles of enthusiasm and regulations, acronyms, fussiness and sanitary arrangements. (Chemical toilets, water coloured Elsan blue with Jeyes Fluid, were new to the market.) Good behaviour enforcement vies for space with battles with local landowners and county councils – as well as a resurgence of folk singing (reintroduced with great success in the 1960s in the club's folk song and dance group). Camping Gaz cookers fuelled by methylated spirits were on sale in 1956 at about the same time as the Pakamac plastic raincoat, which could fold up into a tiny pocket. (This was then outgunned in 1971 by the arrival of the cagoule, with its crucial and capacious front pocket.) For those who didn't have the luxury of caravan refrigeration, there was a hygienic collapsible food safe. Caravans became more and more deviously luxurious, with teak veneer finishes and wipe-easy melamine surfaces. The fantasy 'gipsy' caravan of 1900 now looked more like a suburban bungalow on wheels. Permanent caravans were a source of hot contention. The genuine voice of intra-club exclusivity is heard in the correspondents in the Camping and Caravanning Club magazine: 'Are we losing the best people?' wondered a member in January 1961. 'Let us get away from the mentality which segregates perms from non-perms, and caravans from lightweights, and simply make it radios-and-dogs, and non-radio-and-dogs.'[23]

Campsites also proliferated. The author Stanley Bennett Hough and his wife Justa, keen campers of the old school, set off by motorcycle around France in 1956. Stanley Hough wrote up their adventures in *A Pound a Day Inclusive* (if ever there were a defining word in the lexicon of the postwar holidaymaker it is the word 'inclusive'). Guided by a book they had borrowed from the library called *Europa Camping*, the Houghs headed for the Riviera – until the First World War the preserve of the rich and leisured, and now covered all over with campsites. 'We went down to Antibes. We went with no sense of entering on holy ground. We were not Picasso fans,' wrote Hough. 'It was compulsion, the compulsion of sheer fame, which brought us, hot and dusty, to the cool corridors, the clean grey and white interior, of the museum in the old fort on the battlements that overlook the harbour.'[24] His book captures charmingly the blitheness of a world suddenly made open and possible. Every evening, the Houghs cracked open a bottle of wine or two with fellow middle-aged campers: 'British holidaymakers were on the move. During one conversation, Picasso came up. "Fancy little us," said Mrs Jones suddenly. "Here on the Riviera and talking about Art."'[25]

Even on the continent, the Houghs found campsites fitted to the highest modern specification. In fact, the new sites were very often more hygienic than cheap hotels and certainly more so than public lavatories – for the 'footsteps' of which the British tourist had an almost superstitious horror. 'You walked into a cubicle,' recalled one woman who went in France in the mid-fifties, 'and there was a hole in the ground, the vilest smelling hole you can imagine and each side there was a porcelain footprint and you placed your feet in them. Then there were two metal bars on either side and you lowered yourself over the hole and just hoped that nothing came up and bit you.'[26] But in the new campsites, there was no need ever to rough it Baden-Powell style; this was the great outdoors with modern sanitation. Near Cervo on the Italian Riviera, for example, the Houghs pitched their tent under a specially placed electric light and enjoyed 'a series of showerbaths and lavatories which would have done credit to a grand hotel'. There were 'large mirrors, chromium fittings, clean white paint, and the sinks carefully arranged for washing dishes and washing clothes . . . I noticed at once the carry-through of detail even to the electric razor plugs beside the mirrors, each socket having the voltage marked.'[27]

Camping was also liberation from the fussiness of hotel clothing codes, for a hotel holiday still seemed to demand a great deal of equipment and changes of clothes. As late as 1968, the Letts guide to the Italian Riviera provided a clothing list for men that was still notably comprehensive:

> a dinner jacket is necessary only if you are going to a top-grade hotel in one of the fashionable resorts, or for the opera or a casino. You will need a lightweight lounge suit; lightweight sports jacket and trousers; sports shirt, singlet and shorts; light pullovers and a cardigan; lightweight macintosh; beach sandals and swimwear; a towelling dressing gown or beach robe.

Under 'other necessities' were listed: 'folding clothes hangers and a nylon line for drip-dry washing; detergent, soap, which is not provided in hotels on the Continent, and toothpaste; sunglasses and sunburn lotion; cosmetics; toiletries, sanitary requisites, adhesive plasters; and a continental two-pin adaptor for your electric razor'.[28]

For the camper, however, low-maintenance grooming was de rigueur. In the event of it being too hot to wear a jacket, as well as nylon shirts ('worn with or without a tie'), Hough recommended a 'man bag' in which to carry passports and travellers' cheques: 'a small, light haversack, to be slung from the shoulder, in which to keep papers of the more valuable sort, money, cigarettes, matches and all the impedimenta which fill the pockets of jackets'. The only dress code seemed to have arisen from the enforced intimacy of the queue for the washroom. 'Pyjamas should look presentable in public. Inevitably they will be presented in public. If the female looks slightly daring there is no harm done, but if the male looks like someone who only needs a nightcap, bed-socks and a candlestick to complete him, he hasn't quite achieved the standard.'[29]

It was indeed a new world.

ON THE BEACH

Five hundred years ago the beach was the haunt mainly of fisherfolk or the shipwrecked. The sea was to be feared and on its coastal margins the beaches were rough, wind-parched, desiccated stretches where little flourished: sandy, scrubby, pebbly and, in summer, scorched. But in the seventeenth century, with renewed interest in the health-giving effects of bracing cold water, the sea gradually became thought of as beneficent as well as dangerous: not necessarily merely the edge of the safe world but a place teeming with fertility and primordial life. By the eighteenth century, sea water was thought dizzyingly intoxicating, and it was believed that the immersion of the body in waves administered hefty doses of life-giving oxygen. If the cold sea was associated with the restorative energies of northern mythologies, the dry edges of the Mediterranean were also the ancient origin of European culture.

For Tobias Smollett, always in search of a watery health cure, the saltiness of the sea seemed to have an intoxicatingly thinning effect on the blood. In 1812, following Burke's definition of the sublime, Joseph Addison described in the *Spectator* how the 'agreeable horrour' provoked by watching the fearful waves of the sea was itself health-giving. 'I cannot see the Heavings of this prodigious Bulk of Waters, even in a calm, without a very pleasing Astonishment.'[30] By the 1750s, bathing machines, with their modesty hoods, were common in coastal spas like Scarborough and professionals were on hand to help ease bathers into the therapeutic waters – the sexes strictly separated with 'bathers' for men and 'dippers' for women. With the nineteenth century's surge of enthusiasm for geology and natural history, the beach too, with its rockpools, seaweeds, fossils and stones, provoked reflection on the vaster questions of existence.

There was something almost alarmingly exciting about the effects of immersion in sea water. The quality of 'excitement', according to Frederick Harrington Brett in 1852, could not only ward off contagious diseases such as cholera but also imparted 'a vital energy' which is 'manifested by ruddiness of the complexion, a general glow of the whole nervous and muscular systems, augmentation of the appetite, alertness of the mind, and a stimulating effect on the generative functions of both sexes'.[31] In Dieppe, a visitor marvelled:

I have seen young ladies joining together, holding hands and
performing round dances in the waves, the *baigneurs* ranging
themselves around them, to announce when a wave larger than
the rest is about to break . . . they rediscover, in this marine
dancing, the suppleness of limb and freshness of complexion
which the ball of the previous evening has somewhat
dimmed.'[32]

Doctors, scientists and quacks rushed to profit from the medical
effects of sea-bathing. This dangerous stimulation made the sea
and the beach places of ambivalence, immersion in the waves
another metaphor for emotional and psychological release. But
once vital and uncontrollable forces are the rage, they soon
become associated with dissipation and loucheness. There was less
pathos and lots of pleasure in a seaside holiday. At a seaside resort
strangers from all classes mingled promiscuously, epitomised by
the unrepentantly merry widow Aunt Greenow in Trollope's *Can
You Forgive Her?* and the raggle-taggle bunch of unsuitable suitors
she picks up while staying in Yarmouth. Seaside resorts became
places to be seen in, to be spotted conspicuously taking the air on
promenades made for that purpose alone. Seaside places seemed to
the disapproving to be created solely to facilitate a state of lassitude.
The inventions that belong to the seaside are primarily associated
with comfort and lying about: sun-loungers, windbreaks, deck
chairs and sun-umbrellas.

In *Glaucus; or the Wonders of the Shore*, Charles Kingsley thought
seaside resorts were places to go and rot:

You are going down, perhaps by railway to pass your usual six
weeks at some watering place along the coast, and as you roll
along think more than once, and that not over-cheerfully, of
what you shall do when you get there. You are half-tired, half-
ashamed of making one more in the 'ignoble army of idlers'
who saunter about the cliffs, and sands and quays; to whom
every wharf is but a 'wharf of lethe', by which they rot 'dull as
the oozy weed'. You foreknow your doom by sad experience.

A great deal of dressing, a lounge in the club-room, a stare
out of the window with a telescope, an attempt to take a bad
sketch, a walk up one parade and down another, interminable
reading of the silliest of novels, over which you fall asleep in the
sun, and probably have your umbrella stolen; a mackerel and
the consumption of many cigars . . . and after all, and worst of
all, at night a soulless rechauffe of third-rate London frivolity;
this is the life-in-death in which thousands spend the golden
weeks of summer and in which you confess with a sigh that you
are going to spend them.[33]

On the promenades, respectable and disreputable visitors eyed each
other. Dandies, gamblers, swells and mashers teetered riskily on the
edge of civilised behaviour.

The seaside resort coalesced around three main
developments: the grand hotel, the bathing establishment and
the casino. An 1886 guide to seaside resorts in northern France
shows how efficient over the century these places had become
in the provision of comfort, gambling and swimming. At
Ambleteuse in Normandy, for example, the hotel is said to be
'not picturesque' but 'large, airy and comfortable', and charges
6½ francs a day for 'service', which presumably was full board
(three meals), though did not include 'bougies' – that is, candles
burnt in the bedroom 'of which an account is kept and charged
in the bill with the wine'. The guide noted that the small town of
Cayeux had three hotels and cabins could be hired for 25 cents
and bathing attendants for another 25 cents. At Treport, there
was an 'unpretentious little casino built of wood' situated on the
beach.[34] The resort of Etretat, the guidebook noted, had forty
years before been 'but a little group of small, thatched cottages,
inhabited by a few poor fishermen, but some French artists and
Alphonse Karr the novelist first managed with paper and pen to
make this charming nook known to the world at large'. Now the
fishermen's huts were gone, replaced by hotels and 'pretty villas
in every style of ornamental architecture'. The bathing cabins
were run by Monsieur Tephir, 'who has a large staff of intrepid

swimmers in his establishment in order to assist the bathers in case of accident'. The cost of sea-bathing (which could not be arranged without help) was 90 francs and each beach cabin came equipped with a warm foot bath.[35]

Warm southern resorts, like those on the French Riviera, often seemed much more relaxed than their British counterparts about sex segregation, noted Dr James Bennet in 1878. Bennet observed that 'dipping' had become popular – swimmers who were beginners using corks or gourds tied under the arms for buoyancy. 'Once in the water, all the bathers, male and female, mingle together; the timid remaining near the beach, and the bold and learned in the art of swimming striking out into deep water.' Many French coastal resorts had '*guides baigneurs*' walking up and down the beach to help the nervous bather: 'They take your hand, hold you up and assist you in making the necessary jump so the wave does not go over your head.'[36] They were recognisable by their uniforms of canvas trousers, striped jerseys and hats with their occupation written on.

The Riviera beach itself had become a backdrop for all sorts of popinjay antics and dressing up. 'The gents' dress is a kind of sailor's costume, and as custom gives them more latitude with respect to colour, material and make, great varieties are observed. The exquisites of the place seem to take a pride in showing themselves off thus prepared for their marine gymnastics.' As for bathing, there were outfits for both men and women to hire from the attendant. Swimming costumes for women were modest but hideous – ankle-length black woollen bloomers and a knee-length black tunic fastened with a leather belt. They also wore broad-brimmed straw hats and wide waterproof capes which were discarded at the water's edge, where they were given to the attendant. Bennet reported, however, that no one seemed remotely abashed by being exposed in this way. 'They pass smilingly before their friends and the spectators, appearing to enjoy every stage of the performance.'[37]

The increasing ubiquity of bathing was reflected in the changing fashion of female bathing suits. The diaphanous woollen smocks of the first part of the century made way in the 1890s for wasp-waisted corsetry that showed off the lines of the body rather than concealing them – while remaining completely covered up. In 1910, bathing dresses for women still came below the knee and up to the neck and were generally worn with canvas shoes, thick stockings and a hat. Underneath the main costume was usually some form of corset that would not lose its shape in water. By 1914, the skirts of the costume had risen a bit but were still worn with long bloomers. After the Great War, new stretch materials, and in 1917, the invention of rubberised fabric, revolutionised the bathing dress. A close-fitting, knee-length knitted one-piece appeared in 1918, and was considered so daring that it had to be worn with an overdress that could be removed when safely at the water's edge.

By the 1920s, bathing and parading in beachwear (which was now more or less like any other daywear but a little shorter) had given way to the exercise potential of water – and swimming. The postwar desire for the relaxing warmth and uncerebral pleasures of the coastal resorts sparked a radical abandonment of old proprieties. The beach became celebrated as a place that was the opposite of the violent battlefield; it was the cradle of peace: 'I shall lie on a beach/ On a shore where the rippling waves just sigh/ And listen and dream and sleep and lie,' wrote Max Plowman, who had served on the Western Front.[38] The sun was no longer to be warded off with parasols and sunhats – it was to be actively sought out as a source of gloriously liberating, primal health.

Sunbathing is now such a familiar feature of a summer holiday that it's easy to forget that as a popular (as opposed to weird and esoteric) cultural practice, it is barely a hundred years old. Once, the foreign habit of bathing in the sea in July and August, in the full heat of the summer, would have been considered not only thoroughly suspect but dangerous. Temperate, moderate weather used to be the key to beach enjoyment: 'To our English minds, this seems inconceivable,' wrote Lucy Scott in 1888, astounded at the thought of spending the summer on the Med. 'During those two months the scorching rays of "sol Leone" render the sands a burning desert, the sea is as warm as the hot air above it, and the close lodgings are too stifling to endure. Of what use is a month at the seaside to us if our children cannot dig in the sands, and our boys and girls take long walks, seaweed and sea-anemone hunting?'[39]

Sunbathing began, like sea-bathing, as an aid to health rather than beauty. Warm tonic air was refreshing and revitalising – but tanned skin, associated with the coarsening effects of outdoor labour, was thought ugly. 'The fond and fashionable mother would as soon see green celery on her table,' remarked James Johnson in the 1830s, 'as brown health on the cheek of her daughter. When, therefore, the ladies venture into the open carriage, they carefully provide themselves with parasols to aid the dense clouds of an English atmosphere in preventing the slightest intrusion of the cheerful, but embrowning rays of Phoebus. In short, no mad dog can have a greater dread of water, than has a modern fine lady of the solar beams.'[40]

Like sea, mountains and air, the sun was characterised by violent extremes of both beneficence and malevolence. It was often associated with antiquity, with the naked human body best seen in its classical marble perfection in sunlight. The painter G. W. Watts told Ruskin that: 'Under the influence of the glowing sun every object is presented in a manner so in harmony with my own feelings and the whole language of nature seems to me perfectly intelligible.'[41] And if the human physical form was seen at its peak in a classical statue then pale bodies were like marble statues, and sun-browned bodies were bronze statues. But the effects of extreme heat on the real-life body (particularly in the tropics, where the debilitating climate experienced by colonial officers could be mentally destabilising) was viewed with trepidation. In 1863, Julius Jeffrey, a physician with the Bengal Medical Service, was the first to make a scientific study of the physical effects of exposure to sunlight. Jeffrey recommended the regular use of sunglasses (or what became known as 'blue spectacles') to stop the sun entering through the eyes and inducing 'solar apoplexy'.[42]

Attitudes towards sun were changing, however, and William Morris and his friends in the Art and Crafts movement were among those who began to see pale skin as an indication not of female beauty but of listless indoor lives in overheated, over-furnished parlours. A tan was the product of wholesome outdoors labour. It was now 'sun-kissed' rather than 'sunburnt'. 'Look if I don't need a little sun on my pasty white skin,' cries the heroine of Morris's utopian novel *News from Nowhere*. Paleness came also to be associated with the transparent skin pallor that indicated tuberculosis; it was the colour of the sickbed. It was also increasingly seen as the colour of an effete and degenerate aristocracy, rotten and drained of vigour. Bram Stoker's Count Dracula is probably the most vivid manifestation of this horror of sunlessness: bloodsucking yet also bloodless, a corrupted nobleman who cannot bear the revealing light of day.

It would be several decades, however, before a suntan became popular beyond those radical circles which also favoured rational dress and vegetarianism. But two schools of thought on the nature of female beauty were emerging: a pale face suggested sheltered, ladylike, appropriately timid characteristics; a tanned one was vigorous, healthy and robust. In 1902 the anonymous author of *Requisites for Beauty Care*, 'The Countess', stressed that the ideal complexion could only be achieved by avoiding sunlight altogether: 'There is a very simple method . . . and that is never to go out in the sun or night dew or when the moon is bright, for that tans as quickly as the sun, without covering the face with a fine white, or better still, cream coloured veil, first putting a little glycerine on the face, and then passing a powder puff over it.'[43] Complexion bleaching was popular – with whitening creams readily available – though the taint of inauthenticity hung over them as it did over fake souvenirs. Yet in the same year that the countess counselled sun-avoidance, *The Art of Being Beautiful* by 'The Baroness' took the opposite view: 'The rays of the sun act upon the human being as upon the plant, they bring out the body and brightness of its hue . . . open air life at midday is the only cure for delicacy.'[44]

Among the pioneers of health-giving 'sun baths' was the Swiss physician Auguste Rollier, who in 1903 had opened an 'Institute of Heliotherapy' at Leysin on Lake Geneva. In his 1923 book *Heliotherapy*, Rollier claimed sunbathing was a primal instinct: 'Life is at its lowest ebb when darkness envelopes us, our senses become deadened and dulled and sleep supervenes . . . in all ages there have been Sun-worshippers. It could not be otherwise. Terrestrial life craves for the golden rays. They are the world's great tonic which stimulate and enliven, but in undue excess intoxicate.'[45] In his sanatorium, Rollier's patients were made to lie in rows outside in cold, dry sunlight where a *Times* reporter described them as 'naked, plump and brown as earth itself'.[46]

Rollier's quasi-religious language is typical of the new sun-worshippers, who on a sunny day would wax lyrical about 'the embrowning rays of Phoebus'. Mysterious references were often made to primordial urges and cultish rituals: it was all part of what the writer and Capri-dwelling sybarite Norman Douglas called the 'paganism and nudity and laughter' to be found in hot places. The sun was seen not only a natural source of health but a craving, an adulation: it was associated with freedom and uncomplicated sex and natural physical urges. D. H. Lawrence was naturally a keen proponent of this idea. In his 1925 short story 'Sun', a woman sunbathing on a remote Mediterranean promontory, under doctor's orders, feels that the rays of the sun are 'mating' with her:

> She slid off all her clothes and lay naked in the sun. As she lay she looked up through her fingers at the central sun, his blue, pulsing roundness, whose outer edges streamed brilliance. Pulsing with marvellous blue, and alive, and streaming white fire from his edges, the sun! He faced down to her with his look of blue fire, and enveloped her breasts and her face, her throat, her tired belly, her knees, her thighs and her feet.'[47]

A fanatical quality characterised even the strictly therapeutic sun worshippers. The former Danish army lieutenant J. P. Muller, author in 1908 of *My Sunbathing and Fresh-Air System*, ran a sanatorium at Vjelfjord where the windows were open wide day and night in all weathers. He loathed the stress-inducing confinement of indoor modern life, the polluted air of cities, where smoke and smuts cut off the light of the sun. Urban living, wrote Muller, was killing people and so was new technology. He thought the air in railway carriages was a breeding ground for sickness: 'If there is any poisonous, bacilli laden air anywhere it is to be found in these overfilled, tiny rooms called railway compartments.'[48] Like many obsessives, Rollier too was engrossed by the practical details. He suggested that open windows should be mandatory in all forms of transport and public buildings; for those oddballs who would prefer to have the windows closed a special compartment would be made available like those for smokers.[49] He insisted that sunlight was everywhere: 'Good air is the foundation of all conditions of life.' The British obsession with draughts in their homes could be resolved by simply opening all windows and doors, all the time, so that outside air is not forced through small apertures. 'Exposure of a whole body to air is what is called an air bath,' he wrote in 1923. Muller illustrated the front cover of his book with a photograph of himself skating naked in St Moritz.[50]

Natural urges, nudism, unisex exercise regimes – these ideas suited the postwar mood of the 1920s. J. P. Muller called for a return to a fast-disappearing simple life: 'A pair of shorts, a straw hat and sandals or wooden sabots, are all that is necessary when working in a garden, field or forest. How picturesque and healthy country people would look if they only dressed like this,' he wrote. 'Sun burning does no harm at all, throw off the hat! Join the hatless brigade! It is said that the heart of the sun's rays beating on your head is harmful: this is fancy!'[51] Soon so keen were the residents in the resort of Davos to show off their healthy colour that the British consul observed that 'people who cannot procure a brown skin by natural exposure, get it from a drug store'.[52] Tanned skin, once the sign of hard outdoor occupations, had suddenly become a signifier of the luxury of free time. A suntan now said that its bearer had leisure to enjoy the sun rather than labour under it. It flattered the fashionable to imagine that they were succumbing to the superior values of the 'simple' life – but in deluxe style.

Fashion responded to the 'sun craze' with holiday garments that were easily slipped on and off for maximum exposure. The Art Deco motif of the sun appears everywhere in the graphics and designs of the period, sparked by the 'Egypt craze' that followed the discovery of Tutankhamun's tomb in 1922. Nude sunbathing was recommended by heliotherapists, but as the privacy that this required was, on the whole, inconvenient, costumes (still in one piece) became skimpier to give 'sun-access' to as much of the body as was decently possible. A particularly hot summer in 1928 cemented the popularity of 'the sun bath' and the fashion for clothes designed specifically for lying on the beach. Towelling beach pyjamas were all the rage, as were sailors' sweaters and peasanty straw hats; in more daring circles, stockings gave way to bare legs. In the 1930s, fashionable French men popularised swimming trunks that could be removed by a hand button-opener and shaken down through the trouser leg, saving the embarrassing dance of the towel which was (and still is) such a feature of the beach experience.

'Sunshine is Life' read a British railway poster of the 1920s summoning people to holidays on the French Riviera. In 1922 the American socialites Gerald and Sara Murphy reported that 'at that time no one ever went near the Riviera in summer. The English and the Germans – there were no longer any Russians – who came down for the short spring season, closed their villas as soon as it began to get warm.'[53] But by the middle of the decade, people who once would have gone to the South of France only in winter were now flocking there in pursuit of the sun – and the suntan.

Sunlight's ultra-violet qualities were prescribed for all sorts of skin diseases and other ailments, and electric sun lamps became available from the early 1920s. Research now showed how beneficial sunlight was for the cure of rickets. During the Second World War, German doctors had found that sun baths could be a treatment for 'deficiency diseases' in children: they thus became part of a hearty, outdoor style of recreation for all classes. It wasn't until 1956 that over-exposure to sun was found to be related to skin cancer: in the decades of the mid-twentieth century basking in the midday heat was thought to be the very essence of pleasure and relaxation. As a doctor remarked in 1930: 'The sunbather who is benefitting from insolation is always cheerful and happy. None are brighter in spirits than those who are sun-worshippers.'[54]

Sunning oneself was viewed as partly therapeutic ('insolation'), partly hedonistic. An untanned body not only began to look unhealthy, but it denoted someone who couldn't afford a foreign holiday. Sunbathing nude was still regarded the best possible way to do it, and helio-therapists advised being unclothed as much of the time as possible (including while asleep, 'like our forefathers') before heading to the beach to prepare oneself by exposure to 'surrounding air'.[55] According to the *Daily Mail* in 1931, 'sunbathing is to be encouraged at all the popular holiday resorts'. Even the high-minded motives of the Polytechnic Touring Association were soon adapted to the call of the sun: in their brochures, the chief attraction of a 1930 Poly all-in package to the Mediterranean is flagged up as 'all-day sunshine'. The Poly even offered a guarantee of heat or your money back: 'We have arranged free weather insurance for travellers to Menton. If it should rain for as little as half an hour between 8 a.m. and 8 p.m., your hotel fees will be repaid to you on the spot.'[56]

Sun*burning*, however, was advised against, and with beaches increasingly covered with roasting bodies, this led to the speedy development of 'browning oils' – including, most famously, the one produced by the founder of L'Oréal, Eugène Schueller. L'Oréal's laboratories created the first sun-protection cream that promised to prevent the skin from burning while encouraging it to tan. Schueller called his concoction Ambre Solaire and it launched in 1935. Guidebooks began to include whole sections of advice on sunbathing – where best to go and how to do it safely. Many of the anti-burn potions recommended seem now better suited to putting on salad than protecting skin. In Robert Trimnell's 1954 guide to Majorca, he issues dire warnings about sunburn: 'The worst damage from the sun is not to your skin. Certain rays go right through into the meat, and can cause nausea, violent headaches and absolute prostration that will put you in bed for days.'[57] Trimnell recommended a 'native' tip of olive oil and lemon juice as suntan lotion. Warren Hall, holidaying in Cannes in 1952, thought Ambre Solaire was perfectly efficient, but even better was his own thrifty concoction: 'It's very easy to prepare a homemade sun lotion. Mix equal parts of olive oil and vinegar and add a dash of iodine afterwards.'[58]

The poet Robert Graves, Majorca's most famous British resident, had settled in the hot south in 1929, in the village of Deià. Graves was as much enamoured of the simple living and sun-engendered spontaneity as any bohemian creative of the 1920s. But in the postwar years, he found the Majorcan beaches increasingly debased by rows of passive sun-tanners: Graves reflected that they had no idea that it was really all about sex. In 1958, in a talk called 'The Sun Seekers' he summoned up an imaginary 'pretty typist' 'stretched out like a plump white plaice on the grill, trying to collect a tan worthy of that tremendous solar male'. As something of a sun-cultist himself, he deplored the way that it had seeped into popular culture and there been cheapened by mere self-indulgence. It ruined the view for everyone. 'The average emancipated Englishwoman associates the Sun with an idyll of lying scantily clad on a nice hot sandy beach, while a bronzed lover – and incarnation of the Sun – mutters fiery and unintelligible endearments in her chaste ear. Probably she has been reading that crazy D. H. Lawrence, England's most fanatical Sun-cult revivalist.'[59]

A HERMETICALLY SEALED WORLD

In the mid-1920s, the author Ada Harrison visited Majorca and discovered that it had 'fallen to Britain'. Majorca had 'become one of those places which, the English say, are being ruined by the English'. The result was that the Hotel Continental in the Majorcan capital Palma was largely occupied by suspicious guests demanding 'a diet of roast beef and rice pudding'.[60]

Harrison herself, however, like most tourists, thought the island most palatable when its amenities were also comfortable. In 1855, George Sand, accompanied by her lover Chopin and her two children, had spent a challenging winter in what she called the 'green Switzerland' of Majorca's interior. Sand found the food scarce and disgusting and the locals hostile because Sand's daughter wore trousers and the family didn't go to Mass. But although she did not frame her idea so specifically, Sand thought that with its wild and craggy beauty, Majorca had potential as a tourist destination. All it needed was reliable infrastructure and a regular boat service from France, and 'the time will doubtless come when frail dilettantes and even lovely women will be able to visit Palma with no more exhaustion and discomfort than Geneva'.[61]

A half-century later, Sand's prediction proved right. Improved maritime communications after 1910 led to the island becoming a stopover for cruise liners and longer-distance shipping lines. By 1918, Palma had an agency, Short's (established by the island's former Thomas Cook representative F. G. Short), which specialised in supplying home comforts and accommodation to the British. In 1930, 20,000 tourists were recorded in the island's hotels, and nearly 15,000 cruise passengers came ashore. By 1931, there was an air service with two daily flights to Palma from mainland Spain and another from Marseilles. According to the 1933 *Lindo* guide, the journey from London, by air with two stopovers, now took less than forty-eight hours – even though at the airport, even in the 1950s, the passengers' luggage was collected by horse and cart and taken to their hotel. By 1935, with 135 hotels on the island, seventy-one of them in Palma, the number of tourists had more than doubled: there were 40,000 hotel stays and 50,000 cruise visitors.[62]

The *Lindo* guide is packed with advertisements for English hotels and English villa rental agents. 'Go to Short's,' reads one, 'for a house, a servant, a nurse, a doctor, a guide, an interpreter, a motor-car.' Short's also ran a tea room and a lending library, and there was an 'English American cake and teashop'. With an eye perhaps to picnicking British tourists undeterred by wet weather, the Casa Medina store specialised in rubber goods – galoshes, hot-water bottles, rainproof knapsacks, plus waterproof sheets.

Robert Graves, from his eyrie in the village of Deià, looked on with dismay. 'About 1931, a small tourist boom began, which troubled me despite such advantages as being now able to buy in Palma cow's milk, beef, butter, teapots, kettles, beer and ready-made sheets, none of which had hitherto been procurable,' he wrote. 'Several new hotels were added to the six; a small golf course was laid out at Aloudia; blurred pictures of film stars appeared in the local press, the Duke of Westminster anchored his yacht

off the Palma *mole*, and the Prince of Wales himself put up at the
Formentor Hotel where he composed a bagpipe march, "Mallorca",
for the Scots Guards pipers.'[63]

In the 1920s, Ada Harrison had found Palma, with its stone
buildings, cobbles and pantile roofs, 'a tiny provincial capital, a little
bustling thriving sea-port where the ancient Majorcan tradition
of ship-building and navigation is still kept green. It has all the
adjuncts of the city, but it is too small and too much circumscribed
by its nature ever to lose connection with the simple life.'[64] She
observed the famous 'windmills' of the interior, 'which are in fact
pumps for groundwater owing to the lack of permanent rivers', but
only a few years later, these would prove inadequate to meet the
water demands of the new influx of tourists with their golf courses
and sanitary mod cons. The local food, which George Sand had
thought so execrable, 'dominated by peppers and garlic', Harrison
enjoyed – especially the membrillo, the sweet cakes and the 'long
crisp radishes' with the rind pared back and curled like wings.

Yet Harrison noticed too the encroachment of a feature that was
soon to dominate coastal villages all over the Mediterranean: the
dispiriting, damp melancholy of the off-season holiday home. In
Palma, El Terreno was a 'strip of holiday houses reaching westward
along the coast'. The English rented these villas in the winter, the
Spanish in the summer. 'It is a quarter quite singularly unattractive . . .
there is something extremely painful about Mediterranean holiday
houses. They have a uniform air of being built of stucco and white
cardboard, and they attempt to look as sumptuous as they succeed
in looking collapsible.'[65]

It took a while after 1945 for the Majorcan tourist economy to
re-establish itself. Majorca had been occupied by Mussolini's forces
since the end of the civil war, and by the end of the Second World
War, the capital was looking battered. In 1949, a visitor to Palma
would have found the hotels rather tired, and there was only one, ill-
attended nightclub. By the mid-1950s, however, the holidaymakers had
returned in force, and Palma's economy was soon entirely dependent
on tourists and villa-dwelling retirees. Nightlife was flagged up (as
well as booze) as being one of the chief attractions of the town.

The guidebook-writer and Palma resident Robert Trimnell ('What you need is Trim') wrote his first guide to Palma in 1955 and it remained so popular that it was regularly updated until the late 1970s. Trimnell's guidebooks captured the style of the postwar middle-class English expatriatism: easy-going, blazer-wearing, louche but resolutely *un*bohemian. It was boozy and jovial, at ease with a bit of undemanding culture but more at home on the golf course: retirement in the sun with every amenity. When Graves had moved to Deià in 1929, there was already a small colony of British exiles in El Terreno, in flight from thrifty budgeting and rain, and he described them as 'retired civil servants from Asian and African dependencies, who had not dared face either the English climate or the high cost of domestic help at home'.[66] By the time Robert Trimnell set out the island delights in his guidebook, Deià itself had become a destination for the more intrepid tourist: 'The home of bearded artists, Swedish artists and wild-eyed artists.' Trimnell's 1955 guide even suggests a post-prandial stroll up into the hills there, perhaps to spot the reclusive Robert Graves. His Majorca is a hotchpotch of consumable local characteristics, from markets ('we're bugs about markets') to 'quaint' regional festivals and shopping (glassware, embroidery, olivewood trinkets and a bottle or several of the local liquor).

By this time tourists didn't even have to make do with just Majorcan culture: there was a wide range of other cultures on tap. In the 1964 edition of the guide, Trim notes that you can buy in Palma Italian silk ties and Pringle jumpers; you can 'drink your draught beer in a bullring' in the El Toro bullfighter-themed bar. Or what about the South African-owned 'Africa Bar' where, in a typical bit of touristic cultural dissonance, you can eat 'the best pizza, spaghetti, lasagne and Italian salads in town'? There's the Tres Coronas, owned by Swedes, which offered a weekend 'smorgasbord', and an Indonesian restaurant called Casa Bambu. Then there was the Bar Rodeo ('where you can drink all day') owned by expats Vera and Betty ('Vera from Southend has been on television and stage and the same cockney charm prevails here as it did in London. You're sure of a really warm welcome from her and assistant hostess Betty Mack, late of the Corkscrew Club'). Trim's guides were among the first to give 'nightlife' a whole section to itself – along with shopping and eating, churches and museums. Trim's Palma is a theme park of pseudo-Balearic experience carefully tailored to feel, with its hair salons, pubs and golf courses, almost like home – but cheaper, boozier and warmer. In this enclosed world, everything is provided, and little demanded of the tourist except ready cash.

No one figure, however, quite embodies the new, hermetically sealed holiday package experience as much as the Russian émigré Vladimir Raitz, the founder of Horizon Holidays. Raitz was in his late twenties and working for Reuters, when in 1949 he travelled to the remote coastal village of Calvi in Corsica. His friend Dimitri Filipoff was running a water polo club for White Russians there and had created on Calvi's deserted beach a tented holiday village called Club Olympique. Conditions were primitive: army surplus tents and camp beds, no mains drainage and only one washing and showering cubicle. There was, however, a dance floor, and two bars which, Raitz noted, 'functioned beautifully' by means of coupons purchased, Cook-style, from the bartender. Snorkelling equipment was available to hire and, as in Palma, where Trim noted that water-skiing, go-karting and 'Li-los' were increasingly popular, the residents of Club Olympique were looking for new toys and new sporting (but not necessarily competitive) diversions.

Raitz was impressed by Club Olympique, despite (perhaps even because of) its rudimentary nature. He saw possibilities: an all-in kind of holiday in which sun, sea and beach were the main components; all that this vision required was a really fine beach. 'My own holiday had finished but my enthusiasm for the concept of holidays was just beginning,' he wrote.[67]

The story of the early years of Raitz's Horizon Holidays empire is also the story of social and national displacement in a changing postwar Europe. Raitz returned to Calvi a year after his first visit, determined to transform the Corsican coast into an established holiday destination for a new kind of tourist. In 1950, the main obstacle he faced was the journey, which involved taking a train and a boat, then another train and boat, and took days each way. The only solution was for Raitz to charter his own planes and fly

them to the deserted runway near the beach which had been left
there by American forces stationed on the island in 1943. Using
a £3,000 legacy from his grandmother, Raitz persuaded a firm of
air brokers to provide him with several 32-seater converted DC-3s.
Then he opened an office for Horizon in London's Fleet Street.

For that first holiday, Raitz needed 350 tourists simply to break
even, but regulations on flights abroad meant that he could only
use the decommissioned DC-3s if their passengers were students
or teachers. The holiday camp was therefore advertised in *Teachers'
World*, the *Nursing Mirror* and the *New Statesman*. Raitz offered
accommodation under canvas and blazing sun, with 'delicious
meat-filled meals' and unlimited local wine, for an all-inclusive deal
of £32 10s. What irresistible temptation for austerity-weary workers
from a country which was not only still under rationing but had
just experienced two years of freakishly cold and wet weather! In
May 1950, the first plane set off from Gatwick (a small airport that
had been decommissioned after the war but still served some civil
flights). There were 180 passengers and the plane refuelled at Lyons.
When the group disembarked at Calvi it was greeted by a municipal
brass band and local villagers bearing garlands of flowers.

Air travel meant saving time. And on a beach holiday that
was time saved to do nothing. There was very little that was
educative or high-minded about the new kind of holiday - no jolly
character-building while roughing it or tramping over the hills
singing 'Strawberry Fair'. The new beach holiday meant doing
nothing but basking and getting a tan, perhaps a little swimming,
certainly a lot of eating and drinking. In 1951, Thomas Cook's air
tours assured customers of 'extra hours to laze in the sun on sandy
beaches'. Travel agencies recommended air travel for 'fatigue-free
holidaymaking . . . By spending the minimum time in travelling,
guests derive the maximum from their hols.' Aeroplanes were
comfortable, reliable and mostly punctual; their disadvantages
were relatively minor (one airline warned passengers: 'Because the
reduction of atmospheric pressure often causes fountain pens to
leak it would be wise to empty your pen if you are rather fond of
your suit'). They made holidays abroad easier, quicker, smoother.

In 1950, Raitz's Camp Franco-Britannique at Calvi was composed of tents, an open-air dining room, a primitive sanitary block, a dance floor and a bar built out of bamboo canes (which became for years to come the very model of the idea of a beach bar). By 1951, the student/teacher clause in flight regulations having been abolished, Horizon Holiday flights were full. By 1952, they had expanded operations to Majorca, where Raitz employed the same formula. He avoided the towns and instead headed for a small village in the north-west, on a remote bay called Puerto de Soller. There was one hotel there, the Costa Brava, run by a British woman, Noreen Harbord, a hard-drinking escapee who'd lived there for years. Raitz bought the hotel and employed Noreen to manage it on Horizon's behalf. Harbord's 'salty language' was disapproved of by some of Raitz's punters (she called them the 'Horizontals') but the first holidays were nonetheless a success.

By 1954, there were Horizon encampments in Alghero in Sardinia and Spain's Costa Brava. The spectacular uninhabited beaches of Sardinia were ripe for a takeover by the company's bamboo bars, particularly since the malarial mosquito that had made the island inhospitable to visitors for centuries had been successfully wiped out. In Spain, the Horizontals established themselves in two sleepy fishing villages called Tossa de Mar and Sant Feliu de Guixols. 'The locals', noted Vladimir Raitz, 'had no concept whatsoever of this form of tourism.'[68] Raitz was not alone. The Belgian agent of Club Olympique, Gérard Blitz, in 1950 founded Club Méditerranée, which by 1965 had twenty-six outposts. Co-operative Tours also ventured to the Costa Brava in search of beaches to conquer. 'El Estartit is a small, unspoiled fishing village nestling at the foot of the pine-clad hills of the Cost Brava, the picturesque and rugged costs that extends from the Franco-Spanish border towards Barcelona,' read a Co-op brochure. 'It possesses one of the finest beaches in this part of Spain, its beautiful sands stretching for several miles. The sardine boats, which lend so quaint a charm to the beach by day, as they lie dotted along the shore, present an even more attractive picture as they put to sea at night, each with a lighted lamp at its prow to attract the fish into the nets.'[69]

The all-inclusive new holidays in the sun, devoid of any expectations of culture, made acceptable the notion of two weeks of self-indulgence and pure enjoyment. Respectable mores could be left behind on a Horizon holiday, where the sexes mingled freely on the beach in revealing bathing costumes ('Don't be so bloody silly,' easy-going Noreen Harbord was said to have replied when an engaged couple asked for separate rooms in Puerto de Soller). The all-you-can-eat buffets were an almost unimaginable luxury after rationing. Punter Harry Ritchie remembered the thrill of being 'whisked' by plane to completely new places and experiences. The heat, the swimming, and the 'new foodstuffs like peaches' were part of the experience, but for tourists coming from an urbanised Britain still emerging from rationing, it was also deliriously romantic and mind-expanding. He stared up at the Milky Way, Ritchie remembered, and stepped 'onto your balcony (a balcony!)' ready to 'start another day in paradise.'[70]

The travel agents were a new type too – not so much the descendants of Thomas Cook but of UK holiday pioneers Fred Pontin and Billy Butlin. East Ender Harry Chandler, for example, had been in charge of arranging the homeward passage of British POWs from Changi prison in Singapore at the end of the war – and he went on to use this experience to found the Travel Club of Upminster. Chandler was the first to develop the beaches of the Portuguese Algarve. Five years after Raitz moved into Sardinia, Fred Pontin himself established an overseas branch of his popular holiday camps. He called it Pontinental Holidays, and situated its flagship camp at the Pineta Beach Hotel, Sardinia. As air travel prices were coming down fast and former wartime aircraft could be rapidly converted into passenger planes, Pontin was soon able to offer two weeks in Sardinia for the same price as a fortnight in his celebrated holiday camp in Torquay.

Above all it was about sun – hot, soothing, reliable sun. Pontinental's camps were self-contained pleasure palaces, requiring for their existence not much more than clear skies, a blue sea, a decent stretch of sandy beach and a reliable supply chain for basic necessities. They were instant villages. 'One remarkable feature of the sun-cult', Robert Graves had written in the early 1960s, 'is the truly religious nowhere-ness of many tourist camps or hotels: built on a deserted headland far away from the nearest village, and supplied with all necessities by long distance lorry or motorboat.'[71]

In 1964, the first Pontinental camp in Majorca opened at Cala Mesquida – using for accommodation and infrastructure, as Raitz had done, deserted military facilities. Fred Pontin looked on it with pride: it was approached via a long, rough track and though it had been transformed by adding 142 brick-built chalets, kitchen, dining room, primitive shower and bars, it lacked any modern facilities. But it was the 'lovely bay, clear blue water and wide beach which captivated new arrivals.'[72]

Although Thomas Cook still ran seven of Palma's hotels, increasingly, other agencies were crowding in with all-inclusive packages of sun, sea and sand, as the primary purpose of any holiday. In 1958, Cosmos advertised a holiday package to Majorca for 'those whose principal requirement is to lie in the sun and who wish for no reminders of the bustle of life at home'.[73]

By 1953, two million British a year were holidaying abroad – half a century later, in 2000, the figure would be 30 million. In 1938, the Holidays with Pay Act had mandated a week's paid annual leave for all industrial workers. Wages had gone up sharply during the postwar labour shortages: average weekly earnings between 1955 and 1960 rose by 34 per cent. The 1944 Education Act had raised the school leaving age to fifteen and with it raised aspirations. Television now introduced images of foreign destinations into living rooms. At the end of 1950, economy-priced seats were introduced on planes.

Although the cultural tourist may have viewed the sealed encampments of the sun-seekers with dismay, the new, airline-driven tourism brought new jobs to old watering holes. In 1952, the writer Warren Hall, revisiting Cannes after twenty years, met up with his friend from the French tourist office, Mme Pourrière, once known as 'Madame Welcome of the Côte d'Azur'. 'Chic and blonde, this time a blue parting and eyebrows matched trimmings on her dress . . . now she has joined Pan American airlines.'[74] Hall found Cannes now given over completely to tourist entertainment and services. 'Apart from fishing, which has almost degenerated into a pastime for local boys and a hobby for visitors, Cannes has no industry of any kind except the tourist industry,' he wrote. 'The beaches, packed with sun-bathing crowds and everything from a deckchair and a cup of tea to a speed boat and a six-course lunch, the restaurants, the cafes, the shops, the hotels, the coach tours, the cinemas, the casinos – everything caters for, and relies on, the tourist.'[75]

In many places, notably Franco's Spain, cultural clashes were inevitable. The distinctiveness of ordinary life was made artificial by being constantly watched and photographed – or was simply erased. The nature of the traditional evening *paseo* in Spain, for example, when the local young men and women dress up and walk out to view each other, was altered by the presence of British and German tourists wearing skimpier clothes. In the early 1950s women exposing too much flesh (bathing costumes had to have skirts) were sent home by the Guardia Civil. Robert Graves's daughter Lucia went to school in England in early 1950s; when she left Majorca, the local girls were kept strictly at home until they became mothers but on her return a few years later she was amazed to see that under the influence of the tourists, they were now out on the beach wearing tiny bikinis. 'Real' travellers were in retreat. The writer Norman Lewis recalled a Spanish village ('Farol' – actually a composite of several villages on the Costa Brava) where he'd spent three summer seasons just after the war, when lone travelling was difficult. The inhabitants of 'Farol', except for a priest, a shopkeeper and a Civil Guard, lived wholly by fishing: 'They were neither rich nor poor, and even the charming old aristocrat who owned most of the land grew on it no more than a few meagre vegetables, and stole out at night to put down pots from which once in a while he recovered a lobster.' The only entertainments in that first summer were fiestas, dancing to a wind-up phonograph, composing poetry and telling stories. Like Robert Graves and many before him, Lewis saw in this life a natural balance lost in the discordant modern world. 'Above all, it seemed to me, the villagers lived in harmony.'[76]

When Lewis returned the next year, there was a sprinkling of other visitors: some young French women staying in a room over the bar who moved on quickly – 'but their brief presence left an extraordinary effect'. The fishermen's wives, he wrote, 'who spent most of their day mending nets spread out on the beach had been much impressed by their clothes and had copied them carefully. Within a matter of weeks, still busy with torn netting, they were clad in reasonable imitations of French fashions.' The couple who owned the bar added to the establishment an annexe with two more rooms. Soon these were occupied by more French tourists, 'and a developer attracted as if by magic to the scene put in plans for a 3-storey hotel'.[77]

By the third summer, there was yet more change. All the main roads were resurfaced, the potholes in local ones filled in, the swamp had been drained and the bridge repaired. A new hotel, 'modernistic' in design, 'dominated the mild contours of the old village like an army strongpoint and was full of English and French and the foundations of two new hotels were already in place'. Lewis wrote that many of the young men had abandoned fishing and were now working as barmen and waiters, making more from tips than the most experienced old fishermen. There were plans for a marina, a car park, a seafront promenade and more hotels. Farol is, of course, a romantic allegory of touristic destruction, of the bringing of the uniform to the particular, the smoothing out of pleasing irregularity – and, worst of all, the end of that harmonious coexistence that is perceived to exist only in isolation from the outside world.

Lewis returned to 'Farol' in 1984, for the first time in thirty-four years. 'I had suspected that I should find it unrecognisable and this proved to be the case.' The old streets he found 'had been blasted and bulldozed into a uniform width with buildings of a standard design'. There were traffic lights and a one-way system, burger restaurants and amusement arcades; the sea was invisible behind hoardings. Most of the beach was a car park with notices warning of the danger of theft. 'Fishing was at an end, but fishermen who could not bring themselves wholly to abandon the sea had fitted glass bottoms to their boats and took tourists on trips to 'explore the beauties of the coral gardens.'[78]

Robert Graves had seen it coming in 1958: in Norman Lewis's loss of 'harmony', Graves saw the destruction of *baraka*, the 'spirit of generations, of place and inheritance and custom but also of kneeling, of divine inspiration, lightning rapture'. Something 'real' was being swamped by its own shadow – unreal tat simulating real craftsmanship: fake 'gypsies' playing flamenco in bars and 'bullfighting posters on which tourists could have their own names printed between those of El Litri and Jaime Ostos'.[79]

Like attitudes to Cook's tourists in the nineteenth century, Graves saw 'real' Majorca collapsing under the weight of the incoming crowd, with its chatter, its megaphones and its loud motor vehicles: 'The [tourist] business now brings 5,000 planes a month every summer to a new and vastly enlarged Palma airport, and has encouraged the building of over a thousand new hotels. Spain I am told expects twenty million tourists this year, and I can see nothing [standing] against the exploitation of these derelict foreshores as "throw-away" tourist resorts.'[80] In 1975, the sociologists John Ash and Louis Turner observed that the 'promise of sun' had 'inverted the work-leisure relationship', symbolising a 'vital reaction against the eleven months of grey weather not spent on holiday'. Now the holiday was the reward for work rather than simply its absence. 'People began to work eleven months of the year to go on holiday, while before they went to the sea when their work was done.'[81]

By the 1970s, the uniformity of the sun, sea and sand package-tour experience had become a ubiquitous shorthand for uncultured jollification, the descendant of the naughty seaside postcard of the twenties and thirties. In the *Carry On* films, Spain was seen as simply a sunny backdrop against which a motley group of merry British can shed their sexual inhibitions until it's time to go home. *Carry on Abroad* (1972) is set on the island resort of 'Elsbels'. Spanish women are frighteningly seductive and Spanish men (mostly waiters) wickedly predatory. 'Steady on chaps,' say the Brits as they succumb (temporarily). Inhibitions are happily shed behind coy 'do not disturb' signs and, at the end of the holiday, the coach returns everyone home to Britain – there to dream of the same thing, same time next year.

Coda

This book was completed in early 2021, when the Covid-19 global pandemic had effectively shut down international travel. Tourism, which the economic historian Hartmut Berghoff once described as 'the world's largest single industry', ground almost totally to a halt. The statistics for economies entirely or even partly dependent on the tourist trade from the last two years were devastating: according to the United Nations World Tourism Organisation (UNWTO), tourist arrivals in January 2021, worldwide, were down 85 per cent from the preceding January.

Not being able to go abroad focused attention on what the foreign holiday stood for in the national imagination. The field of choice for the holidaymaking British has expanded since 1815, of course: once it took two days simply to get to Paris and now it takes less than one to get to Bali. But the impulses behind the twenty-first-century holiday, which include variety, climate, views, status, stories and shopping, would have been more or less recognisable to the Regency traveller. The aspirations of the British tourist (and perhaps all tourists) seem to have altered very little. The origins of the modern continental holiday are clearly visible in the Victorian groups who stepped off steam packets, trains and ferries. Tourism is a defining feature of social mobility over two centuries. Roy Hattersley has observed that it was televisions, washing machines and continental holidays that helped to 'blur the boundaries of class struggle': the domestic world was transformed by labour-saving technology and the idea of labour itself was changed by the idea of leisure, once a privilege and now considered a right.[1]

Transport is faster and (for the most part) more comfortable, and distant places perhaps look slightly less unfamiliar than they might have done now that we have Google Images to look at before we go. However, little in the mood and experience of holiday travel, independent in spirit but also strangely passive in actuality, seems to have altered. Even the most ubiquitous features of the submission to systems beyond the traveller's control are recognisable today. When Catherine Braithwaite, for example, returned home from her first trip to the continent in 1892, her group found the trains from Folkestone to London had been delayed by snow on the line. Four hours and an omnibus replacement service later, they arrived at Holborn faint with hunger after a station buffet that could only provide three oranges and a macaroon to sustain them.[2]

The prevailing paradox of tourism is that it so often destroys what it seeks. This book has shown how tourism can preserve cultures and landscapes; but it also flattens and contains them beneath the standardisation that the tourist business demands. Take the Alps: the tourist groups, the view-seekers, mountaineering clubs and winter sports enthusiasts that Ruskin so hated have not diminished appreciation of the magnificence of the mountains but they have nonetheless tamed the experience. The opening in 1912 of the funicular railway that led from Grindelwald to Jungfraujoch in the Swiss Alps meant it was possible to go direct from Geneva to the highest point on the Eiger glacier. Yet before long, Jungfraujoch station had acquired the melancholy blandness. The station restaurant was evocatively described in 1921 by the British mountaineer Dorothy Pilley as 'an odd place, a cross between a cowshed and the Trocadero, with flavours of the Bakerloo tube and the Caverns of Cheddar'.[3] Now, a hundred years later, Grindelwald and Jungfraujoch are linked by a cable car ('tricable gondola'), which promises passengers a 'multimedia experience', including a stopover on a specially constructed viewing platform on which 'to take your own personal souvenir picture'. At the top, the Jungfraujoch, the visitor is greeted by the 'highest Lindt chocolate shop in the world'.

What would Albert Smith, the Victorian showman, make of the Eiger Express? I think he would have enjoyed it. He surely would have relished the possibilities the internet has plumbed for virtual travel: they are in many ways the natural descendants of his 3D panoramas. He might even have applauded the chutzpah with which social media packages the scenery of the world as status-enhancing backdrops. A recent guide for aspiring Instagram influencers suggested the regular use of water in posts ('lakes, rivers etc.') because not only was 'nature' popular but pictures with lots of blue in them got 24 per cent more likes.

Owing more to advertising than literature, the language of modern guidebooks seems more purple than would have been approved of by Mariana Starke or John Murray III. But the spirit of the guides, with their reassuring appeal to the familiar, their lists of consular addresses and vocabulary ('please', 'thank you' and 'where is the chemist?') remains the same. The jaunty nightlife sections that Robert Trimnell included in his 1950s books on Majorca are now standard across the genre. Adventurous eating, which was generally the activity of the least interest to the author of a Murray's handbook, is now a defining (often *the* defining) tourist experience. The current Lonely Planet pocket guide to Tuscany (published in 2014) gives equal billing to the region being an 'artistic powerhouse' as it does to it being a centre of 'sensational slow food', which apparently 'trumps every other regional characteristic'. But it is still flagging the 'postcard-perfect landscape' well into the age when the actual postcard has been replaced by the digital image delivered by smartphone snaps in seconds.

Shopping is of course still key. A Club Med survey published in 2021 found that although souvenirs have changed in minor particulars – alcohol is now by far the most popular purchase and tattoos and fridge magnets are recent entries in the top ten – old favourites such as keyrings and decorative shot glasses still hold their own. A surprising traditionalism still dominates the market for national stereotypes. The most popular British souvenir is an umbrella, and models of the Eiffel Tower have only just (after one hundred years) been toppled by felt berets as the most popular souvenir purchased in Paris.[4]

The industry grinds it way through historical experience. A response is invited of the visitor, but what? Now the Nazi extermination camp of Auschwitz-Birkenau in Poland is a Unesco World Heritage Site which, in 2019, had 2.3 million visitors. But how many years must pass before a place of horror can truly be considered a visitor destination? Dylan Harris, the founder of Lupine Travel, which specialises in that holy grail - 'unique destinations' - was 'taken aback' when he visited Auschwitz for the first time:

> I was shocked but not in the way one expects to be, having travelled with the perhaps naive expectation that the place would be a museum piece, remaining exactly as it was when liberated in 1945. The last thing I expected was a visitors' centre, a cafeteria serving dinner options, and a noisy reception area pushing audio guides onto visitors. It felt crass and commercialised. This wasn't the way it should be . . . Wandering around the site, I became overwhelmed with grief.[5]

The preserving but destructive drive of tourism raises many questions. Venice, open again to vast cruise ships like floating cities, is sinking. The sprinkler-fed golf courses of southern Spain are causing a disastrous water shortage. Popular beaches in Europe have to be artificially topped up with sand imported from across the world. All night in the Alps, machines push displaced snow back uphill for skiers the next morning, consuming every hour enough fuel to drive a Range Rover from Britain to East Africa.

Dr Johnson once observed that we travel to 'regulate imagination with reality'. Today tourism, which has in the course of two centuries so gloriously opened up the world and also closed it, now regulates reality with artifice.

Acknowledgements

I am grateful for the help of several people in the writing of this book, among them Piers and Vyvyan Brendon, Steven Gerrard, Marius Kociekowski, Brian Murray, Francesca and Nigel Oakley, Jane O'Grady and Peter Scott. My agent, Catherine Clarke, has been a staunch support and ally.

My thanks also to the team at Bloomsbury, who have made sure it all came together in the end. Michael Fishwick set the book in motion and Elisabeth Denison brilliantly saw it through to its final destination. My thanks, too, to Kieron Connolly, Robert Davies and Alan Rutter. And my most particular gratitude to Kate Johnson for her gimlet-eyed editing and her warm encouragement.

My family have been, as ever, unfailingly supportive, in particular my sister, Anna, who is my most perspicacious reader.

Notes

INTRODUCTION

1 John Carr, *A Stranger in France: A Journey from Devonshire to Paris*, 1803, p. 14.

2 *Westminster Review*, October 1826.

3 Richard Lassels, *A Compleat Journey Through Italy*, London, 1670, preface.

4 Samuel Taylor Coleridge, 'The Delinquent Travellers' (1824), *The Complete Poems of Samuel Taylor Coleridge*, ed. William Keach, Penguin, London, 1997, p. 378.

5 Coleridge, 'Travellers'.

6 Marquis of Normanby, *The English in Italy*, London, 1825, vol. II, p. 221.

7 *The Essays, Articles and Reviews of Evelyn Waugh*, ed. Donat Gallagher, Little Brown & Co., London, 1984, p. 170.

8 Coleridge, 'Travellers', p. 378.

9 Nicholas Cooper, *The Opulent Eye: Late Victorian and Edwardian Taste in Interior Design*, Architectural Press, London, 1976, p. 12.

10 Erik Cohen, 'Nomads from Affluence: Notes on the Phenomenon of Drifter-Tourism', in *The International Journal of Comparative Sociology*, 1973, XIV, 1–2, pp. 89–103.

I 'WHERE SHALL WE GO NEXT?'

1 *Miss Jemima's Swiss Journal: The First Conducted Tour of Switzerland*, Putnam & Co., London, 1963, p. xi.

2 Charles Dickens, 'Some Account of an Extraordinary Traveller', *Household Words*, April 1850, p. 110.

3 Ralph Hyde, *Panoramania! The Art and Entertainment of the 'All-Embracing' View*, Barbican Art Gallery Publications, London, 1988, p. 21.

4 See Judith Flanders, *Consuming Passions: Leisure and Pleasure in Victorian Britain*, HarperPress, London, 2006, pp. 263–4.

5 Quoted in Richard D. Altick, *The Shows of London*, Harvard University Press, Cambridge, Mass., 1978, p. 274.

6 Anon. [Mary Browne], *Diary of a Young Girl in France*, N. Shore, London, 1883, p. 5.

7 Raymond Fitzsimons, *The Baron of Piccadilly: The Travels and Entertainments of Albert Smith, 1816–1860*, Geoffrey Bles, London, 1967, p. 99.

8 Edmund Yates, *Recollections and Experiences*, R. Bentley & Son, London, 1884, p. 142.

9 Flanders, *Consuming Passions*, p. 286.

10 Yates, *Recollections*, p. 146.

11 Fitzsimons, *Albert Smith*, p. 44.

12 Yates, *Recollections*, p. 142.

13 Fitzsimons, *Albert Smith*, p. 81.

14 Ibid.

15 Fitzsimons, *Albert Smith*, pp. 94–7.

16 Albert Smith, *Mont Blanc*, Ward, Lock & Tyler, London, 1852, p. 20.

17 Fitzsimons, *Albert Smith*, p. 119.

18 Henry Vizetelly, *Glances Back Through Seventy Years: Autobiography and Other Reminiscences*, Kegan, Paul & Co., London, 1893, vol. 1, p. 321.

19 Yates, *Recollections*, pp. 140–1.

20 Frederick Harrington Brett, *The Gems of Tuscany: A Fragment for the Invalid and the Tourist in Italy by a Fellow of the Royal Society of Surgeons*, Ackerman & Co., London, 1852, p. 12.

21 Fitzsimons, *Albert Smith*, p. 13.

22 Yates, *Recollections*, p. 277.

23 Vizetelly, *Glances Back*, vol. 1, p. 319.

24 *The Genius of John Ruskin: Selections from his Writings,* ed. John D. Rosenberg, Allen & Unwin, London, 1964, p. 308.

25 Herman Merivale, in the *Edinburgh Review*, 104, 1856, p. 446.

26 Vizetelly, *Glances Back*, vol. 1, p. 371.

27 Ibid., p. 320.

28 Ibid., p. 318.

29 *The Times*, 6 October 1856.

30 Albert Smith, *The Adventures of Mr Ledbury and his Friend Jack Johnson*, Richard Bentley & Sons, London, 1882, p. 342.

31 Yates, *Recollections*, p. 144.

32 C. P. Brand, *Italy and the English Romantics: The Italianate Fashion in Nineteenth-Century England*, Cambridge University Press, Cambridge, 1957. p. 24.

33 *Miss Jemima's Swiss Journal*, p. xii.

34 *Miss Jemima's Swiss Journal*, p. xiii.

35 Piers Brendon, *Thomas Cook: 150 Years of Popular Tourism*, Secker & Warburg, London, 1991, p. 72.

36 Simon Bradley, *The Railways: Nation, Network and People*, Profile Books, London, 2016, p. 89.

37 Brendon, *Thomas Cook*, p. 83.

38 Leicestershire, Leicester and Rutland Archives, TC/5/1/1/14.

39 Ibid.

40 Brendon, *Thomas Cook*, p. 48.

41 Susan Barton, *Working-Class Organisations and Popular Tourism, 1840–1970*, Manchester University Press, Manchester, 2005, p. 30.

42 *Southampton Herald*, 11 December 1869.

43 Gaze archive: material available at http://sotonopedia.wikidot.com/:gaze-henry.

44 Henry Gaze, *Belgium and Holland: How to See Them for Seven Guineas*, Letts & Co., London, 1864, p. 51.

45 Alexander Innes Shand, *Old Time Travel*, London, 1903, p. 39.

46 'W. E. F. and his journals of travelling on the Continent', Nottinghamshire County Archives: DD 125/1–3.

47 Shand, *Old Time Travel*, p. 40.

48 Letter, Mariana Starke to John Murray, John Murray Archive, National Library of Scotland, Edinburgh, MS.41151.

49 Ibid.

50 Starke, *Information and Direction for Travellers on the Continent*, John Murray, London, 1820, p. 77.

51 'Verses Written in a Blank Leaf of Mrs Starke's Guide to Travellers', John Bull, 27 June 1836.

52 John Murray Archive, MS. 41151.

53 Richard Mullen and James Munson, 'The Smell of the Continent', *North of England Magazine*, July 1843, p. 113.

54 Bodleian Library, Oxford, Special Collections, Ms.Top.Gen.e.77.

55 Susan Horner's Journal, 1829–1867, Archives of the British Institute, Florence, Horner Collection (HOR).

56 Galignani's *Traveller's Guide to Switzerland*, A. & W. Galignani, Paris, 1818, p. iii.

57 Galignani's *Switzerland*, p. xxiii.

58 Ibid., p. xxvii.

59 Ibid., A. & W. Galignani, Paris, 1819, p. 67.

60 *Murray's Magazine* (vol. 6, July–December 1889), p. 625.

61 Humphrey Carpenter, *The Seven Lives of John Murray: The Story of a Publishing Dynasty*, John Murray, London, 2008, p. 166.

62 Letter from John Murray, 1834, in Carpenter, *Seven Lives*, p. 169.

63 Carpenter, *Seven Lives*, p. 173.

64 Ibid.

65 Ian Robertson, *Richard Ford: Hispanophile, Connoisseur and Critic*, Michael Russell Publishing, Wilby, 2004, p. 178.

66 Ibid., p. 184.

67 Quoted in introduction by John R. Gretton to William Lister, *A Bibliography of Murray's Handbooks to Travellers and Biographies of Authors, Editors, Revisors and Principal Contributors*, Dereham Books, Norfolk, 1993, p. 228.

68 James Buzard, *The Beaten Track: European Tourism, Literature and the Ways to Culture, 1800–1918*, Oxford University Press, Oxford, 1993, pp. 65–6.

69 Arthur O'Leary [pseudonym of Charles Lever], *His Wanderings and Ponderings in Foreign Lands*, Henry Colburn, London, 1845, p. 35.

70 Alan Sillitoe, *Leading the Blind: A Century of Guidebook Travel 1815–1911*, Macmillan, London, 1997, p. 38.

71 Emily Birchall, *A Wedding Tour: January–June, 1873*, Sutton Publishing, Stroud, 1989, p. 23.

72 Alfred Bishop, *Fifty Years of Globetrotting*, Society of Friends, London, 1929, p. 18.

73 Birchall, *Wedding Tour*, p. 54.

74 Anon., from *Mr Punch on the Continong*, Punch Publications, London, 1906, p. 88.

75 Richard Mullen and James Munson, *The Smell of the Continent*, Macmillan, London, 2009, p. 122.

76 John Murray Archive, MS.41151.

77 *Murray's Magazine*, vol. 6, July–December 1889.

78 Lillias Campbell Davidson, *Hints to Lady Travellers at Home and Abroad*, Royal Geographical Publications, London, 2011, p. 104.

79 H. Ellen Browning, *A Girl's Wanderings in Hungary*, Longman, Green & Co., London, 1896, p. 90.

80 Jill Steward, 'Grant Allen and the Business of Travel', in *Literature and Cultural Politics at the Fin de Siecle*, edited by William Greenslade and Terence Rodgers, Taylor & Francis, Abingdon, 2017, p. 167.

81 Hugh and Pauline Massingham, *The Englishman Abroad*, Sutton Publishing, Stroud, 1984, p. 12.

82 Galignani, *Switzerland*, p. xxcvii.

83 Sillitoe, *Leading the Blind*, p. 37.

84 M. L'Abbaye Bussut, *The Italian and English Phrase-Book, Serving as a Key to Italian Conversation* (1830), Kessinger Legacy Reprints, Whitefish, Mont., 2011, p. 12.

85 W. Pembroke Fetridge, *Harper's Phrase-Book, or Hand-Book of Travel Talk for Travellers or Schools*, Sampson, Low & Son, London, 1873, p. 37.

86 Steward, 'Grant Allen and the Business of Travel', p. 157.

87 Ibid., p. 161.

88 Ibid., p. 163.

89 Ibid., p. 160.

90 Brendon, *Thomas Cook*, p. 11.

91 Ibid., p. 16.

92 *Cook's Excursionist*, June 1854.

93 Edmund Yates, 'My Excursion Agent', in *All the Year Round*, 7 May 1864.

94 Arthur Sketchley [pseud. George Rose], *Out for a Holiday with Cook's Excursion Through Italy and Switzerland*, London, 1870, p. 17.

95 Brendon, *Thomas Cook*, p. 92.

96 Arthur Sketchley [pseud. George Rose], *Mrs Brown on the Grand Tour*, George Routledge & Sons, London, 1869, pp. 9–10.

97 Anthony Trollope, *Travelling Sketches* (reprinted from the *Pall Mall Gazette*), London, 1866, p. 12.

98 Albert Smith, *The Adventures of Mr Ledbury and His Friend, Jack Johnson*, Richard Bentley, London, 1844, pp. 185–6.

99 *Punch*, Vols 4–7 (1841–1843), Punch Publications, London, 1843, p. 119.

100 Helen Dufferin [pseud. Helen Blackwood], *Lispings from Low Latitudes: Extracts from the Journal of the Hon. Impulsia Gushington*, John Murray, London, 1863, p. 2.

101 Mrs Gore, 'The Travelled Man', *Bentley's Miscellany*, vol. XIX, Richard Bentley, London, 1846, pp. 176-7.

102 R. S. Surtees, *Jorrocks's Jaunts and Jollities*, Routledge & Sons, London, 1871, p. 216.

103 Brendon, *Thomas Cook*, p. 114.

104 Jeremy Black, *The British Abroad: The Grand Tour in the Eighteenth Century*, History Press, Cheltenham, 2003, p. 150.

105 Jane Robinson, *Unsuitable for Ladies: An Anthology of Women Travellers*, Oxford University Press, Oxford, p. 47.

106 William Cole, *A Journal of My Journey to Paris*, 1765, Constable & Co., London, 1931, p. 64.

107 *Cook's Excursionist*, 23 September 1873.

108 'The Smell of Continent', *North of England Magazine*, July 1843, p. 262.

109 Nathaniel Newnham Davis and Algernon Bastard, *The Gourmet Guide to Europe*, Grant Richards, London, 1903, p. 211.

110 Private collection, with thanks to Vivien Brendon.

111 *Cook's Excursionist*, 28 August 1864.

112 Kenneth Clegg (editor), *Chronicles of a Journey 1839–40: The Diaries of Mary and Tom Beswick of Gristhorpe of their Travels to Malta, Egypt, Naples, Rome, Florence, Lyon, Paris and London*, Kenneth Clegg, 1997, p. 11.

113 Olivia Stone, *Tenerife and its Six Satellites*, Marcus Ward & Co., London, 1889, p. 37.

114 Quoted in Marjorie Morgan, *National Identities and Travel in Victorian Britain*, Palgrave Macmillan, London, 2001, p. 123.

115 Catherine Braithwaite, 'First Journey on the Continent', Library of the Society of Friends, MS/vol. 298, p. 56.

116 Mullen and Munson, *Smell of the Continent*, p. 268.

117 *The Edinburgh Edition of the Collected Works of Katherine Mansfield: Volume 2, The Collected Fiction of Katherine Mansfield, 1916–1922*,

  eds Gerri Kimber and Vincent O'Sullivan (Edinburgh: Edinburgh
  University Press, 2012), p. 290.

118 Trollope, *Travelling Sketches*, p. 18.

119 Charles Edwardes, 'Health Resort Vignettes', *Temple Bar*, vol. 83
  (1888), p. 205.

120 Birchall, *Wedding Tour*, p. 62.

121 Charles Lever, 'Continental Excursionists', *Blackwood's Magazine*,
  97 (February 1865), p. 230.

122 Yates, 'My Excursion Agent', p. 24.

123 W. H. Russell, *A Diary in the East*, Routledge, London, 1869,
  pp. 45–46.

124 Thomas Cook, 'Letters to his Royal Highness the Prince of Wales
  and to the Right Honourable the Earl of Clarendon, Foreign
  Secretary of State', Thos. Cook & Son, London, 1870.

125 Ibid.

126 Thomas Cook, 'Letters from the Sea and from Foreign Lands:
  Descriptive of a Tour Round the World', *History of Tourism*, vol. 3,
  edited by Paul Smith, Routledge, London, 1999, p. 104.

127 H. Rider Haggard, *A Winter Pilgrimage*, Longmans & Co., London,
  1904, p. 201.

128 Evelyn Waugh, *Labels: A Mediterranean Journal*, Penguin Classics,
  London, 1995, pp. 35–6.

11 WATER, AIR AND MOVEMENT

1 Thomas Hardy, *The Hand of Ethelberta*, Penguin Classics, London,
 1997, p. 363.

2 Maria Frawley, *Invalidism and Identity in Nineteenth-Century
 Britain*, University of Chicago Press, Chicago, 2004, p. 56.

3 George Eliot, *Adam Bede*, Penguin Classics, London, 2008, p. 298.

4 Anna Maria Twigg diary, BL MSs RP 9225 (box 254), British Library,
 London.

5 Bradley, *The Railways*, p. 89.

6 Erasmus Wilson, *A Three-Week Scamper Through the Spas of
 Germany*, J. Churchill, London, 1858, p. 5.

7 John Ruskin, *The Stones of Venice*, vol. 2, Smith, Elder & Co.,
 London, 1853, p. 5.

8 John Ruskin, *Praeterita*, Oxford University Press, Oxford, 2012,
 p. 72.

9 *The Railway Traveller's Handy Book*, Old House Books, London, 2012, p. 81.

10 E. F. Benson, *Our Family Affairs 1867–1896*, Cassell, London, 1920, p. 77.

11 'Journal of a Tour of the Rhine 1861 – Brightwen Family of Great Yarmouth', MC2847/G12 Norwich Archives.

12 E. S. Turner, *Taking the Cure*, Michael Joseph, London, 1967, p. 128.

13 Quoted in Helen Bynum, *Spitting Blood: The History of Tuberculosis*, Oxford University Press, Oxford, 2012, p. 67.

14 Charles Dickens, *Sketches by Boz*, Penguin Classics, London, 1996, p. 400.

15 Browne, *Diary of a Girl in France*, p. 11.

16 Rev. Greatorex, 'London to Spain and Back, Diaries, Vols 1 and 2', TH/8833, Tower Hamlets Local History Library.

17 Nona Bellairs, *Going Abroad*, 1857, quoted in Morgan, *National Identities*, p. 33.

18 Osborne Collection, Beinecke Library, OSB d388, Yale University.

19 Michael Heafford (ed.), *Two Victorian Ladies on the Continent*, Postilion Books, Cambridge, 2008, p. 2.

20 Geoffrey Trease (ed.), *Matthew Todd's Journal*, Heinemann, London, 1968, p. 56.

21 James Johnson, *Change of Air or A Philosopher in Pursuit of Health and Recreation Illustrating the Beneficial Influence of Bodily Exercise, Change of Scene and Temporary Relaxation from the Wear and Tear of Education and Avocation*, S. Higheley, London, 1829, p. 2.

22 Gustav Jaeger, *Health-Culture*, Waterlow & Son, London, 1887, p. 292.

23 R. T. Claridge, *Every Man His Own Doctor: A Medical Handbook*, James Madden, London, 1849, p. 32.

24 Anon., *A Hot Water Cure Sought out in Germany in the Summer of 1844*, London, 1845, p. 27.

25 Henry Matthews, *Diary of an Invalid*, John Murray, London, 1820, p. 44.

26 Frawley, *Invalidism*, p. 14.

27 Johnson, *Change of Air*, p. 281.

28 *Railway Travellers Handy Book*, p. 6.

29 Frawley, *Invalidism*, p. 230.

30 Edward Sparks, *The Riviera: Sketches of the Health Resorts of the North Mediterranean Coast of France and Italy from Hyeres to Spezia*, J. & A. Churchill, London, 1879, p. 154.

31 Turner, *Taking the Cure*, p. 128.

32 Johnson, *Change of Air*, p. 310.

33 Thomas Burgess, *The Climate in Italy in Relation to Pulmonary Consumption*, Longman & Co., London, 1879, p. 51.

34 Sketchley, *With Cook's Excursionists*, p. 12.

35 Johnson, *Change of Air*, p. 25.

36 J. M. Dent, *The House of Dent 1888–1938*, J. M. Dent & Sons, London, 1938, p. 51.

37 Ibid., pp. 51–3.

38 Johnson, *Change of Air*, p. 4.

39 *Pall Mall Gazette*, 4 January 1882.

40 Peter Thorold, *The British in France: Visitors and Residents Since the Revolution*, Continuum, London, 2008, p. 60.

41 Anon., *Three Weeks in Wet Sheets: Being the Diary and Doings of a Moist Visitor to Malvern*, Hamilton, Adams & Co., London, p. 78.

42 Turner, *Taking the Cure*, p. 116.

43 Francis Harrington Brett, *Gems of Tuscany: Being a Fragment for the Invalid and Tourist in Italy*, Ackerman & Co., London, 1852, p. 82.

44 Anon, *Three Weeks in Wet Sheets*, p. 17.

45 Pierre Lafagne, *Spa and the English*, Association for the Promotion of Tourism, Spa, 1948, p. 2.

46 Quoted in Turner, *Taking The Cure*, p. 97.

47 Shand, *Old Time Travel*, p. 88.

48 Ibid., p. 34.

49 Wilson, *A Three-Week Scamper*, p. 37.

50 Turner, *Taking the Cure*, p. 131.

51 David Clay Large, *The Grand Spas of Central Europe*, Rowman & Littlefield, Lanham, Md., 2015, p. 61.

52 Edwin Lee, *Notes on Italy and Rhenish Germany*, Edinburgh, 1870, p. 99.

53 Shand, *Old Time Travel*, p. 114.

54 Granville, *Spas of Germany*, p. 110.

55 Lee, *Notes on Italy and Rhenish Germany*, p. 111.

56 Turner, *Taking the Cure* p. 268.

57 Wilson, *A Three-Week Scamper*, p. 19.

58 Granville, *Spas of Germany*, p. 288.

59 Brett, *Gems of Tuscany*, p. 3.

60 'An Old Man' [Sir Francis Bond Head], *Bubbles from the Brunnen of Nassau*, London, 1866, p. 262.

61 Mary Eyre, *A Lady's Walks in the South of France*, London, 1865, p. 385.

62 Anon., *Confessions of a Hypcondriac in Search of Health*, London, 1849.

63 Thomas Linn, *The Health Resorts of Europe*, H. Kimpton, London, 1893, pp. 12–13.

64 Anon., *A Hot Water Cure*, p. 90.

65 'Old Man', *Bubbles*, p. 271.

66 Wilson, *A Three-Week Scamper*, p. 58.

67 Anon., *A Hot Water Cure*, p. 4.

68 'Old Man', *Bubbles*, p. 31.

69 Granville, *Spas of Germany*, p. xiii.

70 Brett, *Gems of Tuscany*, p. 17.

71 'Old Man', *Bubbles*, p. 33.

72 'Old Man', *Bubbles*, pp. 193–5.

73 Brett, *Gems of Tuscany*, p. 30.

74 Quoted in Turner, *Taking the Cure*, p. 125.

75 Granville, *Spas of Germany*, p. 201.

76 Linn, *Health Resorts*, p. 129.

77 Richard Claridge, *The Cold Water Cure, as Practised by Vincent Preissnitz*, J. Madden & Co., London, 1842, p. 10.

78 'Old Man', *Bubbles*, p. 66.

79 Jaeger, *Health-Culture*, pp. 12–13.

80 Dr James Freeman, *Medical Reflections on the Water Cure*, Saunders & Otley, London, 1842, p. 14.

81 Brett, *Gems of Tuscany*, p. 25.

82 Large, *Grand Spas*, p. 176.

83 Quoted in Turner, *Taking the Cure*, p. 39.

84 Newnham Davies, *A Gourmet's Guide to Europe*, p. 288.

85 Shand, *Old Time Travel*, p. 107.

86 Thorold, *The British in France*, p. 72.

87 Ibid., p. 63.

88 James Johnson MD, *Pilgrimages to the Spas in Pursuit of Health and Recreation with an Inquiry into the Comparative Merits of Different Mineral Waters,* London, 1841, p. 66.

89 Shand, *Old Time Travel*, p. 100.

90 Ibid., p. 101.

91 Ibid., pp. 88–90.

92 Ibid., p. 101.

93 Ibid., p. 102.

94 Wilson, *Three Weeks*, p. 66.

95 'A Medical Practitioner', *Quacks and Quackery*, London, 1844, p. 18.

96 William Chambers, *Wintering at Mentone*, W. & R. Chambers, Edinburgh, 1870, p. 4.

97 Baron Londesborough, *Wanderings in Search of Health*, privately printed, London, 1849, p. 1.

98 Turner, *Taking the Cure*, p. 7.

99 Jeremy Lewis, *Tobias Smollett*, Jonathan Cape, London, 2003, p. 241.

100 Quoted in Fawley, *Invalidism and Identity*, p. 126.

101 Burgess, *Climate of Italy*, p. 1.

102 Jaeger, *Health-Culture*, p. 19.

103 Linn, *Health Resorts of Europe*, p. 202.

104 Quoted in John Pemble, *The Mediterranean Passion: Victorians and Edwardians in the South*, Faber & Faber, London, 2009, p. 86.

105 R. H. Otter, *Winters Abroad, Some Places Visited by the Author on Account of his Health*, John Murray, London, 1882, p. 124.

106 Evangeline Whipple, *A Famous Corner of Tuscany*, Jarrolds, Norwich, 1928, p. 238.

107 Margaret Maria Brewster, *Letters from Cannes and Nice*, Constable & Co., Edinburgh, 1857, p. 10.

108 Brewster, *Letters from Cannes and Nice*, p. 31.

109 Sidney Colvin (ed.) *The Letters of Robert Louis Stevenson*, Methuen, London, 1901, pp. 83–4.

110 Charles Nottage, *In Search of Climate*, Sampson & Low, London, 1894, p. 340.

111 Otter, *Winters Abroad*, p. 2.

112 Richard Colt Hoare, *Recollections Abroad*, Bath, 1819, p. 36.

113 Mary and Anne Wilson, *A European Journal: Two Sisters Abroad in 1847*, Bloomsbury, London, 1987, p. 144.

114 Susan Horner's Journal.

115 Linn, *Health Resorts of Europe*, p. 204.

116 John Altrayd Wittitterley [Pseud. Elizabeth Carne], *Three Months Rest at Pau*, London, 1860, p. 14.

117 Isaac Burney Yeo, *Climate and Health Resorts*, Chapman & Hall, London, 1885, p. 346.

118 C. Home Douglas, *Searches for Summer: The Anti-winter Tactics of an Invalid*, William Blackwood, London and Edinburgh, 1874, p. 39.

119 William Chambers, *Wintering in Mentone*, Edinburgh, 1870, p. 37.

120 Sparks, *The Riviera*, p. 154.

121 Ibid., p. 156.

122 Ibid., p. 154.

123 James Henry Bennet, *Mentone and the Riviera as a Winter Climate*, John Churchill, London, 1861, p. 214.

124 *Pall Mall Gazette*, 4 January 1882.

125 Maquay Collection, archives of the British Institute, Florence.

126 Massinghams, *Englishman Abroad*, p. 8.

127 *Pall Mall Gazette*, 4 January 1882.

128 Edmund Hobhouse, ed., *Health Abroad: A Medical Handbook of Travel*, Smith, Elder & Co., London, 1899, p. 234.

129 T. Wemyss Reid, *The Life, Letters and Friendships of Richard Monckton Milnes*, vol. 2, Cassell, London, 1890, p. 122.

130 Bennet, *Mentone and the Riviera*, p. 218.

131 Home Douglas, *Searches for Summer*, p. 22.

132 Matilda Houstoun, *Texas and the Gulf of Mexico*, John Murray, London, 1844, p. 31.

133 Bennet, *Mentone and the Riviera*, p. 37.

134 Shand, *Old Time Travel*, p. 115.

135 Claire Harman, *Robert Louis Stevenson: A Biography*, HarperCollins, London, 2006, p. 204.

136 Burney Yeo, *Climate and Health Resorts*, p. 47.

137 Quoted in Jim Ring, *How the English Made the Alps*, John Murray, London, 2008, p. 124.

138 *Cook's Excursionist*, 15 May 1870. Leicester, Leicestershire and Rutland Record Office, TC/S/1/1/14.

139 Quoted in Harman, *Robert Louis Stevenson*, p. 205.

140 Johnson, *Change of Air*, p. 28.

141 Otter, *Wintering Abroad*, p. 17.

142 Ring, *How the English Made the Alps*, p. 126.

143 William Lockett, *Robert Louis Stevenson at Davos*, Hurst & Blackett, London, 1934, p. 31.

144 Ibid., p. 45.

145 Ibid., p. 46.

146 Harman, *Robert Louis Stevenson*, p. 207.

147 Lockett, *Robert Louis Stevenson at Davos*, p. 84.

148 *The Fortnightly Review*, vol. 37, 1882, p. 640.

III THE OCEAN IN A SEASHELL

1 Dickens, *Little Dorrit*, Penguin Classics, London, 2003, p. 499.

2 Osborn Collection, d313.

3 *The History of the Business of a Diary Publisher*, privately published, p. 4.

4 Hannah Wills, 'Pre-printed diaries and almanacs: an aid to managing the disease of modern life?' (www.web.diseasesofmodernlife.ox.ac.uk).

5 Quoted in ibid.

6 Richard Colt Hoare, *Hints to Travellers in Italy*, p. 7.

7 *Chronicles of a Journey 1839–40: The Diaries of Mary and Tom Beswick of Gristhorpe of their Travels to Paris, Malta, Egypt, Naples, Rome, Florence, Lyon, Paris and London*, transcribed by Kenneth Clegg, 1997, p. 9.

8 Ibid., p. 30.

9 Ibid., p. 31.

10 Anthony Trollope, *Travelling Sketches*, p. 67.

11 Special Collections, Bodleian Library, Oxford, MS Eng.c 7099.

12 Browne, *The Diary of a Girl in France in 1821*, p. 8.

13 Ibid., p. 87.

14 Johnson, *Change of Air*, p. 39.

15 See Kate Summerscale, *Mrs Robinson's Disgrace: The Private Diary of a Victorian Lady*, Bloomsbury, London, 2012, p. 150.

16 *Women's Travel Writings in Post-Napoleonic France*, vol. 1, Pickering & Chatto, London, 2011, p. 27.

17 Osborn Collection, Beinecke Library, D.56 1–2.

18 Anna Jameson, *Diary of an Ennuyée*, Henry Colburn, London, 1826, p. 4.

19 Alison Chapman and Jane Stabler, *Unfolding the South: Nineteenth-Century British Women Writers and Artists in Italy*, Manchester University Press, Manchester, 2003, p. 2.

20 Frances Anna Kemble, *Records of a Girlhood*, vol. 2, H. Holt, London, 1879, p. 127.

21 Kathryn Walchester, *Our Own Fair Italy: Nineteenth-Century Women's Travel Writing*, Peter Lang, Frankfurt, 2007, p. 7.

22 Dufferin, *Lispings from Low Latitudes*, p. 2.

23 Dufferin, *Lispings from Low Latitudes*, p. 7.

24 Catherine Gore, *Sketches of English Character*, Richard Bentley, London, 1848, p. 260.

25 Quoted in Heafford (ed.), *Two Victorian Ladies*, p. iii.

26 Catherine Taylor, *Letters from Italy to a Younger Sister*, John Murray, London, 1840, p. xii.

27 Joseph Fox, *Holiday Memories*, L. Tozer, London, 1908, p. 88.

28 Osborn Collection, Beinecke Library, Ms. D56.

29 Oscar Wilde, *The Importance of Being Earnest*, Dover Editions, New York, 2000, p. 22.

30 Mary Elizabeth Herbert, *Impressions of Spain in 1866*, Richard Bentley, London, 1867, p. 1.

31 Churnjeet Mahn, *British Women's Travel to Greece 1840–1914*, Routledge, London, 2016, p. 99.

32 Trease, *Journal of Matthew Todd*, p. 75.

33 Augustus Hare, *The Story of My Life*, G. Allen, London, 1896, p. 460.

34 *A Tale of Two Journeys: The Fry Diaries: France and Belgium in the Early 1800s*, ed, Richard Pelly, Disley, Millrace, 2005, p. 17.

35 Fitzsimons, *Albert Smith*, p. 57.

36 Beswick, *Chronicles of a Journey*, p. 15.

37 Charles Dickens, *Pictures from Italy*, Penguin Classics, London, 2006, p. 76.

38 Sarah Goldsmith, *Masculinity and Danger on the Eighteenth Century Grand Tour,* Institute of Historical Research, London, 2020, p. 46.

39 Letter to Richard West, *From St James to St Peters, Horace Walpole's and Thomas Gray's Letters from the Grand Tour, 1739–1741*, Malthouse Press, Stoke on Trent, 1996, p. 8.

40 Adrian Tinniswood, *The Polite Tourist*, National Trust, Swindon, 1999, pp. 116–17.

41 Ian Ousby, *The Englishman's England: Taste, Travel and the Rise of Tourism*, Cambridge University Press, Cambridge, 1990, p. 191.

42 John Chetwode Eustace, *A Classical Tour Through Italy: vol. 2: Rome, Naples and Etruria*, J. Mawman, London, 1814, p. 100.

43 Anthony Kenny (ed.), *Mountains, an Anthology*, John Murray, London, 1991, p. 113.

44 William Combe, *The Tour of Dr Syntax in Search of the Picturesque*, London, 1812, p. 5.

45 Roland Barthes, *Mythologies*, Vintage Classics, London, 2009, p. 74.

46 'Old Man', *Bubbles*, p. 313.

47 Henry Gaze, *Switzerland, How to See it for Ten Guineas*, London, 1863, p. 19.

48 Advertisement in *Murray's Handbook to Switzerland*, John Murray, London, 1853.

49 Heafford (ed.), *Two Victorian Ladies*, p. 73.

50 Brendon, *Thomas Cook*, p. 89.

51 *Selected Letters of Leslie Stephen*, vol 1: 1864–1882, (ed.) John Bicknell, Ohio University Press, Athens, Ohio, 1996, p. 51.

52 *Diary of a Cook's Tourist from Rochdale*, private collection, p. 217.

53 Chloe Chard, 'From the Sublime to the Ridiculous: The Anxieties of Sightseeing', in Hartmut Berghoff, Barbara Korte, Ralf Schneider, Christopher Harvie (eds) *The Making of Modern Tourism: the Cultural History of the Modern Experience*, Palgrave Macmillan, London, 2002, p. 47.

54 Fergus Fleming, quoted in *Killing Dragons: The Conquest of the Alps*, Granta, London, 2000, P. 140.

55 Robinson, *Unsuitable for Ladies*, pp. 11–12.

56 Ronald Clark, *The Victorian Mountaineers*, B. T. Batsford, London, 1953, p. 176.

57 Rosalind Vallance (ed.), *Dickens in Europe*, Folio Society, London, 1975, pp. 108–9.

58 Brendon, *Thomas Cook*, pp. 217–18.

59 Johnson, *Change of Air*, p. 51.

60 Special Collections, Bodleian Library, Oxford, Ms Eng Misc f24.

61 De Beer, *Travellers in Switzerland*, p. 20.

62 Olivia Stone, *Tenerife*, p. 16.

63 Jenny Uglow, *In These Times*, Faber & Faber, London, 2014, p. 620.

64 *Days of Battle or Quatre Bras and Waterloo* by 'an Englishwoman resident in Brussels in June 1815', London 1818, p. 123.

65 Ibid. p. 124.

66 John Scott, *Journal of a Tour to W'loo and Paris in company with Sir Walter Scott 1815*, London, 1842, pp. 45–6.

67 Osborn Collection, Beinecke Library, Ms. d.11.

68 Scott, *Journal of a Tour*, p. 46.

69 Mullen and Munson, *Smell of the Continent*, p. 60.

70 Finetta Staley, *Autumn Rambles; Fireside Recollections*, E. Wrigley & Son, Rochdale, 1863, p. 13.

71 David Lloyd, *Battlefield Tourism: Pilgrimage and the Commemoration of the Great War in Britain, Australia and Canada 1919–1939*, Bloomsbury, London, 1998, p. 26.

72 Elizabeth Nitchie, *The Reverend Colonel Finch*, New York, 1940, p. 32.

73 Patrick Anderson, *Over the Alps: Reflections on Travel and Travel Writing with Special Reference to the Grand Tours of Boswell, Beckford and Byron*, Hart Davis, London, 1969, p. 25.

74 See Andrew Wilton and Ilaria Bignamini (eds), *Grand Tour: The Lure of Italy in the Eighteenth Century*, Tate Publishing, 1996, pp. 282–302.

75 Viccy Coltman, *Fabricating the Antique: Neo-classicism in Britain, 1760–1800*, University of Chicago Press, Chicago, 2006, p. 2.

76 Dickens, *Little Dorrit*, p. 188.

77 *Railway Travellers' Handy Book*, p. 17.

78 Edmund Yates, *Recollections*, vol. 1, p. 28.

79 Ibid., p. 47.

80 Wilsons, *A European Journal*, p. 39.

81 Asa Briggs, *Victorian Things*, Penguin, London, 1990, p. 243.

82 *Women's Travel Writings in Post-Napoleonic France*, p. 34.

83 Brand, *Italy and the English Romantics*, p. 19.

84 Giles St Aubyn, *Victorian Eminence: The Life and Works of Henry Thomas Buckle*, Barrie Books, London, 1958, pp. 79–80.

85 Diane Fortenberry, *Souvenirs and New Ideas: Travel and Collecting in Egypt and the Near East*, Oxbow Books, Oxford, 2013, p. 63.

86 Ibid., p. 64.

87 Alison Cunningham, *Cummy's Diary: A Diary Kept by R. L. Stevenson's Nurse*, Chatto & Windus, London, 1926, p. 126.

88 Ann Hilker, unpublished phD thesis: 'A biography of the American snow globe: from memory to mass production, from souvenir to sign', Parsons/Cooper Hewitt, New York, 2014.

89 Quoted in Liz Wells, *Photography: A Critical Introduction*, Taylor & Francis, Abingdon, 2015, p. 16.

90 See Briggs, *Victorian Things*, p. 227.

91 J. G. Links, *The Ruskins in Normandy*, John Murray, London, 1968, p. 15.

92 Ibid., p. 3.

93 Ian Jeffrey, *Photography: A Concise History*, Thames & Hudson, London, 1981, p. 31.

94 Katarzyna Michalkiewicz and Patrick Vincent, 'Victorians in the Alps: A Case Study of Zermatt's Hotel Guest Books and Registers', in Kate Hill (ed.), *Britain and the Narration of Travel in the Nineteenth Century*, Taylor & Francis, Abingdon, p. 189.

95 Osborne, *Travelling Light: Photography, Travel and Visual Culture*, Manchester University Press, Manchester, 2000, p. 58.

96 Special Collections, Bodleian Library, Oxford, MS. Top. Gen. e.77.

97 Naomi Schor, 'Collecting Paris' in Roger Cardinal (ed.), *The Cultures of Collecting*, Reaktion, London, 2004, p. 266.

98 Richard Carline, *Pictures in the Post: The Story of the Picture Postcard*, Gordon Fraser, London, 1971, p. 57.

99 Ibid., p. 9.

100 Naomi Schor, 'Collecting Paris', p. 262.

101 Martin Willoughby, *A History of Postcards*, Bracken Books, London, 1994, p. 143.

102 Kate Hill (ed.), *Britain and the Narration of Travel in the Nineteenth Century: Texts, Images and Objects*, Routledge, Abingdon, 2016, p. 138.

103 Vita Sackville-West, *Passenger to Tehran*, HarperCollins, London, 1990, p. 13.

104 Gilles Dorfles, *Kitsch, an Anthology of Bad Taste*, Studio Vista, London, 1975, p. 154.

105 Warren Hall, *Azure Coast: A Diary of the French and Italian Rivieras*, Neville Woodbury Publishing, London, 1952, p. 218.

106 Ibid., p. 219.

107 William Chambers, *Wintering at Mentone*, p. 79.

108 Penny Sparke, 'The Straw Donkey: Tourist Kitsch or Proto-Design? Craft and Design in Italy, 1945–1960, *Journal of Design History*, vol. 11, No 1, 1998, pp. 59–69.

109 Susan Stewart, *On Longing: Narratives of the Miniature, the Gigantic, the Souvenir, the Collection*, Duke University Press, Durham, N.C., 1984, p. 135.

IV VALEDICTIONS

1 Dickens, *Letters from Rome*, pp. 12–13.

2 E. M. Forster, *A Room with a View*, Penguin Classics, London, 2000, p. 13.

3 Edward Austen Knight, Grand Tour Journal (1790), Beinecke Library, Yale University, no ref.

4 See Pen Vogler, *Scoff: A History of Food and Class in Britain*, Atlantic Books, London, 2020, p. 203.

5 Birchall, *Wedding Tour*, p. 80.

6 Wilsons, *European Journal*, p. 121.

7 Captain M. J. Jousiffe, *A Road Book for Travellers in Italy*, Meline, Cans & Co. Brussels, p. 147.

8 Browne, *Journal of a Tour in France*, p. 95.

9 John William Cunningham, *Cautions to Continental Travellers*, Ellerton & Henderson, London, 1818, p. 58.

10 *Spectator*, 13 September 1879, vol. 52, p. 1161.

11 Quoted in *English Miscellany*, British Council, London, 1956, p. 256.

12 Ibid.

13 Brendon, *Thomas Cook*, p. 98.

14 Susan Horner's Diary, archives of the British Institute, Florence.

15 Heafford (ed.), *Two Victorian Ladies*, p. 153.

16 Pemble, *The Mediterranean Passion*, p. 212.

17 Quoted in Mullen and Munson, *Smell of the Continent*, p. 288.

18 Private diary, thanks to Vivienne Brendon.

19 Wittitterley, *Three Months Rest at Pau*, p. 41.

20 Starke, *Information and Directions*, p. 87.

21 Sillitoe, *Leading the Blind*, p. 140.

22 Starke, *Information and Directions*, p. 305.

23 Birchall, *Wedding Tour*, p. 142.

24 Susan Horner's diary.

25 *Miss Jemima's Swiss Journal*, 1864, pp. 48–9.

26 Greatorex, 'London to Spain and Back', TH/8833.

27 Starke, *Information and Directions*, p. 80.

28 David Wills, *The Mirror of Antiquity: British Twentieth-Century Travellers in Greece*, Cambridge Scholars Publishing, Cambridge, 2007, pp. 81–90.

29 *Murray's Handbook to Denmark, Norway, Sweden and Iceland* (1853), p. xi.

30 Quoted in Angela Byrne, *Geographies of the Romantic North: Science, Antiquarianism and Travel, 1790–1830*, Palgrave Macmillan, Basingstoke, 2013, p. 52.

31 Andrew Wawn, *The Vikings and the Victorians: Inventing the North in Nineteenth Century Britain*, D. S. Brewer, Woodbridge, 2002, p. 287.

32 *Murray's Handbook to Denmark, Norway, Sweden and Iceland*, p. 104.

33 Ibid., p. 95

34 Ibid., p. 100.

35 Ibid., p. 90.

36 Ibid.

37 Wawn, *The Vikings and the Victorians*, p. 283.

38 Martin Graebe, introduction to Sabine Baring-Gould, *Iceland, its Scenes and Sagas* Signal Books, Oxford, 2007, p. xxi.

39 Ibid., pp. xxvii–xxviii.

40 Baring-Gould, *Iceland, its Scenes and Sagas*, p. 86.

41 John Purkis, *The Icelandic Jaunt: A Study of the Expeditions made by William Morris to Iceland in 1871 and 1873*, William Morris Society, London, 1962, p. 21.

42 *The Collected Letters of William Morris* (ed. Norman Kelvin), vol. 1, Princeton University Press, Princeton, N.J. 2014, p. 142.

43 *Northern History* XLVIII, 1 March 2011, p. 166.

44 *Lock's Guide to Iceland* (1882), p. 87.

45 *Murray's Hand Book to Icelancd*, 1888, p. 123.

46 J.A. Hammerton, *Wrack of War*, London, 1918, p. 17.

47 'A Drawback to Southern Sunshine', *Pall Mall Gazette*, 4 Jan. 1882.

48 Quoted in Pemble, *The Mediterranean Passion*, p. 168.

49 Christopher Woodward, *In Ruins*, Chatto & Windus, London, 2001, p. 261.

50 Michael Felmingham and Graham Rigby, *Ruins*, Feltham, Country Life Books, 1972, p. 7.

51 Coltman, *Fabricating the Antique*, p. 51.

52 Peter Quennell, *The Colosseum*, TBS Publishers, New York, 1971, p. 126.

53 Ibid., p. 148.

54 Dickens, *Pictures from Italy*, p. 168.

55 Frederic Harrison, in *Fortnightly Review*, 53, pp. 702–21.

56 Maurice Hewlett, *The Road in Tuscany*, Macmillan, London, 1904, p. 160.

57 Brand, *Italy and the English Romantics*, p. 24.

58 Wilfied Scawen Blunt, *My Diaries, Part Two*, Martin Secker, London, 1920, p. 93.

59 Nottinghamshire County Archives, Ms. DD 1251/1–3.

60 *Murray's Handbook to South Italy and Naples*, 1853, p. 140.

61 Osborn Collections, Beinecke Library, ms. C319.

62 Norwich Archives, MC2784/H/10.

63 Cunningham, *Cummy's Diary*, p. 8.

64 Sillitoe, *Leading the Blind*, p. 2.

65 Adam Blenkinsop, *A Hot Water Cure*, Saunders & Otley, London, 1845, p. 15.

66 Journal FC Amherst 'A tour of Holland and the Netherlands'. Kent Archives, U13050/F5/

67 *Observer*, 31 July 1870.

68 *The Times*, 6 April 1900.

69 Lloyd, *Battlefield Tourism*, p. 279.

70 Brendon, *Thomas Cook*, p. 255.

71 Lloyd, *Battlefield Tourism*, p. 20.

72 Ibid., pp. 41–2.

73 Ibid., p. 41.

74 Graham Seton Hutchison, *Pilgrimage*, Rich & Cowan, London, 1935, p. 2.

75 P. B. Clayton, *Tales of Talbot House*, Toc H, London, 1934, p. 11.

V 'WHOLESOME AND EXCELLENT'

1 Quoted in Nicholas Faith, *The World the Railways Made*, Head of Zeus, London, 2014, p. 96.

2 Quoted in Hugh Cunningham, *Time, Work and Leisure: Life Changes in England from 1700*, Manchester University Press, Manchester, 2016, p. 76.

3 Barton, *Working-Class Organisations and Popular Tourism*, p. 60.

4 London Metropolitan Archives, A/TOY/12/1.

5 Ibid.

6 Ibid.

7 T. Arthur Leonard, *Adventures in Holidaymaking: Being the Story of the Rise and Development of a People's Holiday Movement*, Holiday Fellowship, Manchester, p. 13.

8 Ibid., p. 14.

9 Ibid., p. 19.

10 *Over the Hills*, Spring 1973, vol. 2, No. 32.

11 Leonard, *Adventures in Holidaymaking*, p. 137.

12 University of Westminster archives: ACC2005/1 PTA 2/1/11.

13 R. G. Studd, *The Holiday Story*, Percival Marshall, London, 1950, p. 10.

14 Ibid., p. 34.

15 Gavin de Beer, *Travellers in Switzerland*, p. 476.

16 University of Westminster archives: PTA/4/STE/17.

17 Studd, *Holiday Story*, p. 34.

18 Ibid., p. 57.

19 University of Westminster archive Polytechnic Holiday Supplement in November 1914.

20 Leonard, *Adventures in Holidaymaking*, p. 68.

21 Ibid.

22 Ibid., p. 135.

23 Ibid., p. 166.

24 Francis Williams, *Journey into Adventure: the Story of the Workers' Travel Association*, Odhams Press, London, 1960, p. 14.

25 Williams, *Journey into Adventure*, p. 14.

26 Harry Gosling, *Up and Down Stream*, London, 1927, p. 210.

27 Kent County Records, WTA Box U2543/C.

28 Kent County Records, U2543/Z/1/1.

29 *Yorkshire Observer*, 24 August 1923.

30 Ibid.

31 *Daily Herald*, 12 January 1924.

32 Kent Archives/Box U2543/C.

33 *Daily Herald*, 1 November 1932.

34 *Morning Star*, 1 November 1932.

35 Robert Graves and Alan Hodge, *The Long Weekend: A Social History of Britain 1918–1939*, Faber & Faber, London, 1940, p. 276.

36 Kent Archives: WTA/ U2543/Z1/3.

37 Ibid.

38 Studd, *Holiday Story*, p. 120.

39 *Over the Hills,* no 55 1937: Coooperative Archives, Manchester.

40 Studd, *Holiday Story*, p. 158.

41 Ibid., 157.

42 Ibid., 158.

43 University of Sussex, Mass Observation archive, Box 58–2–4 (1947–51).

44 D. H. Lawrence, *Twilight in Italy*, Penguin, London, 1997, p. 147.

45 Ibid., p. 120.

46 Ibid., p. 150.

47 Miriam Akhtar and Steve Humphries, *Some Liked it Hot*, Virgin Publishing, London, 2000, p. 79.

48 Kenneth Grahame, *Wind in the Willows*, Scribners, London, 1908, p. 30.

49 D. Goffe (ed.), *Camping on the Wye*, Bloomsbury, London, 2017, p. 33.

50 *Camping Quarterly*, September 2010.

51 Charles Loch Mowat, *Britain Between the Wars*, Methuen, London, 1976, p. 501.

52 Hazel Constance, *First in the Field: A History of the Camping and Caravanning Club*, CCC, London, 2001, p. 24.

53 Ibid., p. 37.

54 Editions of the Campers Quarterly from 1901 accessible through Adam Matthew Digital Archive/ Leisure and Mass Tourism.

55 Ibid.

56 Ibid.

57 Ibid.

58 Ibid.

VI 'I WANT A HOLIDAY MORE THAN EVER'

1 Brendon, *Thomas Cook*, p. 269.

2 University of Westminster Archive, PTA/2//9.

3 Brendon, *Thomas Cook*, p. 274.

4 Studd, *Holiday Story*, p. 200.

5 Ibid., p. 201.

6 PTA Archives: 2/1/25.

7 PTA Archives: 2/1/21.

8 Barton, *Working Class Organisations and Popular Tourism*, p. 15.

9 Julia Boyd, *Travellers in the Third Reich: The Rise of Fascism through the Eyes of Everyday People*, Elliott & Thompson, London, 2017, p. 154.

10 Brendon, *Thomas Cook*, p. 276.

11 Studd, *Holiday Story*, p. 155.

12 Nigel West: *Spycraft Secrets: An Espionage A–Z*, History Press, London, 2016, p. 250.

13 Studd, *Holiday Story*, p. 157.

14 Elizabeth Bowen, *To the North*, Vintage, London, 1999, pp. 23–4.

15 Sussex University, Mass Observation archives, S8–1–c.

16 University of Sussex Library, TC 58, Holidays 1937–51: SxMOA1/2/58.

17 Ibid.

18 Ibid.

19 Ibid.

20 Studd, *Holiday Story*, p. 179.

21 University of Sussex Library, TC38, Holidays 1937–51: SxMOA1/2/58.

22 Constance, *First in the Field*, p. 181.

23 Ibid., p. 193.

24 S. B. Hough, *A Pound a Day Inclusive: The Modern Way to Holiday Travel*, Hodder & Stoughton, London, 1957, p. 27.

25 Ibid., p. 89.

26 Akhtar and Humphries, *Some Liked it Hot*, p. 93.

27 Hough, *A Pound a Day*, p. 99.

28 *Letts Guide to the Italian Riviera*, p. 40.

29 Hough, *A Pound a Day*, p. 84.

30 Alain Corbin, *The Lure of the Sea: The Discovery of the Seaside, 1750–1840*, Penguin, London, 1995, p. 123.

31 Brett, *Gems of Tuscany*, p. 101.

32 Simona Pakenham, *Sixty Miles from England: The English at Dieppe, 1814–1914*, Macmillan, London, 1967, p. 19.

33 Christiana Payne, 'Seaside Visitors: Idlers, Thinkers and patriots in Mid-Nineteenth-Century Britain', in Susan Anderson and Bruce Tabb (eds), *Water, Leisure and Culture: European Historical Perspectives*, Berg, Oxford, 2010, p. 88.

34 Rosa Baugham, *The Northern Watering Places of France: A Guide for English People to the Holiday Resorts of the Coast*, London, 1880, p. 9.

35 Ibid., p. 21.

36 Pakenham, *Sixty Miles from England*, p. 19.

37 Bennet, *Mentone and the Riviera*, p. 609.

38 Paul Fussell, *Abroad: British Literary Travelling Between the Wars*, Oxford University Press, Oxford, 1982, p. 6.

39 Leader Scott, *Tuscan Studies and Sketches*, T. Fisher Unwin, London, 1888, p. 195.

40 Johnson, *Change of Air*, p. 286.

41 Simon Carter, *Rise and Shine: Sunlight, Technology and Health*, Bloomsbury, London, 2007, pp. 22–3.

42 Ibid., p. 12.

43 Ibid., p. 18.

44 Ibid., p. 18.

45 Auguste Rollier, *Heliotherapy*, H. Frowde, London, 1923, p. 18.

46 Carter, *Rise and Shine*, p. 62.

47 D. H. Lawrence, 'Sun', from *The Woman Who Rode Away and Other Stories*, Martin Secker, London, 1928, p. 28.

48 J. P. Muller, *My Sunbathing and Fresh-Air System*, Athletic Publications, London, 1927, p. 6.

49 Rollier, *Heliotherapy*, p. 20.

50 Ibid., p. 27.

51 Muller, *My Sunbathing System*, p. 8.

52 Lockett, *Robert Louis Stevenson at Davos*, p. 213.

53 Louis Turner and John Ash, *The Golden Hordes: International Tourism and the Pleasure Periphery*, Constable, London, 1975, p. 74.

54 Carter, *Rise and Shine*, p. 100.

55 Ibid, p. 101.

56 University of Westminster Archives: ACC2005/1 PTA 2/1/11.

57 Robert Trimnell, *Trim's Guide to Majorca*, Mossen Alcover Press, Palma, 1958, p. 38.

58 Hall, *Azure Coast*, p. 34.

59 Robert Graves, 'The Sun Seekers' (unpublished MS), St John's College, Oxford, RG/G/CESS.

60 Ada Harrison, *A Majorca Holliday*, G. Howe, London, 1927, p. 16.

61 Stephen A. Royle, 'Tourism Changes on a Mediterranean Island: Experiences from Mallorca' in *Island Studies Journal*, vol. 4, No. 2, p. 229.

62 See, 'Paradise Lost and Found: Tourists and Expatriates in El Torreno, Palma de Mallorca from the 1920s to the 1950s' in John Walton (ed), *Histories of Tourism: Representation, Identity and Conflict*, Channel View Publications, Clevedon, 2005, p. 181.

63 Robert Graves, 'The Phenomenon of Mass-Tourism', (unpublished MS), 1964, St John's College, Oxford Archives, RG/H/PMT.

64 Harrison, *A Majorca Holiday*, p. 21.

65 Ibid., p. 293.

66 *Trim's Guide to Majorca* 1958.

67 Roger Bray and Vladimir Raitz, *Flight to the Sun: The Story of the Holiday Revolution*, Continuum, London, 2001, p. 4.

68 Ibid., p. 20.

69 Adam Matthews Digital: Travel, Leisure and Mass Culture https://www.amdigital.co.uk/.

70 Sue Wright, 'Sun, Sea, Sand and Self-Expression: Mass Tourism as Individual Epression', in Berghoff et al, *The Making of Modern Tourism*, p. 195.

71 Graves, 'The Sun Seekers'.

72 Wright, 'Sun, Sea, Sand and Self-Expression', p. 95.

73 See Adam Matthews Digital, Leisure, Travel and Mass Culture.

74 Hall, *Azure Coast*, p. 35.

75 Ibid., p. 26.

76 Norman Lewis, *The Happy Ant Heap*, Picador, London, 1999, pp. 54–5.

77 Ibid., p. 56.

78 Ibid., p. 57.

79 Graves, 'The Phenomenon of Mass Tourism'.

80 Ibid.

81 Turner and Ash, *The Golden Hordes*, p. 81.

CODA

1 Roy Hattersley, 'New Blood', in Gerald Kaufman (ed.), *The Left: a Symposium*, Anthony Blond, London, 1966, p. 153.

2 Braithwaite, *My Continental Journey*.

3 Dorothy Pilley, *My Climbing Days*, G. Bell & Sons, London, 1935, p. 163.

4 Club Med survey from ClubMed.co.uk.

5 Dylan Harris, foreword to H. E. Sawyer, *I am the Dark Tourist*, Headpress, London, 2018, pp. 1–2.

Select Bibliography

ARCHIVES

Robert Graves Collection, St John's College, Oxford; Bodleian Collections, Oxford; Kent Record Office, Maidstone; Norfolk Record Office, Norwich; National Cooperative Archive, Manchester; Adam Matthew Digital Archive (www.amdigital.co.uk); Workers Travel Association Archives, University of Westminster, London; Tower Hamlets Record Office, London; Thomas Cook Archive; Osborn Collection, Beinecke Library, Yale University.

PUBLISHED SOURCES

Akhtar, Miriam, Belford, Ros, and Humphries, Steve, *Some Liked It Hot: The British on Holiday at Home and Abroad*, London, 2000
Anderson, Patrick, *Over the Alps*, London, 1969
Anon., *Days of Battle or Quatre Bas and Waterloo by an Englishwoman Resident in Brussels in June 1815*, London, 1818
————— *Quacks and Quackery, A Remonstrance*, London, 1844
————— *Diary of a Girl in France in 1821*, London, 1905
Baring-Gould, Sabine, *Iceland, its Scenes and Sagas*, edited by Martin Graebe, Oxford, 2007
Barthes, Roland, *Mythologies*, Paris, London, 1957
Barton, Susan, *Working-Class Organisations and Popular Tourism, 1840–1970*, Manchester, 2005
Baugham, Rosa, *The Northern Watering Places of France*, London, 1880

Bennet, James Henry, *Winter and Spring in the Mediterranean*, London, 1861

Beswick, Mary and Tom, *Chronicles of a Journey 1839–1840: The Diaries of Mary and Tom Beswick of Gristhorpe*, London, 1997

Birchall, Emily, *A Wedding Tour*, London, 1873

Bishop, Alfred, *Fifty Years of Globetrotting*, London, 1929

Black, Jeremy, *The Grand Tour in the Eighteenth Century*, London, 2003

Blenkinsop, Adam, *A Hot Water Cure Sought Out in Germany*, London, 1845

Borsay, Peter, and Walton, John. K., (eds), *Resorts and Ports: European Seaside Towns since 1700*, Bristol, 2011

Bowen, Elizabeth, *To the North*, London, 1933

Boyd, Julia, *Travellers in the Third Reich: The Rise of Fascism Through the Eyes of Everyday People*, London 2017

Bradley, Simon, *The Railways: Nation, Network and People*, London, 2015

Brand, C. P., *Italy and the English Romantics*, London, 1957

Brendon, Piers, *Thomas Cook: 150 Years of Popular Tourism*, London, 1991

Brett, Frederick Harrington, *Gems of Tuscany: Being a Fragment for the Invalid and Tourist in Italy*, London, 1852

Brewster, Margaret Maria, *Letters from Cannes and Nice*, London, 1857

Briggs, Asa, *Victorian Things*, London, 1988

Browning, Ellen H., *A Girl's Wanderings in Hungary*, London, 1897

Burgess, Thomas, *The Climate in Italy in Relation to Pulmonary Consumption*, London, 1852

Buzard, James, *The Beaten Track, European Tourism, Literature and the Ways to 'Culture', 1800–1918*, Oxford, 1993

Bynum, Helen, *Spitting Blood: The History of Tuberculosis*, Oxford, 2012

Campbell-Davidson, Lillias, *Hints to Lady Travellers at Home and Abroad*, London, 1889

Carpenter, Humphrey, *The Seven Lives of John Murray: The Story of a Publishing Dynasty*, London, 2009

Carter, Simon, *Rise and Shine: Sunlight, Technology and Health*, London, 2007

Chambers, William, *Wintering at Mentone*, London, 1870

Chapman, Alison, and Stabler, Jane, *Unfolding the South: Nineteenth-Century British Women Writers and Artists in Italy*, Manchester, 2003

Claridge, R. T., *Every Man His Own Doctor: A Medical Handbook*, London, 1840

Clark, Ronald, *The Victorian Mountaineers*, London, 1953

Clayton, P. B., *Tales of Talbot House*, London, 1934

Cole, William, *A Journal of My Journey to Paris*, 1765.

Coltman, Viccy, *Fabricating the Antique: Neo-Classicism in Britain, 1760–1800*, Chicago, 2006

Colvin, Sidney, (ed.), *Selected Letters of Robert Louis Stevenson* (vol. 2), London, 1912

Combe, William, *The Tour of Doctor Syntax, In Search of the Picturesque*, London, 1823

Constance, Hazel, *First in the Field: A Century of the Camping and Caravanning Club*, London, 2001

Cooper, Nicholas, *The Opulent Eye: Late Victorian and Edwardian Taste in Interior Design*, London, 1976

Corbin, Alain, *The Lure of the Sea: The Discovery of the Seaside 1750–1840* (trans. Jocelyn Phelps), Paris, 1988

Cunningham, Alison, *Cummy's Diary: A Diary Kept by R. L. Stevenson's Nurse*, London, 1926

Cunningham, Hugh, *Time, Work and Leisure: Life Changes in England since 1700*, Manchester, 2014

Davies, Nathaniel Newnham, *A Gourmet's Guide to Europe*, London, 1901

De Beer, Gavin, *Early Travellers in the Alps*, London, 1967

Dent, J. M., *Memoirs, 1849–1926*, London, 1954

Dickens, Charles, *Sketches by Boz*, London, 1836

————*Pictures from Italy*, London, 1846

————*Little Dorrit*, London, 1868

Dorfle, Gillo, *Kitsch: The World of Bad Taste*, New York, 1969

Dufferin, Helen, *Lispings from Low Latitudes*, London, 1863

Eastlake, Charles, *Hints on Household Taste*, London, 1878

Eisner, John, and Cardinal, Roger, (eds), *The Cultures of Collecting*, London, 2004

Eustace, John Chetwode, *A Classical Tour Through Italy*, London, 1815

Eyre, Mary, *A Lady's Walks in the South of France*, London, 1865

Felmingham, Michael, and Rigby, Graham (eds), *Ruins*, London, 1972

Fitzsimons, Raymond, *Baron on Piccadilly: The Travels and Entertainments of Albert Smith 1816–1860*, London, 1967

Flanders, Judith, *Consuming Passions: Leisure and Pleasure in Victorian Britain*, London, 2007

Fleming, Fergus, *Killing Dragons: The Conquest of the Alps*, London, 2002

Fortenberry, Diane, *Souvenirs and New Ideas: Travel and Collecting in Egypt and the Near East*, Oxford, 2013

Frawley, Maria, *Invalidism and Identity in Nineteenth-Century Britain*, Chicago, 2004

Freeman, James, *Medical Reflections on the Water Cure*, Edinburgh, 1842

Goffe, D., *Camping on the Wye*, edited by S. K. Baker, London, 2017

Goldsmith, Sarah, *Masculinity and Danger on the Eighteenth-Century Grand Tour*, London, 2020

Granville, Augustus Bozzi, *The Spas of Germany*, London, 1837

Greenslade, William, and Rodgers, Terence, (eds) *Grant Allen: Literature and Cultural Politics at the Fin de Siècle*, Aldershot, 2017

Hall, Warren, *Azure Coast: A Diary of the French and Italian Rivieras*, London, 1952

Hammerton, J. A., *Wrack of War*, London, 1918

Hanley, Keith, and Walton, John. K. (eds), *Constructing Cultural Tourism: John Ruskin and the Tourist Gaze*, Bristol, 2010

Hardy, Thomas, *The Hand of Ethelberta*, London, 1876

———*The Return of the Native*, London, 1878

Harmon, Claire, *Robert Louis Stevenson: A Biography*, London, 2006

Harrison, Ada, *A Majorca Holiday*, London, 1927

Head, Francis Bond, *Bubbles from the Brunnen of Nassau*, London, 1841

Heafford, Michael (ed.), *Two Victorian Ladies on the Continent 1844–45*, London, 2008

Hewison, Robert, *John Ruskin: The Argument of the Eye*, London, 1976

Hilker, Ann, (unpublished thesis), 'A Biography of the American Snow Globe, from Memory to Mass Production, from Souvenir to Sign'.

Hill, Kate, *Britain and the Narration of Travel in the Nineteenth Century*, Oxford, 2017

Hoare, Richard Colt, *Hints to Travellers in Italy*, London, 1815

Hobhouse, Edmund (ed.), *Health Abroad: A Medical Handbook of Travel*, London, 1899

Hough, Stanley Bennett, *A Pound a Day Inclusive: The Modern Way to Holiday Travel*, London, 1957

Jaeger, Gustav, *Health Culture* (trans. Lewis Tomalin), London, 1884

Jameson, Anna, *Diary of an Ennuyée*, London, 1826

Jennings, Humphrey, *Pandaemonium 1660–1886: The Coming of the Machine as Seen by Contemporary Observers*, London, 1985

Johnson, James, *Change of Air, or the Pursuit of Health; an Autumnal Excursion through France, Switzerland & Italy in the Year 1829*, London, 1832

————*Pilgrimages to the Spas in Pursuit of Health and Recreation with an Inquiry into the Comparative Merits of Different Mineral Waters*, London, 1841

Jousiffe, Captain M. J., *A Road Book to Italy*, 1839

Keates, Jonathan, *The Portable Paradise*, London, 2011

Kenny, Anthony (ed.), *Mountains: An Anthology*, London, 1991

Korte, Barbara, Harvie, C., and Berghoff, Hartmut (eds), *The Making of Modern Tourism: The Cultural History of the British Experience, 1600–2000*, London, 2002

Lafagne, Pierre, *Spa and the English*, Brussels, 1948

Large, David Clay, *The Grand Spas of Central Europe*, Lanham, Md., 2015

Lasansky, Medina, and McLaren, Brian (eds), *Architecture and Tourism: Perception, Performance and Place*, New York, 2008

Lawrence, D. H., *Twilight in Italy*, London, 1916

Leonard, T. Arthur, *Adventures in Holidaymaking, Being the Story of the Rise and Development of a People's Holiday Movement*, London, 1934

Letts Keep a Diary: A History of Diary Keeping in Great Britain from the 16th to the 20th Century, London, 1990

Lewis, Jeremy, *Tobias Smollett*, London, 2003

Lewis, Norman, *The Happy Ant Heap*, London, 2013

Links, J. G., *The Ruskins in Normandy: A Tour in 1848 with Murray's Hand-book*, London, 1968

Linn, Thomas, *A Medical Guide to the Mineral Springs and Climatic Mountain and Health Resorts*, London, 1902

Lippard, Lucy, *On the Beaten Track: Tourism, Art and Place*, New York, 1999

Lloyd, David, *Battlefield Tourism: Pilgrimage and the Commemoration of the Great War in Britain, Australia and Canada, 1919–1939*, London, 2014

Lockett, William George, *The British at Davos*, London, 1920

Mahn, Churnjeet, *British Women's Travel to Greece, 1840–1914*, London, 2016

Massingham, Hugh and Pauline (eds), *The Englishman Abroad*,
     London, 1984

Matthews, Henry, *Diary of an Invalid: Being the Journal of a Tour in
     Pursuit of Health in Portugal, Italy, Switzerland and France in the Years
     1817, 1818 and 1819*, London, 1822

'A Moist Man', *Three Weeks in Wet Sheets*, Malvern, 1851

Miss Jemima's Swiss Journal: The First Conducted Tour of Switzerland,
     London, 1967

Morgan, Marjorie, *National Identities and Travel in Victorian Britain*,
     London, 2001

Mowat, C. L., *Britain Between the Wars 1918–1940*, London, 1955

Muller, J. P., *My Sun-Bathing and Fresh Air System*, Denmark, 1906

Munson, James, and Mullen, Richard, *The Smell of the Continent: The
     British Discover Europe*, London, 2009

Murray's Hand-book to Switzerland, London, 1853

Murray's Hand-book to Spain, London, 1855

Murray's Handbook for Travellers in Denmark, with Sleswig and Iceland,
     London, 1875

Nottage, Charles, *In Search of Climate*, London, 1894

Otter, R. H., *Winters Abroad: Some Information Respecting Places Visited
     by the Author on Account of his Health*, London, 1883

Ousby, Ian, *The Englishman's England: Taste, Travel and the Rise of
     Tourism*, London, 2002

Pakenham, Simona, *Sixty Miles from England: The English at Dieppe,
     1814–1914*, London, 1967

Pemble, John, *The Mediterranean Passion: Victorians and Edwardians in
     the South*, Oxford, 1987

Pimlott, J. A. R., *The Englishman's Holiday: A Social History*,
     London, 1976

Purkis, John, *The Icelandic Jaunt: A Study of the Expeditions Made by
     William Morris to Iceland in 1871 and 1873*, London, 1962

Quennell, Peter, *The Colosseum*, London, 1971

Raitz, Vladimir, and Bray, Roger, *Flight to the Sun: The Story of the
     Holiday Revolution*, Boston, 2001

Ring, Jim, *How the English Made the Alps*, London, 2011

Robertson, Ian, *Richard Ford, 1796–1858: Hispanophile, Connoisseur and
     Critic*, London, 2004

Robinson, Jane, *Unsuitable for Ladies: An Anthology of Women Travellers*, Oxford, 2001

Rollier, Auguste, *Heliotherapy*, London, 1923

Ruskin, John, *The Stones of Venice*, London, 1858

————*Sesame and Lilies*, London, 1865

————*Praeterita*, London, 1885

Scott, John, *Journal of a Tour to Waterloo and Paris*, London, 1816

Scott, Lucy, *Tuscan Studies*, London, 1888

Shand, Alexander Innes, *Old Time Travel*, London, 1903

Sillitoe, Alan, *Leading the Blind: A Century of Guidebook Travel*, London, 1995

Sketchley, Arthur, *Out for a Holiday with Cook's Excursionists in Switzerland*, London, 1870

Smith, Albert, *The Adventures of Mr Ledbury*, London, 1944

Sparks, Edward, *The Riviera: Sketches of the Health Resorts of the North Mediterranean Coast of France and Italy from Hyeres to Spezia*, London, 1879

Staley, Finetta, *Autumn Rambles*, London, 1863

Starke, Mariana, *Travels on the Continent: Written for the Use and Particular Information of Travellers*, London, 1820

Stewart, Susan, *On Longing: Narratives of the Miniature, the Gigantic, the Souvenir, the Collection*, New York, 1984

Stone, Olivia, *Tenerife and its Six Satellites*, London, 1889

Studd, Ronald Granville, *The Holiday Story*, London, 1950

Summerscale, Kate, *Mrs Robinson's Disgrace: The Private Diary of a Victorian Lady*, London, 2012

Thorold, Peter, *The British in France: Visitors and Residents Since the Revolution*, London, 2016

Tinniswood, Adrian, *The Polite Tourist: Four Centuries of Country House Visiting*, London, 1998

Trease Geoffrey, *Matthew Todd's Journal: A Gentleman's Gentleman in Europe, 1814–1820*, London, 1968

Trollope, Anthony, *The Complete Short Stories (vol. 3): Tourists and Colonials*, London, 1981

Turner, E. S., *Taking the Cure*, London, 1967

Turner, Louis, and Ash, John, *The Golden Hordes: International Tourism and the Pleasure Periphery*, London, 1975

Uglow, Jenny, *In These Times: Living in Britain Through Napoleon's Wars*, London, 2014

Vizetelly, Henry, *Glances Back Through 70 Years: Autobiography and Other Reminiscences*, London, 1890

Walchester, Kathryn, *Our Own Fair Italy: Nineteenth-Century Women's Travel Writing and Italy 1800–1844*, Bristol, 2007

Walton, John. K., *Histories of Tourism: Representation, Identity and Conflict*, Bristol, 2005

Waugh, Evelyn, *Labels: A Mediterranean Journal*, London, 1930

Wawn, Andrew, *The Vikings and the Victorians: Inventing the Old North in Nineteenth-Century Britain*, Woodbridge, 2002

Williams, Edward, Francis, *Journey into Adventure: The Story of the Workers Travel Association*, London, 1960

Willoughby, Martin, *A History of Postcards*, London, 1994

Wills, Hannah, *Pre-Printed Diaries and Almanacs: An Aid to Managing the Disease of Modern Life?* (www.web.diseaseofmodernlife.ox.ac.uk)

Wilson, Erasmus, *A Three Weeks' Scamper Through the Spas of Germany and Belgium*, London, 1856

Wilson, Mary and Anne, *A European Journal: Two Sisters Abroad in 1847*, London, 1987

Wilton, Andrew and Bignamini, Iliaria, *Grand Tour: The Lure of Italy in the Eighteenth Century*, London, 1996

Wittiterley, John Altrayd, *Three Months Rest at Pau*, London, 1860

Woodward, Christopher, *In Ruins*, London, 2002

Yates, Edmund, *The Business of Pleasure*, London, 1879

————*Recollections*, London, 1884

Yeo, Isaac Burney, *Climate and Health Resorts*, London, 1890

Image Credits

Index

Page numbers in **bold** refer to illustrations.

A Note on the Type

The text of this book is set Adobe Garamond. It is one of several versions of Garamond based on the designs of Claude Garamond. It is thought that Garamond based his font on Bembo, cut in 1495 by Francesco Griffo in collaboration with the Italian printer Aldus Manutius. Garamond types were first used in books printed in Paris around 1532. Many of the present-day versions of this type are based on the *Typi Academiae* of Jean Jannon cut in Sedan in 1615.

Claude Garamond was born in Paris in 1480. He learned how to cut type from his father and by the age of fifteen he was able to fashion steel punches the size of a pica with great precision. At the age of sixty he was commissioned by King Francis I to design a Greek alphabet, and for this he was given the honourable title of royal type founder. He died in 1561.